OXFORD WORLD'S CLASSICS

ALEXANDRE DUMAS *fils*

La Dame aux Camélias

Translated with an Introduction and Notes by
DAVID COWARD

OXFORD
UNIVERSITY PRESS

OXFORD
UNIVERSITY PRESS

Great Clarendon Street, Oxford OX2 6DP

Oxford University Press is a department of the University of Oxford.
It furthers the University's objective of excellence in research, scholarship,
and education by publishing worldwide in

Oxford New York

Athens Auckland Bangkok Bogotá Buenos Aires Calcutta
Cape Town Chennai Dar es Salaam Delhi Florence Hong Kong Istanbul
Karachi Kuala Lumpur Madrid Melbourne Mexico City Mumbai
Nairobi Paris São Paulo Singapore Taipei Tokyo Toronto Warsaw

with associated companies in Berlin Ibadan

Oxford is a registered trade mark of Oxford University Press
in the UK and in certain other countries

Published in the United States
by Oxford University Press Inc., New York

Translation, Introduction, Notes and
editorial matter © David Coward 1986

The moral rights of the author have been asserted

Database right Oxford University Press (maker)

First issued as a World's Classics paperback 1986
Reissued as an Oxford World's Classics paperback 2000
Reissued 2008

British Library Cataloguing in Publication Data

Data available

Library of Congress Cataloging in Publication Data

Dumas, Alexandre, 1824–1895.
La dame aux camélias.
(Oxford world's classics)
Bibliography: p.
I. Title. II. Series.
PQ2231.D2E5 1986 843'.7 86–5239

ISBN 978–0–19–954034–1

2

Printed in Great Britain by
Clays Ltd, St Ives plc

CONTENTS

INTRODUCTION

La Dame aux Camélias has never been a novel for which persons of taste and discernment have been able to confess outright enthusiasm. When it appeared in 1848, stern judges declared its subject to be indelicate. Nowadays the blushes spring from a reluctance to admit openly that a four-hankie novel can claim to be literature or even have a serious call on our attention. By any standards, it is not a particularly good book: at most, it falls into G. K. Chesterton's category of 'good bad books'. Yet the judgement of history is clear. However embarrassed some readers have been by her, the Lady has had far more friends than enemies. Since 1848, she has never been much further away than the nearest bookstall, always in print, always available, bound or papercovered, with or without illustrations, annotated or left to speak for herself. Seventy separate editions in her published life—twenty-one since 1945—may be regarded as a sorry commentary on public taste, but countless copies sold are at least evidence of her longevity. It should not be thought, however, that it is merely the French who stand accused. The British were first off the mark with a translation in 1856, followed by the Spaniards in 1859. Since then, Marguerite Gautier has lived, loved and died to the evident satisfaction of Russians, Germans, Hungarians, Italians, the Japanese and others besides, who should all perhaps have known better.

But this is only part of the story. Dumas turned the novel, which he wrote in a month, into a play, which took him a week: Act II was dashed off one day in 1849 between lunch and tea. It was blocked at first for commercial reasons and then ran foul of the censor. It was not finally performed until February 1852 when it started its career as the greatest dramatic success of the century. It is impossible to say how many times it has been played throughout the world, but its status may be gauged by the fact that, as each generation has its Hamlet, so Eugénie Doche (the first Marguerite), Bernhardt (who took the play to London and the United States),

Duse (who toured in it throughout Europe and South America), Cécile Sorel, Ida Rubenstein, Blanche Dufrène, Marie Bell, Ludmilla Pitoëff all left their mark in the role. Edwige Feullière played Marguerite over a thousand times between 1939 and 1952. More recently, the challenge has been taken up memorably by Loleh Bellon in Paris in the '60s and, in London in 1985, by Frances Barber.

But even this does not exhaust the list of Ladies. There have been over twenty screen adaptations, the earliest made by a Dane in 1909. Sarah Bernhardt was Marguerite on celluloid in 1913; Lubitsch directed Pola Negri in 1920; Abel Gance made the first sound version in 1934, with Yvonne Printemps. Cukor's *Camille* (1937)—which, like the first American stage version in 1856, retitled the story after the flowers worn by its heroine—was hugely successful, and for a generation the face of Garbo symbolized noble suffering and tragic self-sacrifice. In 1981, Isabelle Huppert, in Pierre Bolognini's loose rendering, was the first actress to add nudity to the role. Marcel Pagnol adapted the novel for television in 1962 for Ludmilla Tcherina, and Kate Nelligan starred in a BBC serialization in 1976 . . . Marguerite has had many faces.

And voices. Verdi attended the first performance of the play in Paris in 1852 and immediately saw its musical potential. The first production of *La Traviata*, in Venice in 1853, was a hurried affair which its composer described as a 'fiasco'. It was restaged, however, in 1854, and proved to be an immense success. Christine Nilsson sang Violetta in the first Paris production in 1856 and her successors—from Patti, Melba and Pons, to Callas, Sutherland, and Kiri Te Kanawa—include all the great *divas*. Since the war, there have been four notable ballet versions. And strip cartoons in newspapers. According to estate agents, she lived in as many houses in Paris as Cromwell built castles in the British Isles. Whatever view we might take of Dumas's merits as novelist and dramatist, it is clear that Marguerite Gautier has been much more than a character in a book or a play: she is a cultural phenomenon.

Part of the explanation lies in the public's eternal fascination with the private lives of great people in general, and of great sinners in particular. Marguerite was drawn from life, where she was Alphonsine Plessis, who was born at Nonant, in Normandy, on 16 January 1824. Her father was a pedlar, Marin Plessis (1790–1841), the illegitimate son of a priest and a peasant girl with a weakness for cider and men. Her mother, Marie Deshayes (1795–1830) was the daughter of Anne du Mesnil d'Argentelle, last of a noble but impoverished line, who had married a servant. Marin Plessis was a brutal man and, leaving Alphonsine and her sister Delphine (who was two years older) with an aunt, Marie Deshayes found employment as the companion of an English noblewoman. She died in Geneva when Alphonsine was six and already sufficiently difficult for her aunt to return her to her father. It is possible that Marin Plessis started offering her to men by the time she was twelve.

In 1838 she travelled to Paris, either with her father or with a band of gypsies to whom he had sold her, and lived for a time with relatives who ran a grocer's shop. For a while, shop-girl on weekdays, and dance-hall flirt on Sundays, she remained within the ranks of the grisettes. But she quickly caught the eye of a restaurateur who made her his mistress, and then passed through the hands of a succession of lovers. In 1840 her much publicized affair with Agénor de Guiche (who was later to be, for a brief period, Napoleon III's foreign minister) launched her on her career, and, at sixteen, she was one of the most celebrated courtesans of her day. Agénor installed her at a fashionable address and paid for piano and dancing lessons. It was now that Marie Duplessis, as she styled herself, learned to write and began to read the two hundred books which she owned at the time of her death.

She was loved by many men, and it was said that the 'lions' of the Jockey Club banded together to ensure that every day of her week was reserved for one of their number. She was given vast amounts of money which she spent recklessly. When she left Agénor she moved to 22 rue d'Antin, an even more fashionable address, and soon met Comte Édouard de Perregaux, a wealthy army officer. Of all her suitors, Perregaux appears to have been the most truly in love with her.

He took her to Germany and bought her a house at Bougival. When Marie wearied of him, he was no longer wealthy.

By 1844, Marie's protector was the eighty-year-old Comte de Stackelberg, a Russian diplomat, who, it was believed, had been struck by the uncanny resemblance she bore to his dead daughter. He set her up in style in an apartment at 11 Boulevard de la Madeleine where she was to live until her death. He paid the rent and engaged a cook, a maid and a coachman. Marie was not faithful to him—Dumas claimed that Stackelberg's interest in her was purely sexual—and she was frequently seen in the theatres and the gaming rooms where she won or lost with indifference. The 'lions' of the Jockey Club and the 'loge infernale' came to her apartment where she also received Musset, Eugène Sue and others; after her death, one newspaper called her 'the most elegant of women, having the most aristocratic taste and the most exquisite tact: she set the tone for a whole area of society'.

By general consent, Marie Duplessis was exceptionally beautiful. According to her passport, she was five feet six tall, with auburn hair, brown eyes, well-shaped nose, round chin and an oval face. Dumas, in the 1867 Preface to the play, was less prosaic: 'She was tall, very slim, with black hair and a pink and white face. Her head was small, and she had long, lustrous, Japanese eyes, very quick and alert, lips as red as cherries and the most beautiful teeth in the world.' After her death in 1847, which was widely reported, journalists spoke of her 'exquisite' and 'miraculous' beauty, and of her 'natural elegance and distinction'; she had, said one family paper, 'an indefinable but genuine air of chastity about her'. Albert Vandam, an Englishman who frequented fashionable and literary circles and talked to Marie occasionally between 1843 and her death, recalled 'her marvellously beautiful face, her matchless figure'. Like many others, he agreed that she was 'no ordinary girl'. She possessed 'a natural tact, and an instinctive refinement which no education could have enhanced. She never made grammatical mistakes, no coarse expressions ever passed her lips. Lola Montès could not make friends; Alphonsine Plessis could not make enemies.' According to Vandam, Dr Véron, the newspaper publisher, was equally impressed: 'She is, first of all, the best dressed woman in Paris; second, she neither flaunts nor hides her vices; thirdly, she is not always talking or hinting about money; in short, she is a wonderful courtesan.' The literary critic Jules Janin also remembered 'her young and supple waist', 'the beautiful oval of her face', and 'the grace which she radiated like an indescribable fragrance'. But Janin also detected a sense of *ennui* in her, the result of too many pressing loves. It is a view to be treated with scepticism, for *ennui* was fashionable ('La France s'ennuie', Lamartine had declared). For while a great deal is known about her conduct, little is known about her soul. Her surviving letters, brief undated notes for the most part, do not speak of her soul, and are pointed and direct.

She was Dumas's mistress for eleven months, between September 1844 and August 1845. How much she loved him is difficult to say, though she was very close to him at first. After the break, however, there is nothing to suggest that she pined for him. Her continuing extravagance led her back to her lovers, while her consumption was making her only too familiar with doctors. Late in 1845, at a concert, she met Liszt who appears to have been the only man she ever genuinely loved. 'She was the most absolute incarnation of Woman who has ever existed', he wrote subsequently, and for a while they were happy. Then, inexplicably, on 21 February 1846, she married Perregaux at the Kensington Register Office. The marriage, while valid in England, was not legal in France, and the couple separated at once, Marie returning to Liszt in Paris. Whatever her reasons for marrying Perregaux, she now felt able to sign herself 'la comtesse du Plessis' and to add a coronet to her plate.

Liszt left Paris in the spring, promising to return in the autumn when he would take her with him to Constantinople. She was now increasingly ill and, in June, left to take the waters in Belgium and Germany. She maintained contact by letter with Perregaux who was now attempting to return to the army. Marie was back in Paris by mid-September, but her condition deteriorated steadily. Drs

Davaine, Manec and Chomel saw her frequently, and she consulted Dr Koreff, a fashionable charlatan, but their prescriptions of asses' milk, fumigations, frictions, their warnings against over-use of her voice and the recommendation that she sleep on a horse-hair mattress, made little difference. Liszt did not return and Marie dropped out of circulation. In late December, she paid her last visit to the theatre, 'the shadow of a woman', one journalist reported, sitting in her box like 'something white and diaphanous'.

Cared for by her maid, Clotilde, who tried to shield her against her creditors, she grew weaker and died on 3 February 1847 at the age of twenty-three. She did not die in poverty, however, as some newspapers suggested, nor was she quite alone, for the faithful Perregaux returned. A service was held for her at the Church of La Madeleine which attracted fashionable society and a cohort of journalists who filled their columns for days with anecdotes of her life. She was buried in a temporary grave in Montmartre cemetery and was exhumed on 16 February, at the order of Perregaux, who paid for a permanent plot for her remains. Her possessions were auctioned in her apartment between 24 and 27 February: Eugène Sue bought her prayer-book, and society ladies outbid each other for her combs and trinkets. The sale realized 89,017 francs, of which her creditors took nearly 50,000.

According to Dickens's friend John Forster, Marie 'left behind her the most exquisite furniture and the most voluptuous and sumptuous bijouterie. Dickens wished at one time to have printed the moral of this life and death of which there was great talk in Paris while we were together.' The same idea also occurred to Dumas who, however, had more pressing motives for doing so.

Dumas, younger than Marie by six months, was the illegitimate son of a famous father who, unwittingly and almost singlehandedly, made his boyhood unhappy and furnished him with that obsessiveness without which there is no literature. In 1831 Dumas *père* removed him from his mother, to whom he always remained attached, and sent him to a succession of *pensions* where taunts about his

illegitimacy made him wretched: a few months before his
death in 1895, he confessed bitterly that 'ever since the age
of seven I have been fighting life'. It was to these years that
he owed his enduring preoccupation with the plight of
illegitimate children and abandoned mothers, and his
general belief that illicit love was a force for evil.

He left school having failed his examinations and was
drawn into the whirling life of Dumas *père*, a roaring man
of great appetites and legendary generosity, who took
immense pleasure in initiating his son into the delights of
Paris. Alexandre was tall, blond and handsome, and he took
readily to what he later called, disapprovingly, the 'paganism
of modern life'. It was said that Victor Hugo warned his son
against associating with the dissolute Dumas *fils* who, in
1843, took his first mistress. He was a familiar figure in the
gaming rooms, cafés and theatres of Paris, and he never paid
his tailor. One day in September 1844, after visiting his
father at Saint-Germain, he met up with Eugène Dejazet,
the son of Mademoiselle Dejazet, of the Théâtre du Palais
Royal. On reaching Paris, they dined and, for want of anything better to do, wandered into the Théâtre des Variétés.
Marie Duplessis was in her usual box. Dumas must have
known her by sight, but it was through Dejazet, who was
acquainted with Marie's neighbour, Clémence Prat, more
go-between than milliner, that they engineered an invitation
to supper in the apartment at 11 Boulevard de la Madeleine.

Dumas became her lover. On the evidence of his straitened
circumstances alone, it may be deduced that Marie returned
his passion. She called him by his initials, and 'Adet' was
granted the status of 'amant de cœur'. But since he was not
rich and her needs were great, his exclusive position did not
last long, and Marie returned to her regular keepers—
Stackelberg, Perregaux and others besides. After eleven
months of increasing suspicion and anxiety, Dumas ended
the affair with a note, dated 30 August 1845, part of which
survives in the letter sent by Armand in Chapter XIV.

It is difficult to say how attached to Marie he was: in
October 1844, he was still trying to free himself of a mistress
he had found during a stay at Marseilles the previous

summer. It is likely that Perregaux loved her more, and certain that Liszt occupied a higher place in her affections. But for a while they had been happy together. After the break, he could not have avoided seeing Marie in the small world of fashionable Paris, but there was to be no further contact between them. Wearying now of the dissolute life, of which he had never really approved, he resolved to earn enough money to pay off the 50,000 francs which he owed: his ambition, he later said, was not to see Naples and die, but to pay his debts and die. He wrote enough poems to fill a volume which, when it appeared in 1847, sold fourteen copies. He wrote a play, and began a novel. He found himself a new mistress.

In October 1846, fourteen months after the end of the affair, he travelled to Spain with his father. It was there that he learned of Marie's illness, and he wrote to her asking for forgiveness and suggesting that they might begin again. No reply to his letter is known, but Dumas did not return to Paris. Instead, he continued on his travels with his father to North Africa, apparently content to go his own way. He returned to France early in January 1847 and on 10 February received news that Marie was dead. Though he left at once for Paris, his reason for travelling was not unconnected with urgent business with his publisher. He arrived on 14 February, may have been the friend who accompanied Perregaux at the exhumation, and certainly attended either the preview of the auction or the auction itself which drew the whole of Parisian society, 'the female part of which—almost without distinction—went to look at her apartment, to appraise her jewels and dresses, etc. "They would probably like to have had them on the same terms," said a terrible cynic. The remark must have struck young Dumas, in whose hearing it was said, or who, at any rate, had it reported to him.' Vandam may have been right in going on to conclude that 'the first idea of the novel was probably suggested to him, not by his acquaintance (with Marie) but by the sensation her death caused among the Paris public'. Yet his first literary response was a rather banal elegy, dedicated to 'M.D.', written soon after the auction, which strikes an anguished note—though whether of personal emotion or of modish lamentation for the waste of youth, it is not easy to say. 'We had quarrelled you and I: what cause?/No cause! For some suspected secret love.' He evokes her 'fevered passion' and their nights of love, and he weeps for her death. 'One man alone was there to close your eyes', and at her graveside, 'Your sometime friends were now but two.'

Exactly when, or why, Dumas resolved to make a novel out of his affair with Marie, cannot be said for certain. He needed money, the story was there to be written, the subject was controversial and Marie was notorious. But whether La Dame aux Camélias was a cynical piece of exploitation or a genuine need to come to terms with his grief, or, more likely, a mixture of the two, Dumas confessed that he wrote the novel quickly, in June 1847. It was published the following summer. 'It was in everyone's hands', reports Vandam, 'and the press kept whetting the curiosity of those who had not read it with personal anecdotes of the heroine.' Vandam exaggerates the impact of the novel on Parisian society which was just emerging from the 1848 Revolution, but he does reflect the commonly held view that Dumas's book was autobiographical and that it revealed the secret mysteries of a courtesan's life.

The notion that La Dame aux Camélias is not simply true to life but actually true clearly helped shape the vogue for the novel which began in earnest after the play was successfully staged in 1852. It even has considerable basis in fact. Gaston R*** was based on Eugène Dejazet, N*** on Perregaux, the 'Duke' on Stackelberg, G*** on Agénor de Guiche, and Prudence is a thinly veiled transposition of Clémence Prat. Marguerite is as intriguing as those who knew Marie say she was, and Armand bears the initials of Dumas himself. The meeting at the theatre and the supper party which followed, Armand's growing jealousy, even the letter he writes, all draw upon reality in the most transparent way. Marie's death, the exhumation, and the auction are similarly factual. In comparison, the changes which Dumas makes—Armand is four years older, Marie's address is disguised, the dates of events occurring between her death and the auction are advanced by seventeen days—are minor and trifling. Few novels between Restif's *Sara* (1783), which was written as the events it chronicles unfolded, and Truman Capote's *In Cold Blood* (1965), reconstructed from official records and interviews, draw quite so brazenly on real life.

Dumas was quite clear in his own mind about the difference between life and art. Of course, he openly acknowledged Marie as his model, but once, after a memorable performance of *La Dame aux Camélias*, he confessed to his father that Armand that night had loved Marguerite more passionately than he himself had ever loved Marie. (Dumas *père* sympathized, and added that, for his part, he knew that D'Artagnan was the man he could never be.) Literature is not a reproduction of reality, it is reality transposed and heightened. Dumas further recalled a revival of his play in 1859 in which Clémence Prat, who was an occasional actress among her other trades, played Prudence, for whom she had unwittingly modelled, and was totally unconvincing in the role. If Dumas's novel, though rooted in fact, is not quite life, then perhaps it is art.

This is a proposition which carried more weight in 1850 than it does today. The impetus of Romanticism was spent and the seeds of a plainer Realism were only beginning to germinate. In historical terms, *La Dame aux Camélias* is a transitional novel which moves away from Romantic excess towards a more restrained presentation of social and psychological realities. Indeed, it impressed its first admirers as a remarkably sober and understated picture of contemporary manners. Modern readers, however, will be impressed rather by its sentimentality and by the melodrama which, in the exhumation scene, verges on the Gothic. Poses are struck, rhetorical flourishes subvert plain speaking, and noble sentiments of stupendous pomposity are paraded without embarrassment. Nor is it possible to venture far into the story without sensing the manipulations of which we are the victims. In spite of the claim that Marguerite will not be shown except as she was, everything is calculated to reveal her in the best light. The Duke's fantasy and her dislike of N*** leave her singularly underemployed in her profession, and Dumas's insistence that she remains 'virginal' in the midst of vice, like his wish to turn her into a saint and martyr, will nowadays strike some readers as a piece of special pleading. Her consumption, a marvellously convenient literary disease, is used to extract our sympathy and to excuse the extravagance of her conduct. If we ever get round to wondering quite why she must have 100,000 francs a year (see Note on Money, p. 203), the question has long since been made tasteless and irrelevant. The fact that she is dead when the novel begins makes it difficult to speak ill of her, and the anecdotes involving Louise, like the behaviour of the public at the auction, remove any wish that we might have to do so. Four first-person narrators tell her story, and each voice is unctuous and persuasive. The first is the voice of our curiosity, and it tantalizes us by giving the view from the outside. Armand, through whose eyes we learn to see Marguerite, tells us part of the inside story, and it is left to Marguerite to take us to the truth. Julie Duprat reads the last rites over the 'unhappy destiny' which we have known was inevitable since Chapter I. That Dumas maintains the suspense of a story having divulged the final outcome at the outset is a considerable achievement, and it suggests that if *La Dame aux Camélias* is not art, then it is at least artful.

Dumas was clearly conscious of the need to package the story for maximum effect. His choice of title, for which he claimed sole responsibility and which has contributed considerably to the notoriety of his novel, was no happy accident. Moreover, he was aware of the basic ground rules for the kind of tale he wished to tell. In the Epilogue to *Antonine* (1849), he deduces from the examples of *Paul et Virginie*, *Werther* and *Manon Lescaut* that an 'histoire de cœur' requires young lovers and that 'death alone can poeticize their young love'. It is likely that if Marie had not died, Dumas would have killed Marguerite. He knew, too, that to succeed, a modern *Manon Lescaut* needed to be solidly anchored in contemporary reality. But his realism—

the careful chronology, the precise locations, the preoccupation with money—is offset by a general mood of hyperbole, and the effect is one of surface without depth. The background characters are vividly realized and, as they were intended to do, they start contrasts designed to give perspective to the hero and heroine. Gaston, the insensitive young man about town, N***, who needs Marguerite to complete his public image, and the Duke, who makes her part of a private fantasy, help to define, by reflection, the sincerity of Armand's love. In the same way, Prudence and Olympe reveal, by implication, how different Marguerite is from the common pattern of the callous courtesan. Yet, though they are nimbly sketched, they remain social and psychological types, uninteresting in their own right and functional in purpose. Even Armand, in spite of occasional moments of self-mockery, fails to rise above the role for which he is typecast. He is a lightweight lover, dense and petulant by turns, a man too preoccupied by his own feelings and pride ever to become truly tragic, and too self-regarding to love anyone but himself. For all his tears and bombast, telling his tale assuages his grief and he 'recovers quickly', much as Dumas himself had done. In this company, Marguerite dominates the novel just as Phèdre dominates Racine's play, for only she escapes the limitations imposed by reality. If Armand and Prudence are reported and chronicled from life, Marguerite was invented.

'Marie', said Dumas in the 1867 preface to the play, 'did not have all the moving adventures which I attribute to Marguerite Gautier, but she would have dearly liked to have them. If she sacrificed nothing to Armand, it was because Armand would not have it.' In life, Marie regularly stopped short of love. As each love died, she began afresh, like Penelope at her loom. In his novel, Dumas takes Marguerite into a 'moving adventure' in which she is not required to unpick the stitches of his imaginative embroidery. He takes her through Worldliness, Love, Renunciation, Atonement and Death, but he also leads her out of reality into fable. The story has survived not merely, as he once said, because 'it will always be replayed throughout the world wherever there are courtesans and young men', though this is probably true. It is rather, as he also said, because it has the qualities of a 'legend'. It scarcely matters if *La Dame aux Camélias*, in spite of its solid carpentry, shrewd dramatic sense and lively dialogue, is no masterpiece, for it is that far rarer thing: a popular myth. Dumas, far from 'poeticizing' Marie, counters our cynicism with his sympathetic and moving portrait of Marguerite, young, hopeful and doomed, who demonstrates that even the souls of outcasts may be redeemed by love. Marguerite Gautier does not properly belong with Emma Bovary or Anna Karenina on the high slopes of literature, but with Juliet, Frankenstein's monster, Madame Butterfly, Tarzan and James Bond at the centre of the collective unconscious. For generations of (especially women) readers, Marguerite symbolized romance and selfless love in the most immediate way. Already in 1867, Dumas reports, women regularly visited her grave. Later in the century, the Comtesse Néra de la Jonchère put fresh camellias on her tomb each day for many years. In 1950, Edith Saunders, Dumas's biographer, surprised her intimidating *concierge* setting off, as she did each Sunday, with a bouquet of azaleas for the Lady of the Camellias in Montmartre cemetery. The Lady has been an ideal, an inspiration, a consolation. Emma Bovary is a luxury; Marguerite Gautier is a necessity.

Watchful observers, however, have pointed out that by turning his skittish courtesan into an ideal of submissive, self-sacrificing womanhood, Dumas did nothing to help to liberate women. Dumas would have taken the criticism as a compliment, for Armand's respectable father—another invention, incidentally, for Dumas *père* was far from respectable—already voices reservations about the 'paganism of modern life' which were to dominate Dumas's later work. As time passed, his interest in illicit love, which he knew from personal experience was a source of personal unhappiness, turned into a concern for the well-being of society. Though he continued to believe that selfless love can move men and women to selfless acts, he gave dire warnings of the dangers presented not only by prostitution but by adultery.

He came to view woman as evil, a force to be mastered by man, to be subjugated for her own good, for woman would be free only when protected against her own destructiveness. He presented a hard, impassive face to the public which knew him as the self-made author of well-made plays. But it is clear that the ever more moralistic Dumas, famous for his wit, grew increasingly pessimistic as he saw the world plunge deeper into the permissiveness which made no one happy. After 1870, when he turned more and more towards a kind of secular religiosity, his popularity waned, though he knew that his position in the history of the theatre was secure. He continued to be interested in the same narrow range of moral and social problems—the problem of illegitimacy, prostitution, adultery, love, marriage and the family—and eventually spoke out in favour of political rights for women, though less out of conviction than from weariness. Other people's opinions, he remarked, are like nails: the harder you hit them, the more immovable they become.

Dumas's literary influence on several generations was profound. Pierre Louÿs called him 'the master of Ibsen and Tolstoy'. If this is excessive, it is undeniable that Dumas the playwright gave a new impetus to the French dramatic tradition and, by making the transition from the merely well-made play to the well-made play of ideas, prepared the way for the modern movement in the theatre. His novels, for all their incipient realism, made less of an impact, though as a novelist Dumas continued to be read and *La Dame aux Camélias* was regularly reprinted. But neither as a novelist nor as a playwright did he ever recapture the mythical quality of the tale he told of Marguerite Gautier. He wrote better novels and more significant plays, but he wrote them with his head. *La Dame aux Camélias* is a young man's book, and it has all the faults and virtues of youth. It was a romantic indiscretion for which Dumas was never moved to apologize.

DAVID COWARD
Leeds

NOTE ON THE TEXT

THE first edition of *La Dame aux Camélias* appeared in July 1848, and was reprinted, with a preface by Jules Janin, in 1851. A number of minor errors were corrected by Dumas in the third edition, published in March 1852. In 1872, he prepared a revised version, of which only 500 copies were printed, which introduced a number of stylistic and formal changes (for example, Chapter XXV is amalgamated with Chapter XXVI) but, more importantly, modified a number of passages in such a way as to reduce the reader's sympathy for Marguerite the courtesan.

The text of this translation is that of the edition of 1852, which is the most commonly reprinted in France.

SELECT BIBLIOGRAPHY

THERE is no general study of the life and work of Dumas fils, and most of what has been written about him deals mainly with his theatre: C. M. Noël, Les idées sociales dans le théâtre de Dumas (Paris, 1912), F. A. Taylor, The Theatre of Alexandre Dumas fils (Oxford, 1937), and Neil C. Arvin, Alexandre Dumas fils (Paris, 1939) are still of value.

On the other hand, a great deal of attention has been given to Dumas, Marie Duplessis and their affair. Among contemporary accounts, that of Albert Vandam (An Englishman in Paris, London, 1892, 2 vols.) is particularly revealing. Among more recent works, the following will be found useful: Johannès Gros, Alexandre Dumas et Marie Duplessis (Paris, 1924), Henri Lyonnet, La Dame aux Camélias d'Alexandre Dumas fils (Paris, 1930), Edith Saunders, The Prodigal Father (London, 1951) and André Maurois, Les Trois Dumas (Paris, 1957; English translation, London, 1958). Marie's story has many times been retold, by novelists (most recently, by Henriette Chaudret, On l'appelait la Dame aux Camélias (Paris, 1973), and Poirot-Delpech, La Dame aux Camélias, une Vie romancée (Paris, 1981)), and by non-specialist biographers: Maurice Rat, La Dame aux Camélias (Paris, 1958; repr. 1982) and Patrick Toussaint, La vraie Dame aux Camélias (Paris, 1958). Christiane Issartel's excellent Les Dames aux Camélias, de l'histoire à la légende (Paris, 1981) is a richly illustrated survey of the three Ladies: Marie Duplessis, Marguerite Gautier and the Marguerite/Violetta of theatre, screen and opera.

Dumas's own prefaces to his plays are to be found in his Théâtre complet (Paris, 1898, 8 vols.), and his accounts of La Dame aux Camélias (vol. I) and La Femme de Claude (vol. VI) are full of interesting facts and valuable insights. Roger Clark's introduction to his edition of the play (Oxford, 1972) will be of interest to readers of the novel which has been edited by Bernard Raffalli (with a preface by André Maurois) for the 'Folio' series (Paris, 1975) and by Antoine Livio (Paris, 1983). La Dame aux Camélias: le roman, le drame, 'La Traviata', edited by Hans-Jorg Neuschäfer and Gilbert Sigaux (Paris, 1981) offers readers the text of the novel, the play, and the opera.

A CHRONOLOGY OF ALEXANDRE DUMAS *fils*

1824 27 July: Birth of Alexandre Dumas, illegitimate son of Alexandre Dumas *père* (1802–70) and Catherine Labay, a seamstress

1831 Dumas *père* legally acknowledges his son (17 Mar.) and takes charge of his education. In a succession of *pensions* 1831–9) where he is taunted for his illegitimacy, Dumas *fils* is thoroughly unhappy

1839–41 Attends the Collège Bourbon (now the Lycée Condorcet). He fails the *baccalauréat*, but is increasingly caught up in his father's social life

1840 To the dismay of his son, Dumas *père* marries the actress, Ida Ferrier. Dumas *fils* continues to see his mother Catherine Labay who now runs a *cabinet de lecture* in the rue de la Michodière

1843 Dumas takes his first mistress, Mme Pradier

1844 In September, he meets Marie Duplessis and becomes her lover

1845 Writes to Marie ending their affair (30 Aug.), and resolves to earn enough money by his pen to pay off debts of 50,000 frs. Writes poems, a one-act play, and begins a novel, *Aventures de quatre femmes et d'un perroquet*, published 1846–7

1846 One private performance of his first play, *Le Bijou de la Reine*. Becomes the lover of Anaïs Liévenne, an actress. Travels to Spain and North Africa with his father (Oct.)

1847 Returns to Marseilles (15 Jan.). Death of Marie Duplessis (3 Feb.). Travels to Paris and attends the auction of her effects, or the preview (24–27 Feb.). Elegy to her memory published in his verse collection, *Péchés de Jeunesse*. Writes *La Dame aux Camélias* at the Auberge du Cheval Blanc at Saint Germain (June)

1848 July: Publication of *La Dame aux Camélias*, followed in August by *Césarine*, his third novel. In the years to 1854, he writes a further fifteen novels, none particularly successful, some historical and romantic, but most devoted to contemporary manners. Béraud, ex-director of the Ambigu theatre, suggests how *La Dame aux Camélias* could be adapted for the stage. Dumas does not consider the subject theatrical

1849 Dumas turns his novel into a play in a week (summer). Though several theatres were interested, it remained unperformed

1850 Start of Dumas's affair with Lydie Nesselrode, wife of the Russian ambassador. *La Dame aux Camélias* (play) banned for immorality

1851 Dumas pursues Lydie across Europe but is refused entry to Russia (Mar.–June) and never saw her again. He used his experience in *Diane de Lys* (1851) and *La Dame aux Perles* (1853). In Poland, he acquires letters written by George Sand to Chopin and returns them to their author. Slow beginning of a long friendship with Sand. *La Dame aux Camélias* reprinted, with a preface by Jules Janin (Dec.)

1852 2 Feb.: First performance of *La Dame aux Camélias*. Publication of third, corrected edition of the novel. Begins liaison with Princess Nadejda Naryschkine, wife of another Russian diplomat. Dumas repays his debts

1853 6 Mar.: First performance of Verdi's *La Traviata* in Venice. It closes after ten performances

1854 6 May: New production of *La Traviata* in Venice. It is immediately successful

1855 *Le Demi-monde* marks Dumas's shift to the theatre where he treats serious themes in a realistic manner. Increasingly he sees himself as a moralistic dramatist with a mission

1857 Chevalier de la Légion d'honneur (Officier, 1867)

1860 Birth of Colette Dumas, illegitimate daughter of Dumas and Nadejda Naryschkine

1861 Stays with George Sand at Nohant. Dumas regulates his life, alternating between bouts of hard work and rest. Occasional recurrence of nervous disorders: during a trip to Naples, he experiences a sudden urge to kill his father asleep in the next room

1864 The failure of *L'Ami des Femmes* leads him to abandon the stage temporarily. In May, Prince Naryschkine dies and Dumas marries Nadejda (Dec.)

1866 *Affaire Clémenceau,* his best novel

1867 Birth of Jeannine Dumas. Dumas's liaison with Mlle Desclée, the Marguerite of a revival of *La Dame aux Camélias*

1868 Death of his mother, Catherine Labay (22 Oct.)

1870 Death of Dumas *père* (5 Dec.)

1871 Publishes several pamphlets on social questions

1872 *La question de la femme* and *L'Homme-Femme,* two more of the series of books and pamphlets on social, moral and literary issues which accelerate from 1870. He grew interested in the occult sciences, typology and chiromancy. He took up the rights of illegitimate children, campaigned for divorce, and argued that while women should have political rights, they should learn to be subordinate to their husbands

1875 Dumas elected to the French Academy (11 Feb.)

1887 Becomes the lover of Henriette Escalier

1891 Nadejda leaves Dumas

1895 Death of Nadejda (2 April). Dumas marries Henriette Escalier (26 June). In October he catches a chill at the unveiling of a statue to Augier and dies on 28 November. He asked that there should be 'no soldiers, no churchmen, no speeches' at his funeral.

La Dame aux
Camélias

I

IT is my considered view that no one can invent fictional characters without first having made a lengthy study of people, just as it is impossible for anyone to speak a language that has not been properly mastered.

Since I am not yet of an age to invent, I must make do with telling a tale.*

I therefore invite the reader to believe that this story is true. All the characters who appear in it, with the exception of the heroine, are still living.

I would further add that there are reliable witnesses in Paris for most of the particulars which I bring together here, and they could vouch for their accuracy should my word not be enough. By a singular turn of events, I alone was able to write them down since I alone was privy to the very last details without which it would have been quite impossible to piece together a full and satisfying account.

It was in this way that these particulars came to my knowledge.

On the 12th day of March 1847, in the rue Laffitte,* I happened upon a large yellow notice announcing a sale of furniture and valuable curios. An estate was to be disposed of, the owner having died. The notice did not name the dead person, but the sale was to be held at 9 rue d'Antin* on the 16th, between noon and five o'clock.

The notice also stated that the apartments and contents could be viewed on the 13th and 14th.

I have always been interested in curios. I promised myself I would not miss this opportunity, if not of actually buying, then at least of looking.

The following day, I directed my steps towards 9 rue d'Antin.

It was early, and yet a good crowd of visitors had already gathered in the apartment—men for the most part, but also a number of ladies who, though dressed in velvet and wearing Indian shawls,* and all with their own elegant broughams standing at the door, were examining the riches set out before them with astonished, even admiring eyes.

After a while, I quite saw the reason for their admiration and astonishment, for having begun myself to look around I had no difficulty in recognizing that I was in the apartment of a kept woman. Now if there is one thing that ladies of fashion desire to see above all else—and there were society ladies present—it is the rooms occupied by those women who have carriages which spatter their own with mud every day of the week, who have their boxes at the Opera or the Théâtre-Italien* just as they do, and indeed next to theirs, and who display for all Paris to see the insolent opulence of their beauty, diamonds and shameless conduct.

The woman in whose apartments I now found myself was dead: the most virtuous of ladies were thus able to go everywhere, even into the bedroom. Death had purified the air of this glittering den of iniquity, and in any case they could always say, if they needed the excuse, that they had done no more than come to a sale without knowing whose rooms these were. They had read the notices, they had wanted to view what the notices advertised and mark out their selections in advance. It could not have been simpler—though this did not prevent them from looking through these splendid things for traces of the secret life of a courtesan of which they had doubtless been given very strange accounts.

Unfortunately, the mysteries had died with the goddess, and in spite of their best endeavours these good ladies found only what had been put up for sale since the time of death, and could detect nothing of what had been sold while the occupant had been alive.

But there was certainly rich booty to be had. The furniture was superb. Rosewood and Buhl-work pieces, Sèvres vases and blue china porcelain, Dresden figurines, satins, velvet and lace, everything in fact.

I wandered from room to room in the wake of these inquisitive aristocratic ladies who had arrived before me. They went into a bedroom hung with Persian fabrics and I was about to go in after them, when they came out again almost immediately, smiling and as it were put to shame by this latest revelation. The effect was to make me even keener to see inside. It was the dressing-room, complete down to the very last details, in which the dead woman's profligacy had seemingly reached its height.

On a large table standing against one wall—it measured a good six feet by three—shone the finest treasures of Aucoc and Odiot.* It was a magnificent collection, and among the countless objects each so essential to the appearance of the kind of woman in whose home we had gathered, there was not one that was not made of gold or silver. But it was a collection that could only have been assembled piece by piece, and clearly more than one love had gone into its making.

I, who was not the least put out by the sight of the dressing-room of a kept woman, spent some time agreeably inspecting its contents, neglecting none of them, and I noticed that all these magnificently wrought implements bore different initials and all manner of coronets.

As I contemplated all these things, each to my mind standing for a separate prostitution of the poor girl, I reflected that God had been merciful to her since He had not suffered her to live long enough to undergo the usual punishment but had allowed her to die at the height of her wealth and beauty, long before the coming of old age, that first death of courtesans.

Indeed, what sadder sight is there than vice in old age, especially in a woman? It has no dignity and is singularly unattractive. Those everlasting regrets, not for wrong turnings taken but for wrong calculations made and money foolishly spent, are among the most harrowing things that can be heard. I once knew a former woman of easy virtue of whose past life there remained only a daughter who was almost as beautiful as the mother had once been, or so her contemporaries said. This poor child, to whom her mother never said 'You are my daughter' except to order her to keep her now that she was old just as she had been kept when she was young, this wretched creature was called Louise and, in obedience to her mother, she sold herself without inclina-

tion or passion or pleasure, rather as she might have followed
an honest trade had it ever entered anyone's head to teach
her one.

The continual spectacle of debauchery, at so tender an
age, compounded by her continuing ill-health, had extin-
guished in the girl the knowledge of good and evil which
God had perhaps given her but which no one had ever
thought to nurture.

I shall always remember that young girl who walked
along the boulevards almost every day at the same hour.
Her mother was always with her, escorting her as assiduously as a true mother might have accompanied her
daughter. I was very young in those days and ready enough
to fall in with the easy morality of the times. Yet I recall
that the sight of such scandalous chaperoning filled me with
contempt and disgust.

Add to all this that no virgin's face ever conveyed such a
feeling of innocence nor any comparable expression of
sadness and suffering.

You would have said it was the image of Resignation
itself.

And then one day, the young girl's face lit up. In the
midst of the debauches which her mother organized for her,
it suddenly seemed to this sinful creature that God had
granted her one happiness. And after all why should God,
who had made her weak and helpless, abandon her without
consolation to struggle on beneath the oppressive burden
of her life? One day, then, she perceived that she was with
child, and that part of her which remained pure trembled
with joy. The soul finds refuge in the strangest sanctuaries.
Louise ran to her mother to tell her the news that had filled
her with such happiness. It is a shameful thing to have to
say—but we do not write gratuitously of immorality here,
we relate a true incident and one perhaps which we would
be better advised to leave untold if we did not believe that
it is essential from time to time to make public the
martyrdom of these creatures who are ordinarily condemned
without a hearing and despised without trial—it is, we say,
a matter for shame, but the mother answered her daughter

saying that as things stood they scarcely had enough for two, and that they would certainly not have enough for three; that such children serve no useful purpose; and that a pregnancy is so much time wasted.

The very next day, a midwife (of whom we shall say no more than that she was a friend of the mother) called to see Louise, who remained for a few days in her bed from which she rose paler and weaker than before.

Three months later, some man took pity on her and undertook her moral and physical salvation. But this latest blow had been too great and Louise died of the after effects of the miscarriage she had suffered.

The mother still lives. How? God alone knows.

This story had come back to me as I stood examining the sets of silver toilet accessories, and I must have been lost in thought for quite some time. For by now the apartment was empty save for myself and a porter who, from the doorway, was eyeing me carefully lest I should try to steal anything.

I went up to this good man in whom I inspired such grave anxieties.

'Excuse me,' I said, 'I wonder if you could tell me the name of the person who lived here?'

'Mademoiselle Marguerite Gautier.'

I knew this young woman by name and by sight.

'What!' I said to the porter. 'Marguerite Gautier is dead?'

'Yes, sir.'

'When did it happen?'

'Three weeks ago, I think.'

'But why are people being allowed to view her apartment?'

'The creditors thought it would be good for trade. People can get the effect of the hangings and the furniture in advance. Encourages people to buy, you understand.'

'So she had debts, then?'

'Oh yes, sir! Lots of 'em.'

'But I imagine the sale will cover them?'

'Over and above.'

'And who stands to get the balance?'

'The family.'

'She had a family?'

'Seems she did.'

'Thank you very much.'

The porter, now reassured as to my intentions, touched his cap and I left.

'Poor girl,' I said to myself as I returned home, 'she must have died a sad death, for in her world, people only keep their friends as long as they stay fit and well.' And in spite of myself, I lamented the fate of Marguerite Gautier.

All this will perhaps seem absurd to many people, but I have a boundless forbearance towards courtesans which I shall not even trouble to enlarge upon here.

One day, as I was on my way to collect a passport from the *préfecture*,* I saw, down one of the adjacent streets, a young woman being taken away by two policemen. Now I have no idea what she had done. All I can say is that she was weeping bitterly and clasping to her a child only a few months old from which she was about to be separated by her arrest. From that day until this, I have been incapable of spurning any woman on sight.

II

THE sale was due to be held on the 16th.

An interval of one day had been left between the viewing and the sale in order to give the upholsterers enough time to take down the hangings, curtains and so forth.

I was at that time recently returned from my travels. It was quite natural that no one had told me about Marguerite's death, for it was hardly one of those momentous news-items which friends always rush to tell anybody who has just got back to the capital city of News. Marguerite had been pretty, but the greater the commotion that attends the sensational lives of these women, the smaller the stir once they are dead. They are like those dull suns which set as they have risen: they are unremarkable. News of their death, when they die young, reaches all their lovers at the same instant, for in Paris the lovers of any celebrated courtesan see each other every day. A few reminiscences are exchanged about her, and the lives of all and sundry continue as before without so much as a tear.

For a young man of twenty-five nowadays, tears have become so rare a thing that they are not to be wasted on the first girl who comes along. The most that may be expected is that the parents and relatives who pay for the privilege of being wept for are indeed mourned to the extent of their investment.

For my own part, though my monogram figured on none of Marguerite's dressing-cases, the instinctive forbearance and natural pity to which I have just admitted led me to dwell on her death for much longer than it perhaps warranted.

I recalled having come across Marguerite very frequently on the Champs-Élysées, where she appeared assiduously each day in a small blue brougham drawn by two magnificent bays, and I remembered having also remarked in her at that time an air of distinction rare in women of her kind and which was further enhanced by her truly exceptional beauty.

When these unfortunate creatures appear in public, they are invariably escorted by some companion or other.

Since no man would ever consent to flaunt by day the predilection he has for them by night, and because they abhor solitude, they are usually attended either by less fortunate associates who have no carriages of their own, or else by elderly ladies of refinement who are not the least refined and to whom an interested party may apply without fear, should any information be required concerning the woman they are escorting.

It was not so with Marguerite. She always appeared alone on the Champs-Élysées, riding in her own carriage where she sat as unobtrusively as possible, enveloped on winter days in a large Indian shawl and, in summer, wearing the simplest dresses. And though there were many she knew along her favourite route, when she chanced to smile at them, her smile was visible to them alone. A Duchess could have smiled no differently.

She did not ride from the Rond-Point down to the

entrance to the Champs-Élysées* as do—and did—all her sort. Her two horses whisked her off smartly to the Bois de Boulogne. There she alighted, walked for an hour, rejoined her brougham and returned home at a fast trot.

These circumstances, which I had occasionally observed for myself, now came back to me and I sorrowed for this girl's death much as one might regret the total destruction of a beautiful work of art.

For it was impossible to behold beauty more captivating than Marguerite's.

Tall and slender almost to a fault, she possessed in the highest degree the art of concealing this oversight of nature simply by the way she arranged the clothes she wore. Her Indian shawl, with its point reaching down to the ground, gave free movement on either side to the flounced panels of her silk dress, while the thick muff, which hid her hands and which she kept pressed to her bosom, was encompassed by folds so skilfully managed that even the most demanding eye would have found nothing wanting in the lines of her figure.

Her face, a marvel, was the object of her most fastidious attentions. It was quite small and, as Musset* might have said, her mother had surely made it so to ensure it was fashioned with care.

Upon an oval of indescribable loveliness, place two dark eyes beneath brows so cleanly arched that they might have been painted on; veil those eyes with lashes so long that, when lowered, they cast shadows over the pink flush of the cheeks; sketch a delicate, straight, spirited nose and nostrils slightly flared in a passionate aspiration towards sensuality; draw a regular mouth with lips parting gracefully over teeth as white as milk; tint the skin with the bloom of peaches which no hand has touched—and you will have a comprehensive picture of her entrancing face.

Her jet-black hair, naturally or artfully waved, was parted over her forehead in two thick coils which vanished behind her head, just exposing the lobes of her ears from which hung two diamonds each worth four or five thousand francs.

Exactly how the torrid life she led could possibly have

left on Marguerite's face the virginal, even childlike expression which made it distinctive, is something which we are forced to record as a fact which we cannot comprehend.

Marguerite possessed a marvellous portrait of herself by Vidal,* the only man whose pencil strokes could capture her to the life. After her death, this portrait came into my keeping for a few days and the likeness was so striking that it has helped me to furnish details for which memory alone might not have sufficed.

Some of the particulars contained in the present chapter did not become known to me until some time later, but I set them down here so as not to have to return to them once the narrative account of this woman's life has begun.

Marguerite was present at all first nights and spent each evening in the theatre or at the ball. Whenever a new play was performed, you could be sure of seeing her there with three things which she always had with her and which always occupied the ledge of her box in the stalls: her opera-glasses, a box of sweets and a bunch of camellias.

For twenty-five days in every month the camellias were white, and for five they were red. No one ever knew the reason for this variation in colour which I mention but cannot explain, and which those who frequented the theatres where she was seen most often, and her friends too, had noticed as I had.

Marguerite had never been seen with any flowers but camellias. Because of this, her florist, Madame Barjon, had finally taken to calling her the Lady of the Camellias, and the name had remained with her.*

Like all who move in certain social circles in Paris, I knew further that Marguerite had been the mistress of the most fashionable young men, that she admitted the fact openly, and that they themselves boasted of it. Which only went to show that lovers and mistress were well pleased with each other.

However, for some three years previously, ever since a visit she had made to Bagnères,* she was said to be living with just one man, an elderly foreign duke* who was fabulously wealthy and had attempted to detach her as far as possible from her old life. This she seems to have been happy enough to go along with.

Here is what I have been told of the matter.

In the spring of 1842, Marguerite was so weak, so altered in her looks, that the doctors had ordered her to take the waters. She accordingly set out for Bagnères.

Among the other sufferers there, was the Duke's daughter who not only had the same complaint but a face so like Marguerite's that they could have been taken for sisters. The fact was that the young Duchess was in the tertiary stage of consumption and, only days after Marguerite's arrival, she succumbed.

One morning the Duke, who had remained at Bagnères just as people will remain on ground where a piece of their heart lies buried, caught sight of Marguerite as she turned a corner of a gravel walk.

It seemed as though he was seeing the spirit of his dead child and, going up to her, he took both her hands, embraced her tearfully and, without asking who she was, begged leave to call on her and to love in her person the living image of his dead daughter.

Marguerite, alone at Bagnères with her maid, and in any case having nothing to lose by compromising herself, granted the Duke what he asked.

Now there were a number of people at Bagnères who knew her, and they made a point of calling on the Duke to inform him of Mademoiselle Gautier's true situation. It was a terrible blow for the old man, for any resemblance with his daughter stopped there. But it was too late. The young woman had become an emotional necessity, his only pretext and his sole reason for living.

He did not reproach her, he had no right to, but he did ask her if she felt that she could change her way of life, and, in exchange for this sacrifice, offered all the compensations she could want. She agreed.

It should be said that at this juncture Marguerite, who was by nature somewhat highly strung, was seriously ill. Her past appeared to her to be one of the major causes of her illness, and a kind of superstition led her to hope that God would allow her to keep her beauty and her health in exchange for her repentance and conversion.

And indeed the waters, the walks, healthy fatigue and sleep had almost restored her fully by the end of that summer.

The Duke accompanied Marguerite to Paris, where he continued to call on her as at Bagnères.

This liaison, of which the true origin and true motive were known to no one, gave rise here to a great deal of talk, since the Duke, known hitherto as an enormously wealthy man, now began to acquire a name for prodigality.

The relationship between the old Duke and the young woman was put down to the salacity which is frequently found in rich old men. People imagined all manner of things, except the truth.

The truth was that the affection of this father for Marguerite was a feeling so chaste, that anything more than a closeness of hearts would have seemed incestuous in his eyes. Never once had he said a single word to her that his daughter could not have heard.

The last thing we wish is to make our heroine seem anything other than what she was. We shall say therefore that, as long as she remained at Bagnères, the promise given to the Duke had not been difficult to keep, and she had kept it. But once she was back in Paris, it seemed to her, accustomed as she was to a life of dissipation, balls and even orgies, that her new-found solitude, broken only by the periodic visits of the Duke, would make her die of boredom, and the scorching winds of her former life blew hot on both her head and her heart.

Add to this that Marguerite had returned from her travels more beautiful than she had ever been, that she was twenty years old and that her illness, subdued but far from conquered, continued to stir in her those feverish desires which are almost invariably a result of consumptive disorders.

The Duke was therefore sadly grieved the day his friends, constantly on the watch for scandalous indiscretions on the part of the young woman with whom he was, they said, compromising himself, called to inform him, indeed to prove

to him that at those times when she could count on his not
appearing, she was in the habit of receiving other visitors,
and that these visitors often stayed until the following
morning.

When the Duke questioned her, Marguerite admitted
everything, and, without a second thought, advised him not
to concern himself with her any more, saying she did not
have the strength to keep faith with the pledges she had
given, and adding that she had no wish to go on receiving
the liberalities of a man whom she was deceiving.

The Duke stayed away for a week, but this was as long as
he could manage. One week later to the day, he came and
implored Marguerite to take him back, promising to accept
her as she was, provided that he could see her, and swearing
that he would die before he uttered a single word of
reproach.

This was how things stood three months after Marguerite's return, that is, in November or December 1842.

III

On the 16th, at one o'clock, I made my way to the rue
d'Antin.

The raised voices of the auctioneers could be heard from
the carriage entrance.

The apartment was filled with inquisitive spectators.

All the famous names from the world of fashionable vice
were there. They were being slyly observed by a number of
society ladies who had again used the sale as a pretext for
claiming the right to see, at close quarters, women in whose
company they would not otherwise have had occasion to
find themselves, and whose easy pleasures they perhaps
secretly envied.

The Duchesse de F*** rubbed shoulders with Mademoiselle A***, one of the sorriest specimens of our modern
courtesans; the Marquise de T*** shrank from buying an
item of furniture for which the bidding was led by Madame
D***, the most elegant and most celebrated adulteress of
our age; the Duc d'Y***, who is believed in Madrid to be

ruining himself in Paris, and in Paris to be ruining himself in Madrid, and who, when all is said and done, cannot even spend all his income, while continuing to chat with Madame M***, one of our wittiest tale-tellers, who occasionally agrees to write down what she says and to sign what she writes, was exchanging confidential glances with Madame de N***, the beauty who may be regularly seen driving on the Champs-Élysées, dressed almost invariably in pink or blue, in a carriage drawn by two large black horses sold to her by Tony for ten thousand francs . . . and paid for in full; lastly, Mademoiselle R***,* who by sheer talent makes twice what ladies of fashion make with their dowries, and three times as much as what the rest make out of their love affairs, had come in spite of the cold to make a few purchases, and it was not she who attracted the fewest eyes.

We could go on quoting the initials of many of those who had gathered in that drawing-room and who were not a little astonished at the company they kept; but we should, we fear, weary the reader.

Suffice it to say that everyone was in the highest spirits and that, of all the women there, many had known the dead girl and gave no sign that they remembered her.

There was much loud laughter; the auctioneers shouted at the tops of their voices; the dealers who had crowded on to the benches placed in front of the auction tables called vainly for silence in which to conduct their business in peace. Never was a gathering more varied and more uproarious.

I slipped unobtrusively into the middle of the distressing tumult, saddened to think that all this was taking place next to the very room where the unfortunate creature whose furniture was being sold up to pay her debts, had breathed her last. Having come to observe rather than to buy, I watched the faces of the tradesmen who had forced the sale and whose features lit up each time an item reached a price they had never dared hope for.

Honest men all, who had speculated in the prostitution of this woman, had obtained a one-hundred per cent return on her, had dogged the last moments of her life with writs, and came after she was dead to claim both the fruits of their honourable calculations and the interest accruing on the shameful credit they had given her.

How right were the Ancients who had one God for merchants and thieves!

Dresses, Indian shawls, jewels, came under the hammer at an unbelievable rate. None of it took my fancy, and I waited on.

Suddenly I heard a voice shout:

'A book, fully bound, gilt-edges, entitled: *Manon Lescaut*.* There's something written on the first page: ten francs.'

'Twelve,' said a voice, after a longish silence.

'Fifteen,' I said.

Why? I had no idea. No doubt for that 'something written'.

'Fifteen,' repeated the auctioneer.

'Thirty,' said the first bidder, in a tone which seemed to defy anybody to go higher.

It was becoming a fight.

'Thirty-five!' I cried, in the same tone of voice.

'Forty.'

'Fifty.'

'Sixty.'

'A hundred.'

I confess that if I had set out to cause a stir, I would have succeeded completely, for my last bid was followed by a great silence, and people stared at me to see who this man was who seemed so intent on possessing the volume.

Apparently the tone in which I had made my latest bid was enough for my opponent: he chose therefore to abandon a struggle which would have served only to cost me ten times what the book was worth and, with a bow, he said very graciously but a little late:

'It's yours, sir.'

No other bids were forthcoming, and the book was knocked down to me.

Since I feared a new onset of obstinacy which my vanity might conceivably have borne but which would have assuredly proved too much for my purse, I gave my name, asked for the volume to be put aside and left by the stairs. I must have greatly intrigued the onlookers who, having witnessed this scene, doubtless wondered why on earth I had gone there to pay a hundred francs for a book that I could have got anywhere for ten or fifteen at most.

An hour later, I had sent round for my purchase.

On the first page, written in ink in an elegant hand, was the dedication of the person who had given the book. This dedication consisted simply of these words:

'Manon to Marguerite,
Humility.'

It was signed: Armand Duval.

What did this word 'Humility' mean?

Was it that Manon, in the opinion of this Monsieur Armand Duval, acknowledged Marguerite as her superior in debauchery or in true love?

The second interpretation seemed the more likely, for the first was impertinently frank, and Marguerite could never have accepted it, whatever opinion she had of herself.

I went out again and thought no more of the book until that night, when I retired to bed.

Manon Lescaut is a truly touching story every detail of which is familiar to me and yet, whenever I hold a copy in my hand, an instinctive feeling for it draws me on. I open it and for the hundredth time I live again with the abbé Prévost's heroine. Now, his heroine is so lifelike that I feel that I have met her. In my new circumstances, the kind of comparison drawn between her and Marguerite added an unexpected edge to my reading, and my forbearance was swelled with pity, almost love, for the poor girl, the disposal of whose estate I could thank for possessing the volume. Manon died in a desert, it is true, but in the terms of the man who loved her with all the strength of his soul and who, when she was dead, dug a grave for her, watered it with his tears and buried his heart with her; whereas Marguerite, a sinner like Manon, and perhaps as truly converted as she, had died surrounded by fabulous luxury, if I could believe

what I had seen, on the bed of her own past, but no less lost
in the desert of the heart which is much more arid, much
vaster and far more pitiless than the one in which Manon
had been interred.

Indeed Marguerite, as I had learned from friends informed
of the circumstances of her final moments, had seen no true
consolation settle at her bedside during the two months
when she lay slowly and painfully dying.

Then, from Manon and Marguerite, my thoughts turned
to those women whom I knew and whom I could see rushing
gaily towards the same almost invariable death.

Poor creatures! If it is wrong to love them, the least one
can do is to pity them. You pity the blind man who has
never seen the light of day, the deaf man who has never
heard the harmonies of nature, the mute who has never
found a voice for his soul, and yet, under the specious
pretext of decency, you will not pity that blindness of heart,
deafness of soul and dumbness of conscience which turn the
brains of poor, desperate women and prevent them, despite
themselves, from seeing goodness, hearing the Lord and
speaking the pure language of love and religion.

Hugo wrote *Marion Delorme*, Musset wrote *Bernerette*,
Alexandre Dumas wrote *Fernande*.* Thinkers and poets
throughout the ages have offered the courtesan the oblation
of their mercy and, on occasion, some great man has brought
them back to the fold through the gift of his love and even
his name. If I dwell on this point, it is because among
those who will read these pages, many may already be about
to throw down a book in which they fear they will see nothing but an apology for vice and prostitution, and doubtless
the youth of the present author is a contributing factor in
providing grounds for their fears. Let those who are of such
a mind be undeceived. Let them read on, if such fears alone
gave them pause.

I am quite simply persuaded of a principle which states
that: To any woman whose education has not imparted
knowledge of goodness, God almost invariably opens up
two paths which will lead her back to it; these paths are
suffering and love. They are rocky paths; women who follow

them will cut their feet and graze their hands, but will at the same time leave the gaudy rags of vice hanging on the briars which line the road, and shall reach their journey's end in that naked state for which no one need feel shame in the sight of the Lord.

Any who encounter these brave wayfarers are duty bound to comfort them and to say to all the world that they have encountered them, for by proclaiming the news they show the way.

It is not a simple matter of erecting two signposts at the gateway to life, one bearing the inscription: 'The Way of Goodness' and the other carrying this warning: 'The Way of Evil', and of saying to those who come: 'Choose!' Each of us, like Christ himself, must point to those paths which will redirect from the second way to the first the steps of those who have allowed themselves to be tempted by the approach roads; and above all let not the beginning of these paths be too painful, nor appear too difficult of access.

Christianity is ever-present, with its wonderful parable of the prodigal son, to urge us to counsels of forbearance and forgiveness. Jesus was full of love for souls of women wounded by the passions of men, and He loved to bind their wounds, drawing from those same wounds the balm which would heal them. Thus he said to Mary Magdalene: 'Your sins, which are many, shall be forgiven, because you loved much'—a sublime pardon which was to awaken a sublime faith.

Why should we judge more strictly than Christ? Why, clinging stubbornly to the opinions of the world which waxes hard so that we shall think it strong, why should we too turn away souls that bleed from wounds oozing with the evil of their past, like infected blood from a sick body, as they wait only for a friendly hand to bind them up and restore them to a convalescent heart?

It is to my generation that I speak, to those for whom the theories of Monsieur de Voltaire* are, happily, defunct, to those who, like myself, can see that humanity has, these fifteen years past, been engaged in one of its boldest leaps forward. The knowledge of good and evil is ours forever;

religion is rebuilding, the respect for holy things has been restored to us, and, if the world is not yet wholly good, then at least it is becoming better. The efforts of all intelligent men tend to the same goal, and all those firm in purpose are yoked to the same principle: let us be good, let us be young, let us be true! Evil is but vanity: let us take pride in Goodness and, above all, let us not despair. Let us not scorn the woman who is neither mother nor sister nor daughter nor wife. Let us not limit respect to the family alone nor reduce forbearance to mere egoism. Since there is more rejoicing in heaven for the repentance of one sinner than for a hundred just men who have never sinned, let us try to give heaven cause to rejoice. Heaven may repay us with interest. Let us leave along our way the charity of our forgiveness for those whom earthly desires have brought low, who shall perhaps be saved by hope in heaven and, as wise old dames say when they prescribe remedies of their own making, if it does no good then at least it can do no harm.

In truth, it must seem very forward of me to seek to derive such great results from the slender subject which I treat; but I am of those who believe that the whole is in the part.* The child is small, and yet he is father to the man; the brain is cramped, and yet it is the seat of thought; the eye is but a point, yet it encompasses leagues of space.

IV

Two days later, the sale was completely over. It had realized one hundred and fifty thousand francs.*

The creditors had divided two thirds among themselves and the family—a sister and a young nephew—had inherited the rest.

The sister's eyes had opened wide when the agent had written telling her that she had come into fifty thousand francs.

It was six or seven years since this young woman had set eyes on her sister who had disappeared one day without anyone ever discovering, either from her or through other people, anything whatsoever about her life from the time of her disappearance.

So she had now arrived post-haste in Paris, and great was the astonishment of those who had known Marguerite when they saw that her sole heir was a hearty, good-looking country girl who, up to that moment, had never set foot outside her village.

Her fortune had been made at a stroke, without her having the least idea of the source from which it had so unexpectedly materialized.

She returned, I have since been told, to her part of the country, bearing away from her sister's death a deep sadness which was, however, eased by an investment at four and a half per cent which she had just made.

All these happenings, which had gone the rounds of Paris, the mother town of scandal, were beginning to be forgotten, and I myself was forgetting quite what my part in events had been, when something occurred which led to my becoming acquainted with the whole of Marguerite's life, and put in my way particulars so affecting that I was seized with an urge to write this story and now do so.

The apartment, empty now of the furniture which had all been auctioned off, had been to let for three or four days when one morning there was a ring at my door.

My servant, or rather the porter who acted as my servant, went to see who it was and brought me a visiting card, saying that the person who had handed it to him wished to speak to me.

I glanced at the card and there I saw these two words: Armand Duval.

I tried to recall where I had seen the name, and then I remembered the fly-leaf of the copy of *Manon Lescaut*.

What could the person who had given the book to Marguerite want with me? I said that the gentleman who was waiting should be shown in at once.

The next moment I saw a young man with fair hair, tall, pale, wearing travelling clothes which looked as though they had not been off his back for several days and which, on his arrival in Paris, he had not even taken the trouble to brush down, for he was covered in dust.

Monsieur Duval, deeply agitated, made no attempt to hide his feelings, and it was with tears in his eyes and a trembling in his voice that he said:

'Please excuse my visit and these clothes; not simply because young men do not stand much on ceremony with each other, but because I wanted to see you so badly today that I have not even taken time to stop off at the hotel where I set my luggage, and have rushed straight here, dreading even so, early as it is, that I should miss you.'

I begged Monsieur Duval to sit down by the fire, which he did, taking from his pocket a handkerchief with which he momentarily hid his face.

'You must be wondering,' he resumed with a melancholy sigh, 'what a stranger can want with you at such an hour, dressed in such clothes and weeping like this. I have come, quite simply, to ask you a great favour.'

'Say on. I am at your service.'

'Were you present at the Marguerite Gautier auction?'

As he said this, the emotion which the young man had held in check was for an instant stronger than he, and he was obliged to put his hands to his eyes.

'I must appear very ridiculous to you,' he added, 'forgive me this too, and please believe that I shall never forget the patience with which you are good enough to listen.'

'Well,' I replied, 'if a service which it seems I can do for you will in some small way ease the pain that you feel, tell me at once in what way I can help, and you will find in me a man happy to oblige.'

Monsieur Duval's grief was affecting and, even had I felt differently, I should still have wished to be agreeable to him.

He then said:

'Did you buy anything at Marguerite's sale?'

'Yes. A book.'

'*Manon Lescaut?*'

'That's right.'

'Do you still have it?'

'It's in my bedroom.'

At this, Armand Duval looked as though a great weight had been taken from his shoulders, and he thanked me as though I had already begun to render him a service simply by holding on to the volume.

I got up, went to fetch the book from my bedroom and handed it to him.

'This is it,' said he, glancing at the dedication on the first page and riffling through the rest, 'this is it.'

And two large tears fell on to the open pages.

'May I ask,' he said, raising his eyes to me and making no effort now to hide the fact that he had wept and was near to tears once more, 'if you are greatly attached to this book?'

'Why do you ask?'

'Because I have come to ask you to surrender it to me.'

'Forgive my curiosity,' I said next, 'but it was you, then, who gave it to Marguerite Gautier?'

'It was I.'

'The book is yours. Take it. I am happy to be able to restore it to you.'

'But,' continued Monsieur Duval with embarrassment, 'the least I can do is to give you what you paid for it.'

'Please take it as a gift. The price fetched by a single volume in a sale like that is a trifle, and I can't even remember how much I gave for it.'

'You gave a hundred francs for it.'

'You are quite right,' said I, embarrassed in my turn, 'how did you know?'

'Quite simple. I hoped to reach Paris in time for Marguerite's sale, but got back only this morning. I was absolutely determined to have something that had been hers, and I went directly to the auctioneer's to ask if I might inspect the list of items sold and of the buyers' names. I saw that this volume had been bought by you, and I resolved to beg you to let me have it, though the price you paid for it did make me fear that you yourself associated some memory with possession of the book.'

In speaking thus, Armand clearly seemed to be afraid that I had known Marguerite in the way that he had known her.

I hastened to reassure him.

'I knew Mademoiselle Gautier by sight only,' I said. 'Her death made the sort of impression on me that the death of any pretty woman he has had pleasure in meeting makes on any young man. I wished to buy something at her sale, and took it into my head to bid for this volume, I don't know why, for the satisfaction of annoying a man who was bent on getting it and seemed determined to prevent it going to me. I repeat, the book is yours, and I beg you once more to accept it. This way it won't come to you as it came to me, from an auctioneer, and it will be between us the pledge of a more durable acquaintance and closer bonds.'

'Very well,' said Armand, extending his hand and grasping mine, 'I accept and shall be grateful to you for the rest of my life.'

I very much wanted to question Armand about Marguerite, for the dedication in the book, the young man's journey, his desire to possess the volume, all excited my curiosity; but I feared that by questioning my visitor, I should appear to have refused his money simply to have the right to pry into his business.

It was as though he sensed my wishes, for he said:

'Have you read the book?'

'Every word.'

'What did you make of the two lines I wrote?'

'I saw straightaway that, in your eyes, the poor girl to whom you had given the book did not belong in the usual category, for I could not bring myself to see the lines simply as a conventional compliment.'

'And you were right. That girl was an angel. Here,' he said, 'read this letter.'

And he handed me a sheet of paper which, by the look of it, had been read many times over.

I opened it. This is what it said:

'My dear Armand, I have received your letter. You are still good, and I thank God for it. Yes, my dear, I am ill, and mine is the sort of illness which spares no one; but the concern which you are generous enough still to show for me greatly eases my sufferings. I expect I shall doubtless not live long enough to have the happiness of grasping the hand which wrote the kindly letter I have just received; its words would cure me, if anything could. I shall not see you, for I am very close to death, and hundreds of leagues separate you from me. My poor friend! the Marguerite you knew is sadly altered, and it is perhaps better that you do not see her again than see her as she is. You ask if I forgive you; oh! with all my heart, my dear, for the hurt you sought to do me was but a token of the love you bore me. I have kept my bed now for a month, and so precious to me is your good opinion, that each day I write a little more of a journal of my life from the moment we parted until the moment when I shall be no longer able to hold my pen.

If the interest you take in me is real, Armand, then on your return, go and see Julie Duprat. She will place this journal in your keeping. In it you will find the reasons and the excuse for what has passed between us. Julie is very good to me. We often talk about you. She was here when your letter came, and we wept together as we read it.

Should I not hear from you, she has been entrusted with seeing that you get these papers on your return to France. Do not be grateful to me. Returning each day to the only happy moments of my life does me enormous good and if, as you read, you find the past exonerated in my words, I for my part find in them a never-ending solace.

I would like to leave you something by which you would always remember me, but everything I own has been seized, and nothing belongs to me.

Do you understand, my dear? I am going to die, and from my bedroom I can hear the footsteps of the watchman my creditors have placed in the drawing-room to see that nothing is removed and to ensure that if I do not die, I shall be left with nothing. We must hope that they will wait for the end before they sell me up.

Oh! how pitiless men are! or rather, for I am wrong, it is God who is just and unbending.

And so, my love, you will have to come to my sale and buy something, for if I were to put aside the smallest item for you and they heard of it, they would be quite capable of prosecuting you for misappropriating distrained goods.

How sad the life I now leave!

How good God would be if He granted that I should see you again before I die! Since the chances are remote, adieu, my dear; forgive me if I do not write more, for those who say they will cure me bleed me to exhaustion, and my hand refuses to write another line.

Marguerite Gautier.'

And indeed, the last few words were scarcely legible.

I gave the letter back to Armand who had doubtless read it over in his thoughts while I had been reading it on the paper, for as he took it he said:

'Who would ever believe that a kept woman wrote that!' And deeply affected by his memories, he stared for some time at the writing of the letter before finally putting it to his lips.

'And when I think,' he went on, 'that she died before I saw her again, and that I shall see her no more; when I think that she did for me what no sister could ever have done—I cannot forgive myself for having let her die like that.

Dead! dead! thinking of me, writing and saying my name, poor dear Marguerite!'

And Armand, giving free expression to his thoughts and tears, held out his hand to me and continued:

'People would think me very childish if they saw me grieving like this for the death of such a woman; but people could not know what I made that woman suffer, how cruel I was, how good and uncomplaining she was. I believed that it was for me to forgive her, and today I find myself unworthy of the pardon she bestows on me. Oh! I would gladly give ten years of my life to be able to spend one hour weeping at her feet.'

It is always difficult to comfort a grief that one does not share, and yet so keenly did I feel for this young man who confided his sorrows with such frankness, that I felt that a few words of mine would not be unwelcome to him, and I said:

'Have you no relatives, no friends? Take hope. Go and see them for they will comfort you, whereas I can only pity you.'

'You are right,' he said, rising to his feet and striding around my bedroom, 'I am boring you. Forgive me, I was forgetting that my grief must mean little to you, and that I trespass upon your patience with a matter which neither can nor should concern you in the slightest.'

'No, you misunderstand me. I am entirely at your disposal; only I regret I am unable to calm your sorrow. If the company of myself and my friends can beguile your thoughts, if you need me in any way, I would like you to know how very happy I would be to help.'

'Forgive me, forgive me,' he said, 'grief magnifies the feelings. Allow me to stay a few minutes more, long enough to dry my eyes so that idlers in the street shall not stare to see a grown man weeping as though he were a freak. You've made me very happy by giving me this book; I'll never know how to repay the debt I owe you.'

'By granting me a little of your friendship,' I told Armand, 'and by telling me the cause of your sorrow. There is consolation in speaking of one's suffering.'

'You are right. But today my need for tears is too great, and what I said would make no sense. Some day I shall acquaint you with the story, and you shall judge whether I am right to mourn the poor girl. And now,' he added, rubbing his eyes one last time and looking at himself in mirror, 'tell me that you do not think me too foolish, and say you give me leave to call on you again.'

The look in the eyes of this young man was good and gentle; I was almost tempted to embrace him.

For his part, his eyes began again to cloud with tears; he saw that I noticed them and he turned his glance away from me.

'Come now,' I told him, 'take heart.'

'Goodbye,' he said.

And, making an extraordinary effort not to weep, he fled rather than left my apartment.

I lifted the curtain at my window and saw him get into the cab which was waiting at the door; but he was hardly inside when he burst into tears and buried his face in his handkerchief.

V

A CONSIDERABLE time elapsed without my hearing a word about Armand, but on the other hand the subject of Marguerite had come up a great deal.

I do not know if you have noticed, but it only takes the name of someone who should in all likelihood have remained unknown or at least of no particular interest to you, to be pronounced once in your hearing, for all sorts of details to collect round that name, and for you then to have all your friends speak about a subject of which they had never spoken to you before. Next thing, you discover that the person in question was there, just out of range, all the while. You realize that your paths have crossed many times without your noticing, and you find in the events which others recount some tangible link or affinity with certain events in your own past. I had not quite reached that point with Marguerite, since I had seen her, met her, knew her by her face and habits. Yet ever since the auction, her name had cropped up so frequently in my hearing and, in the circumstances which I have related in the previous chapter, her name had become associated with sorrow so profound, that my surprise had gone on growing and my curiosity had increased.

The result was that now I never approached any friends, with whom I had never spoken of Marguerite, without saying:

'Did you know someone called Marguerite Gautier?'

'The Lady of the Camellias?'

'That's her.'

'Rather!'

These 'Rather!' sometimes came with smiles which left no possible doubt as to their meaning.

'Well, what kind of girl was she?' I would go on.

'A very decent sort.'

'Is that all?'

'Heavens! I should hope so. A few more brains and perhaps a bit more heart than the rest of them.'

'But you know nothing particular about her?'

'She ruined Baron de G***.'

'Anyone else?'

'She was the mistress of the old Duke de ***.'

'Was she really his mistress?'

'That's what they say: at any rate, he gave her a great deal of money.'

Always the same general details.

But I would have been interested to learn a little about the affair between Marguerite and Armand.

One day, I chanced upon one of those men who live habitually on intimate terms with the most notorious courtesans. I questioned him.

'Did you know Marguerite Gautier?'

The answer was that same 'Rather!'

'What sort of girl was she?'

'A fine-looking, good-hearted type. Her death was a great sadness to me.'

'She had a lover called Armand Duval, didn't she?'

'Tall chap with fair hair?'

'That's him.'

'Yes, she did.'

'And what was this Armand like?'

'A young fellow who threw away the little he had on her, I believe, and was forced to give her up. They say it affected his reason.'

'What about her?'

'She loved him very much too, they also say, but as girls of her sort love. You should never ask more of them than they can give.'

'What became of Armand?'

'Couldn't say. We didn't know him all that well. He

stayed five or six months with Marguerite, in the country. When she came back to town, he went off somewhere.'

'And you haven't seen him since?'

'Never.'

I had not seen Armand again either. I had begun to wonder if, the day he called on me, the recent news of Marguerite's death had not exaggerated the love he had once felt for her and therefore his grief, and I told myself that perhaps, in forgetting the dead girl, he had also forgotten his promise to return to see me.

Such a hypothesis would have been plausible enough with anybody else, but in Armand's despair there had been a note of real sincerity and, moving from one extreme to the other, I imagined that his grief could well have turned into sickness and that, if I had not heard from him, then it was because he was ill, dead even.

Despite myself, I still felt an interest in this young man. It may be that my interest was not without an element of selfishness; perhaps I had glimpsed a touching love story behind his grief, perhaps, in short, my desire to be acquainted with it loomed large in the concern I felt about Armand's silence.

Since Monsieur Duval did not return to see me, I resolved to go to him. A pretext was not difficult to find. Unfortunately, I did not know his address, and of all those I had questioned, no one had been able to tell me what it was.

I went to the rue d'Antin. Perhaps Marguerite's porter knew where Armand lived. There had been a change of porter. He did not know any more than I did. I then asked in which cemetery Mademoiselle Gautier had been buried. It was Montmartre cemetery.*

April had come round again, the weather was fine, the graves would no longer have the mournful, desolate look which winter gives them; in a word, it was already warm enough for the living to remember the dead and visit them. I went to the cemetery, telling myself: 'One quick look at Marguerite's grave, and I shall know whether Armand is still grieving and perhaps discover what has become of him.'

I entered the keeper's lodge and asked him if, on the 22nd of the month of February, a woman named Marguerite Gautier had not been buried in Montmartre cemetery.

The man looked through a fat ledger in which the names of all those who come to their final place of rest are entered and given a number, and he answered that on 22 February, at noon, a woman of that name had indeed been interred.

I asked if he could get someone to take me to the grave for, without a guide, there is no way of finding one's way around this city of the dead which has its streets like the cities of the living. The keeper called a gardener, to whom he gave the necessary details but who cut him short, saying: 'I know, I know . . . Oh! that grave is easy enough to pick out,' he went on, turning to me.

'Why?' I said.

'Because it's got different flowers from all the others.'

'Are you the person who looks after it?'

'Yes, sir, and I could only wish all relatives took as good care of the departed as the young man who asked me to look after that one.'

Several turnings later, the gardener stopped and said:

'Here we are.'

And indeed, before my eyes, were flowers arranged in a square which no one would ever have taken for a grave if a white marble stone with a name on it had not proclaimed it to be so.

This marble block was set upright, iron railings marked the boundary of the plot that had been bought, and every inch of ground was covered with white camellias.

'What do you say to that?' said the gardener.

'It's very beautiful.'

'And every time a camellia withers, my orders are to put another one in its place.'

'And who gave you your orders?'

'A young chap who cried a lot the first time he came. An old gentleman friend of the departed, I'll be bound, because they do say she was a bit of a one, you know. I hear tell she was very bonny. Did you know her, sir?'

'Yes.'

'Like the other chap,' the gardener said with a knowing grin.

'No, I never spoke to her.'

'But you've come to see her here; that's very nice of you, because people who come to see the poor girl don't exactly clutter up the cemetery.'

'So no one comes?'

'Nobody, except that young chap who came once.'

'Just once?'

'Yes, sir.'

'And he never returned?'

'No, but he'll come as soon as he gets back.'

'He's away travelling, then?'

'Yes.'

'And do you know where he is?'

'I do believe he's gone to see Mademoiselle Gautier's sister.'

'What's he doing there?'

'He's going to ask authorization to exhume the body and have it put somewhere else.'

'Why shouldn't he leave her here?'

'You know, sir, people get queer ideas about the departed. See it all the time, we do. This plot was bought for five years only, and that young chap wants a plot in perpetuity and a larger bit of ground: in the new part would be best.'

'What do you call the new part?'

'The new plots that are being sold just now, to your left. If the cemetery had always been kept like it is nowadays, there wouldn't have been another like it in the world; but there's still a lot to do before it's just like it should be. And then, folk are so queer.'

'What do you mean?'

'I mean that there's people who even bring their pride in here. Take this Mademoiselle Gautier. Seems she'd been around a bit, if you'll pardon the expression. She's dead now, is that poor young woman; there's as much left of her as of other women you couldn't say a word against whose resting places we keep watering every day. Well now, when the relatives of them as are buried next to her found out who she was, blow me if they didn't up and say they was against putting her here, and that there ought to be ground set apart for women of her sort, like there is for the poor. Ever hear the like of it? I told them straight, I did; very well-to-do folks who can't even come four times a year to pay their respects to their departed. They bring their own flowers and some flowers they are too, are very particular about arranging upkeep for them as they say they mourn, inscribe on their tombstones the tears they never shed, and are very fussy about who is buried next door. Believe me if you like, sir, I didn't know this young lady, I've no idea what she got up to. But I tell you, I love that poor little girl and I take good care of her, and I let her have the camellias at a very fair price. Of all the departed, she's my favourite. Here, sir, we're obliged to love the dead, for we're kept so busy that we hardly have time to love anything else.'

I looked at this man, and some of my readers will understand, without my having to explain it to them, what I felt as I heard his words.

He sensed my feelings, no doubt, for he went on:

'They say there were gents who ruined themselves for that girl, and that she had lovers who worshipped her; well, when I think that there's not one comes and buys her a single flower, then I say that it's peculiar and sad. Though this one can't complain. She's got a grave, and if there's only one as remembers her, he does right by the others as well. But we've got poor girls here of the same sort and the same age that get thrown into a pauper's grave, and it breaks my heart when I hear their poor bodies drop into the earth. And not a soul looks out for them once they're dead! It's not always very cheery, this job of ours, especially when you've got a bit of feeling left in you. But what do you expect? I can't help it. I got a fine-looking grown-up daughter of twenty, and whenever some dead girl her age is brought in, I think of her, and be it some great lady or a trollop, I can't help being upset.

But I expect I'm wearying you with all this talk, and you didn't come here to listen to me going on. I was told to take you to Mademoiselle Gautier's grave and here you are. Is there anything else I can do for you?'

'Do you know Monsieuer Duval's address?' I asked the man.

'Yes, he lives in the rue de ***, or at least that's where I went to get paid for all the flowers you see here.'

'Thank you, my man.'

I cast a final glance at the flower-strewn grave whose depths, despite myself, I would have gladly plumbed for a sight of what the earth had done with the beautful creature who had been lowered into it, and then I came away, feeling very sad.

'Do you want to see Monsieur Duval, sir?' continued the gardener, who walked at my side.

'Yes.'

'The thing is, I'm pretty near certain that he's not back yet. Otherwise I'd have seen him here already.'

'So you are convinced that he hasn't forgotten Marguerite?'

'Not just convinced, I'd bet anything that this wanting to move her to another grave is his way of wanting to see her again.'

'How do you mean?'

'The first thing he said when he came to the cemetery was: "What do I have to do to see her again?" That can only happen if the body is shifted to another grave, and I told him all about the formalities that have to be gone through to secure a transfer, because, you know, before bodies can be moved from one grave to another, they must be identified, and only the family can authorize the operation which has to be supervised by a police superintendent. It was to get this authorization that Monsieur Duval went to see Mademoiselle Gautier's sister, and his first call will obviously be on us.'

We had arrived at the cemetery gates; I thanked the gardener again, slipping a few coins into his hand, and I went round to the address he had given me.

Armand was not back.

I left a note for him, asking him to come and see me as

soon as he arrived, or to let me know where I might find him.

The following morning, I received a letter from Duval which informed me of his return and asked me to drop by, adding that, being worn out by fatigue, it was impossible for him to go out.

VI

I FOUND Armand in bed.

When he saw me, he held out his hand. It was hot.

'You have a temperature,' I said.

'It won't come to anything—the fatigue of a hurried journey, nothing more.'

'Have you come from Marguerite's sister's?'

'Yes, who told you?'

'I just know. And did you get what you wanted?'

'Yes, again. But who told you about my journey and my reasons for making it?'

'The gardener at the cemetery.'

'You saw the grave?'

I scarcely dared answer, for the tone of these words convinced me that the person who had said them was still in the grip of the same distress I had already witnessed, and that every time his thoughts or something that someone said brought him back to this painful subject, then for a long time to come, his emotions would go on getting the better of his will.

I settled therefore for answering with a nod.

'Has he taken good care of it?' continued Armand.

Two large tears rolled down the sick man's cheeks, and he turned his head away to hide them from me. I pretended not to notice and tried to change the subject.

'You've been away three weeks,' I said.

Armand passed his hand over his eyes and answered:

'Three weeks exactly.'

'It was a long journey, then.'

'Oh! I wasn't travelling all the time. I was ill for a fortnight. Otherwise I would have been back long ago; but I'd only just arrived when a bout of fever got me and I was forced to keep to my room.'

'And you set off again without being fully fit.'

'If I'd stayed another week in that place, I would have died there.'

'But now you're back, you must look after yourself. Your friends will call to see you. And I shall be the first among them, if you'll allow me.'

'In two hours I shall get up.'

'This is most unwise!'

'I must.'

'What have you to do that's so urgent?'

'I have a call to pay on the superintendent of police.'

'Why not let someone else see to a matter that may well make you more ill than you are now?'

'It's the only thing that can make me well. I must see her. Ever since I've known she was dead, and especially since seeing her grave, I haven't been able to sleep. I cannot conceive that the woman I left so young and beautiful can really be dead. I must check for myself. I have to see what God has done with a being I loved so very much, and then perhaps the loathesomeness of the sight will chase away the despair of my memories; you will come with me, won't you . . . unless you'd find it too tiresome?'

'What did her sister tell you?'

'Nothing. She seemed very surprised that a stranger should wish to buy a burial plot and have a headstone put up to Marguerite, and she signed the authorization I asked her for at once.'

'Take my advice: wait until you are properly fit before having the body transferred.'

'Oh! Don't worry: I shall be strong. Anyway I should go mad if I didn't get what I've decided over and done with as quickly as possible: the need to see it through has become part of my grief. I swear to you that I shall not rest easy until I've seen Marguerite. It may be a craving of the fever which burns in me, a dream born of sleepless nights, an effect of my ravings; but even if I have to become a Trappist monk first to manage it, then like Monsieur de Rancé, once I have seen, I shall see.'*

'I can understand that,' I told Armand, 'and you have my complete support. Did you see Julie Duprat?'

'Yes. Oh, I saw her the day I got back, the first time I returned.'

'Did she hand over the papers which Marguerite had left for you?'

'They're here.'

Armand pulled a roll of papers from beneath his pillow, then put it back immediately.

'I know what these papers contain by heart,' he said. 'These last three weeks, I have re-read them ten times each day. You shall read them too, but later, when I'm calmer and can make you understand how much feeling and love this confession reveals. For the moment, I have a favour to ask you.'

'What is it?'

'You have a carriage downstairs?'

'Yes.'

'Well, would you be so good as to take my passport, call at the bureau and ask if they are holding any letters for me poste restante? My father and my sister must have written to me here in Paris, and I left in such a hurry that I didn't take time to see before I set off. When you get back, we'll go together to inform the police superintendent of tomorrow's ceremony.'

Armand handed me his passport and I went round to the rue Jean-Jacques-Rousseau.*

There were two letters in the name of Duval. I picked them up and returned.

When I reappeared, Armand was fully dressed and ready to go out.

'Thank you,' he said, taking the letters. 'Yes,' he added, after glancing at the addresses, 'yes, they are from my father and my sister. They must have been totally mystified by my silence.'

He opened the letters and guessed at, rather than read

their contents, for each was four pages long, and after a moment he folded them up again.

'Let's be off,' he said, 'I'll reply tomorrow.'

We went to see the superintendent of police, and Armand handed over Marguerite's sister's letter of attorney.

In return, the superintendent gave him an advice note for the cemetery keeper; it was agreed that the transfer of the remains should take place the following day at ten in the morning, that I should come and collect him an hour beforehand and that we would drive to the cemetery together.*

I too was curious to be present at the spectacle, and I confess I did not sleep that night.

Judging by the thoughts which assailed me, it must have been a long night for Armand.

When I entered his apartment at nine the following morning, he was horribly pale, but appeared calm.

He smiled at me and held out his hand.

His candles had burned right down and, before leaving, Armand picked up a very thick letter, addressed to his father, which had doubtless been the confidant of the night's reflections.

Half an hour later, we were at Montmartre.

The superintendent was already waiting for us.

We made our way slowly in the direction of Marguerite's grave. The superintendent led the way, Armand and I following a few paces behind.

From time to time, I felt my companion's arm tremble convulsively, as though a series of shudders had suddenly coursed through him. When this happened, I would look at him; he understood my look and smiled at me, but from the time we left his apartment we had not exchanged a single word.

Armand stopped just short of the grave to wipe his face which was streaming with large drops of perspiration.

I took advantage of the halt to catch my breath, for I myself felt as though my heart was being squeezed in a vice.

Why is it that we should find a mixture of pain and pleasure in sights of this kind? By the time we reached the grave, the gardener had taken the pots of flowers away, the

LA DAME AUX CAMÉLIAS   37

iron railings had been removed and two men were digging with picks.

Armand leaned against a tree and watched.

The whole of his life seemed to be concentrated in those eyes of his.

Suddenly ,one of the picks grated on a stone.

At the sound, Armand recoiled as though from an electric shock, and he grasped my hand with such strength that he hurt me.

One grave-digger took a wide shovel and little by little emptied the grave; when there remained only the stones which are always used to cover the coffin, he threw them out one by one.

I kept an eye on Armand, for I was afraid that his sensations, which he was visibly repressing, might get the better of him at any moment; but he went on watching, his eyes fixed and staring like a madman's, and a slight twitching of the cheeks and lips was the only indication of a violent nervous crisis.

For my own part, I can say only one thing: that I regretted having come.

When the coffin was completely exposed, the superintendent said to the grave-diggers:

'Open it up.'

The men obeyed, as though it were the most ordinary thing in the world.

The coffin was made of oak, and they set about unscrewing the upper panel which served as a lid. The dampness of the earth had rusted the screws, and it was not without considerable effort that the coffin was opened. A foul odour emerged, despite the aromatic herbs with which it had been strewn.

'Dear God! Dear God!' Armand murmured, and he grew paler than ever,

The grave-diggers themselves stepped back a pace.

A large white winding-sheet covered the corpse and partly outlined its misshapen contours. This shroud had been completely eaten away at one end, and allowed one of the dead woman's feet to protrude.

I was very near to feeling sick, and even now as I write these lines, the memory of this scene comes back to me in all its solemn reality.

'Let's get on with it,' said the superintendent.

At this, one of the men reached out his hand, began unstitching the shroud and, seizing it by one end, suddenly uncovered Marguerite's face.

It was terrible to behold and it is horrible to relate.

The eyes were simply two holes, the lips had gone, and the white teeth were clenched. The long, dry, black hair was stuck over the temples and partly veiled the green hollows of the cheeks, and yet in this face I recognized the pink and white, vivacious face which I had seen so often.

Armand, helpless to avert his eyes from her countenance, had put his handkerchief to his mouth and was biting on it.

As for me, I felt as though my head was being constricted by an iron band: a mist settled over my eyes, my ears were filled with buzzing noises, and it was as much as I could manage to open a small bottle I had brought with me just in case, and take deep breaths of the salts which it contained.

At the height of my dizziness, I heard the superintendent say to Monsieur Duval:

'Do you identify the body?'

'Yes,' the young man answered dully.

'All right, close it up and take it away,' the superintendent said.

The grave-diggers pulled the shroud back over the dead woman's face, closed up the coffin, took one end each and headed for the spot which had been pointed out to them.

Armand did not move. His eyes were riveted on the empty grave: he was as pale as the corpse which we had just seen . . . He might have been turned to stone.

I saw what would happen when, away from this scene, his grief subsided and would consequently be no longer able to sustain him.

I went up to the superintendent.

'Is the presence of this gentleman,' I said, gesturing towards Armand, 'required for anything else?'

'No,' he said, 'and I would strongly advise you to take him away, for he seems to be unwell.'

'Come,' I said to Armand, taking him by the arm.

'What?' he said, looking at me as though he did not recognize me.

'It's over,' I added, 'you must come away, my friend. You look pale, you're cold, you'll kill yourself with such emotions.'

'You're right, let's go,' he replied mechanically, but without moving one step.

So I took him by the arm and dragged him away.

He allowed himself to be led off like a little child, merely muttering from time to time:

'Did you see the eyes?'

And he turned round as though the sight of them had called him back.

But his stride became jerky; he no longer seemed capable of walking without staggering; his teeth chattered, his hands were cold, violent nervous convulsions took possession of his entire body.

I spoke to him; he did not reply.

It was as much as he could do to allow himself to be led.

At the gate, we found a cab. And none too soon.

He had scarcely sat down inside, when the trembling grew stronger, and he had a severe nervous seizure. Through it, his fears of alarming me made him murmur as he pressed my hand:

'It's nothing, nothing, I simply want to weep.'

And I heard him take deep breaths, and the blood rushed to his eyes, but the tears would not come.

I made him inhale from the smelling bottle which had helped me and, by the time we reached his apartment, only the trembling was still in evidence.

I put him to bed with the help of his servant, ordered a large fire to be lit in his bedroom, and hurried off to fetch my own doctor to whom I explained what had just happened.

He came at once.

Armand was blue in the face. He was raving and stammering disconnected words through which only the name of Marguerite could be distinctly heard.

'How is he?' I asked the doctor when he had examined the patient.

'Well now, he has brain fever, no more and no less, and it's as well for him. For I do believe that otherwise, God forgive me, he would have gone mad. Fortunately, his physical sickness will drive out his mental sickness, and most likely in a month he will be out of danger from both of them.'

VII

ILLNESSES like the one to which Armand had succumbed have at least this much to be said for them: they either kill you at once or let themselves be conquered very quickly.

A fortnight after the events which I have just recounted, Armand was convalescing very satisfactorily, and we were bound by a firm friendship. I had scarcely left his sick room throughout the whole time of his illness.

Spring had dispensed its flowers, leaves, birds, and harmonies in abundance, and my friend's window cheerfully overlooked his garden which wafted its healthy draughts up to him.

The doctor had allowed him to get up, and we often sat talking by the open window at that hour of the day when the sun is at its warmest, between noon and two o'clock.

I studiously avoided speaking to him of Marguerite, for I was still afraid that the name would reawaken some sad memory which slumbered beneath the sick man's apparent calm. But Armand, on the contrary, seemed to take pleasure in speaking of her—not as he had done previously, with tears in his eyes, but with a gentle smile which allayed my fears for his state of mind.

I had noticed that, since his last visit to the cemetery and the spectacle which had been responsible for causing his serious breakdown, the measure of his mental anguish seemed to have been taken by his physical illness, and

Marguerite's death had ceased to present itself through the eyes of the past. A kind of solace had come with the certainty he had acquired and, to drive off the sombre image which often thrust itself into his mind, he plunged into the happier memories of his affair with Marguerite and appeared willing to recall no others.

His body was too exhausted by his attack of fever, and even by its treatment, to allow his mind to acknowledge any violent emotions, and despite himself the universal joy of spring by which Armand was surrounded directed his thoughts to happier images.

All this time, he had stubbornly refused to inform his family of the peril he was in, and when the danger was past, his father still knew nothing of his illness.

One evening, we had remained longer by the window than usual. The weather had been superb and the sun was setting in a brilliant twilight of blue and gold. Although we were in Paris, the greenery around us seemed to cut us off from the world, and only the rare sound of a passing carriage from time to time disturbed our conversation.

'It was about this time of year, and during the evening of a day like today, that I first met Marguerite,' said Armand, heeding his own thoughts rather than what I was saying.

I made no reply.

Then he turned to me and said:

'But I must tell you the story; you shall turn it into a book which no one will believe, though it may be interesting to write.'

'You shall tell it to me some other time, my friend,' I told him, 'you are still not well enough.'

'The evening is warm, I have eaten my breast of chicken,' he said with a smile; 'I am not the least feverish, we have nothing else to do, I shall tell you everything.'

'Since you are so set on it, I'll listen.'

'It's a very simple tale,' he then added, 'and I shall tell it in the order in which it happened. If at some stage you do make something of it, you are perfectly free to tell it another way.'

Here is what he told me, and I have scarcely changed a word of his moving story.

Yes (Armand went on, letting his head fall against the back of his armchair), yes, it was on an evening like this! I had spent the day in the country with one of my friends, Gaston R***. We had returned to Paris in the evening and, for want of anything better to do, had gone to the Théâtre des Variétés.*

During one of the intervals, we left our seats and, in the corridor, we saw a tall woman whom my friend greeted with a bow.

'Who was that you just bowed to?' I asked him.

'Marguerite Gautier,' he replied.

'It strikes me she is very much changed, for I didn't recognize her,' I said with a tremor which you will understand in a moment.

'She's been ill. The poor girl's not long for this world.'

I recall these words as though they had been said to me yesterday.

Now, my friend, I must tell you that for two years past, whenever I met her, the sight of that girl had always made a strange impression on me.

Without knowing why, I paled and my heart beat violently. I have a friend who dabbles in the occult, and he would call what I felt an affinity of fluids; I myself believe quite simply that I was destined to fall in love with Marguerite, and that this was a presentiment.

The fact remains that she made a strong impression on me. Several of my friends had seen how I reacted, and they had hooted with laughter when they realized from what quarter that impression came.

The first time I had seen her was in the Place de la Bourse, outside Susse's.* An open barouche was standing there, and a woman in white had stepped out of it. A murmur of admiration had greeted her as she entered the shop. For my part, I stood rooted to the spot from the time she went in until the moment she came out. Through the windows, I watched her in the shop as she chose what she had come to buy. I could have gone in, but I did not dare. I had no idea what sort of woman she was and was afraid that she would guess my reason for entering the shop and be offended. However I did not believe that I was destined ever to see her again.

She was elegantly dressed; she wore a muslin dress with full panels, a square Indian shawl embroidered at the corners with gold thread and silk flowers, a Leghorn straw hat and a single bracelet, one of those thick gold chains which were then just beginning to be fashionable.

She got into her barouche and drove off.

One of the shop-assistants remained in the doorway with his eyes following the carriage of his elegant customer. I went up to him and asked him to tell me the woman's name.

'That's Mademoiselle Marguerite Gautier,' he replied.

I did not dare ask him for her address and I walked away.

The memory of this vision—for, truly, vision it was—did not fade from my mind like many other visions I had already seen, and I searched everywhere for this woman in white so regal in her beauty.

A few days after this, there was a big production at the Opéra-Comique.* I went along. The first person I saw, in a stage-box in the balcony, was Marguerite Gautier.

The young man I was with recognized her too, for he said, mentioning her by name:

'Take a look at that pretty creature.'

Just then, Marguerite turned her opera glasses in our direction, saw my friend, smiled at him and gestured that he was to come and pay his respects.

'I'll go along and wish her a pleasant evening,' he told me, 'I'll be back in a moment.'

I could not help myself saying: 'You're a lucky man!'

'In what way?'

'Going to see that woman.'

'Are you in love with her?'

'No,' I said, reddening, for I really did not know how I stood in the matter, 'but I would like to get to know her.'

'Come with me, I'll introduce you.'

'Ask her permission first.'

'Oh, nonsense! There's no need to be formal with her. Come on.'

These words of his were hurtful to me. I trembled at the thought that I should learn for certain that Marguerite was not worthy of my feelings for her.

In a book by Alphonse Karr, entitled *Am Rauchen,** there is a man who, one evening, follows a very elegant woman with whom he has fallen in love at first sight, so beautiful is she. Merely to kiss the hand of this woman, he feels he has strength enough for any undertaking, the will to conquer all and the courage to do anything. He scarcely dares glance at the slim ankles which she reveals in her efforts to avoid dirtying her dress as it drags on the ground. As he is dreaming of the things he would do to possess her, she stops him at a street corner and asks if he would like to come upstairs with her.

He turns his head away, crosses the street and returns home sadly.

I now remembered this study and I, who would gladly have suffered for her, was afraid that this woman might accept me too quickly and give me too promptly a love which I should have desired to earn through some long delay or great sacrifice. Of such stuff are we men made; and it is fortunate indeed that the imagination indulges the senses with fancies of this kind, and that the desires of the body make such concessions to the dreams of the soul.

So, had someone said to me: 'You shall have this woman tonight and tomorrow you shall be put to death', I would have accepted. Had I been told: 'Give her ten louis and she's yours', I should have refused and wept like a child who sees the castle which he had glimpsed during the night vanish as he wakes.

However, I wanted to meet her; it was one way, indeed the only way, of knowing how I stood with her.

So I told my friend that I insisted that she should give her permission for him to introduce me, and I loitered in the corridors, reflecting that any moment now she would see me and that I should not know what sort of expression to assume when she looked at me.

I tried to string together in advance the words I would speak to her.

What sublime nonsense love is!

A moment later, my friend came down again.

'She's expecting us,' he said.

'Is she alone?' I asked.

'She's with another woman.'

'There aren't any men?'

'No.'

'Let's go.'

My friend made for the theatre exit.

'Hold on, it's not that way,' I said to him.

'We're going to buy some sweets. She asked for some.'

We went into a confectioner's in the galleries of the Passage de l'Opéra.*

I would have gladly bought the whole shop, and was casting round for what could be made into a selection, when my friend said:

'A pound of sugared raisins.'

'Are you sure she likes them?'

'She never eats any other kind of sweets, it's a well-known fact.'

When we were outside, he went on: 'Now then. Have you any idea what sort of woman I am about to introduce you to? Don't imagine you'll be meeting a duchess, she's just a kept woman—none more kept, my dear fellow. Don't be shy, just say whatever comes into your head.'

'Er, of course,' I stammered, and followed him, telling myself that I was about to be cured of my passion.

When I stepped into her box, Marguerite was laughing uproariously.

I would have preferred her to be sad.

My friend introduced me. Marguerite inclined her head slightly and said:

'Where are my sweets?'

'Here you are.'

As she took them, she looked straight at me. I lowered my eyes and blushed.

She leaned across, whispered something into her companion's ear, and both of them burst out laughing.

It was only too obvious that I was the cause of their mirth: my embarrassment deepened as a result. At the time, I had as a mistress a little middle-class girl, very loving, very cloying, who made me laugh with her sentimentality and sad billets-doux. I realized how much I must have hurt her by the hurt I now felt and, for the space of five minutes, I loved her as never woman was loved.

Marguerite ate her raisins without paying any further attention to me.

Having introduced me, my friend had no intention of leaving me in this ridiculous position.

'Marguerite,' he said, 'you shouldn't be surprised if Monsieur Duval does not speak to you. You have such an effect on him that he cannot think of a thing to say.'

'I rather believe that this gentleman came here with you because you found it tiresome to come alone.'

'Were that true,' I said in turn, 'I would not have asked Ernest to obtain your leave to introduce me.'

'Perhaps it was just a way of putting off the fatal moment.'

Anyone who has spent any time at all in the company of girls of Marguerite's sort is quite aware of what pleasure they take in making misplaced remarks and teasing men they meet for the first time. It is no doubt a way of levelling the scores for the humiliations which they are often forced to undergo at the hands of the men they see every day.

So, if you wish to give as good as you get, you need to have a certain familiarity with their world, and this I did not have. Moreover, the idea that I had formed of Marguerite made her jesting seem worse to me. Nothing about this woman left me indifferent. And so, getting to my feet, I said to her with a faltering in my voice which I found impossible to conceal completely:

'If that is what you think of me, Madame, all that remains for me is to ask you to forgive my indiscretion and to take my leave, assuring you that it will not happen again.'

Thereupon, I bowed and left.

I had scarcely closed the door when I heard a third burst of laughter. I would dearly have wished for someone to try to elbow me out of his way at that moment.

I returned to my seat in the stalls.

The three knocks were sounded for the curtain to rise.

Ernest rejoined me.

'What a way to behave!' he said to me as he took his seat. 'They think you're mad.'

'What did Marguerite say after I left?'

'She laughed, and declared she'd never seen anybody funnier than you. But you mustn't think you're beaten. Just don't do women like that the honour of taking them seriously. They have no idea what good taste and manners are; it's just the same with pet dogs that have perfume poured over them—they can't stand the smell, and go off and roll in some gutter.'

'Anyway, what's it to me?' I said, trying to sound off-hand. 'I shan't ever see that woman again, and even if I liked her before I got to know her, everything is very different now that I have met her.'

'Bah! I wouldn't be at all surprised one of these days to see you sitting in the back of her box and hear people saying how you're ruining yourself on her account. Still, you may be right, she has no manners, but she'd make an attractive mistress all the same.'

Fortunately, the curtain went up and my friend said no more. It would be quite impossible for me to tell you what play was performed. All I remember was that, from time to time, I would glance up at the box I had left so abruptly, and that the shapes of new callers kept appearing in quick succession.

However, I was far from having put Marguerite out of my mind. Another thought now took possession of me. I felt that I had both her insulting behaviour and my discomfiture to expunge; I told myself that, even if I had to spend everything I had, I would have that woman and would take by right the place which I had vacated so quickly.

Some time before the final curtain, Marguerite and her companion left their box.

Despite myself, I rose from my seat.

'You're not leaving?' said Ernest.

'Yes.'

'Why?'

Just then, he noticed that the box was empty.

'Go on, then,' he said, 'and good luck, or rather, better luck!'

I left.

On the stairs, I heard the rustle of dresses and the sound of voices. I stepped to one side and, without being observed, saw the two women walk by me together with the two young men who were escorting them.

In the colonnade outside the theatre, a young servant came up to the two women.

'Go and tell the coachman to wait outside the Café Anglais,'* said Marguerite, 'we shall go as far as there on foot.'

A few minutes later, as I loitered on the boulevard, I saw Marguerite at the window of one of the restaurant's large rooms: leaning on the balcony, she was pulling the petals one by one off the camellias in her bouquet.

One of the two men was leaning over her shoulder and was whispering to her.

I found a seat in the Maison d'Or,* in one of the private rooms on the first floor, and did not take my eyes off the window in question.

At one in the morning, Marguerite got into her carriage with her three friends.

I took a cab and followed.

The carriage stopped outside 9 rue d'Antin.

Marguerite got out and went up to her apartment alone.

No doubt this happened by chance, but this chance made me very happy.

From that day on, I often encountered Marguerite at the theatre or on the Champs-Élysées. She was unchangingly gay and I was unfailingly quickened by the same emotions.

But then a fortnight passed without my seeing her anywhere. I ran into Gaston and asked him about her.

'The poor girl is very ill,' he replied.

'What's the matter with her?'

'The matter with her is that she's got consumption and, because she lives the sort of life which is not calculated to make her better, she's in bed and dying.'

The heart is a strange thing; I was almost glad she was ill.

Every day, I called to have the latest news of the patient, though without signing the book or leaving my card. It was in this way that I learned of her convalescence and her departure for Bagnères.

Then time went by, and the impression she had made on me, if not the memory, seemed to fade gradually from my mind. I travelled; new intimacies, old habits and work took the place of thoughts of her, and whenever I did think back to that first encounter, I preferred to see the whole thing as one of those passions which one experiences in youth, and laughs at in no time at all.

Besides, there would have been no merit in vanquishing her memory, for I had lost sight of Marguerite since the time of her departure and, as I have explained to you, when she passed close to me in the passageway of the Théâtre des Variétés, I did not recognize her.

She was wearing a veil, it is true; but two years earlier, however many veils she had been wearing, I would not have needed to see her to recognize her: I would have known her instinctively.

This did not prevent my heart from racing when I realized that it was her. The two years spent without seeing her, together with the effects which this separation seemed to have brought about, were sent up in the same smoke by a single touch of her dress.

VIII

HOWEVER (Armand went on after a pause), though I realized full well that I was still in love, I felt stronger than I had before and, in my desire to be with Marguerite again, there was also a determination to make her see that I now had the upper hand.

Many are the paths the heart will tread, and many the excuses its finds, that it may reach what it desires!

I could not therefore remain in the corridors any longer, and went back to my seat in the pit, quickly glancing around the auditorium as I did so to see in which box she was sitting.

She was in the stage-box in the stalls, and quite alone. She looked much altered, as I have told you, and I could not detect on her lips her old unconcerned smile. She had been ill; she still was.

Although it was already April, she was still dressed for winter and wore velvet.

I looked at her so insistently that my eye caught hers.

She considered me for a moment or two, reached for her opera-glasses to get a better look, and clearly thought she recognized me, though without being able to say positively who I was. For when she lowered her opera-glasses, a smile —that captivating greeting of women—strayed across her lips in reply to the acknowledgement she seemed to expect from me. But I made no response, as a way of asserting an advantage over her and of appearing to have forgotten while she remembered.

Believing that she was mistaken, she turned her head away.

The curtain went up.

I have seen Marguerite many times in the theatre. I never once saw her pay the slightest attention to what was happening on stage.

For me too, the play was of very little interest, and I had eyes only for her while doing my utmost to ensure that she did not notice.

It was thus that I observed her exchanging looks with the person who occupied the box opposite hers; I raised my eyes to this other box, and in it recognized a woman with whom I was reasonably familiar.

She had once been a kept woman, had tried the stage, had not succeeded and, counting on her contacts among the fashionable women of Paris, had gone into business and opened a milliner's shop.

In her, I saw a way of contriving a meeting with Marguerite, and I took advantage of a moment when she was looking in my direction to wish her a pleasant evening with hands and eyes.

What I had foreseen happened: she summoned me to her box.

Prudence Duvernoy*—such was the apt name of the milliner—was one of those ample women of forty with whom no great diplomatic subtleties are required to get them to say what you wish to know, especially when what you wish to know is as simple as what I had to ask.

Seizing a moment when she was inaugurating a new round of signals with Marguerite, I asked her:

'Who's that you're watching?'

'Marguerite Gautier.'

'Do you know her?'

'Yes, I'm her milliner, and she's a neighbour of mine.'

'So you live in the rue d'Antin.'

'In number 7. The window of her dressing-room looks on to the window of mine.'

'They say she's a charming girl.'

'Don't you know her?'

'No, but I'd very much like to.'

'Do you want me to tell her to come across to our box?'

'No, I'd prefer you to introduce me to her.'

'At her place?'

'Yes.'

'That's more difficult.'

'Why?'

'Because she's under the protection of an old Duke who is very jealous.'

' "Protection", how charming.'

'Yes, protection,' Prudence went on. 'Poor old thing. He'd be hard put to it to be her lover.'

Prudence then related how Marguerite had become acquainted with the Duke at Bagnères.

'And that is why,' I continued, 'she's here on her own?'

'That's right.'

'But who'll drive her home?'

'He will.'

'So he'll come and fetch her?'

'Any minute now.'

'And who's taking you home?'

'Nobody.'

'Allow me.'

'But you're with a friend, I believe.'

'Allow us, then.'

'What's this friend of yours?'

'He's a charming fellow, very witty. He'll be delighted to meet you.'

'Very well, then, it's agreed, all four of us will leave after this play is finished, for I've seen the last one before.'*

'Splendid. I'll go and tell my friend.'

'Off you go.'

I was on the point of leaving when Prudence said: 'Ah! there's the Duke just coming into Marguerite's box.'

I looked.

And indeed, a man of seventy had just sat down behind the young woman and was giving her a bag of sweets which, with a smile, she began to eat at once, and then she pushed them across the front ledge of her box with a sign to Prudence which could be translated as:

'Do you want some?'

'No,' was Prudence's reply.

Marguerite retrieved the bag and, turning round, began chatting to the Duke.

So exact an account of all these detailed happenings must seem very childish, but anything connected with that girl is so present in my recollection that I cannot help but remember it all now.

I went down to let Gaston know what I had just arranged for him and me.

He was game.

We left our seats in the stalls and made for Madame Duvernoy's box.

We had barely opened the door leading out of the orchestra stalls when we were forced to stop and make way for Marguerite and the Duke who were leaving.

I would have given ten years of my life to have been in that old man's shoes.

When he reached the boulevard, he handed her up into a phaeton, which he drove himself, and they disappeared, borne away at a trot by two superb horses.

We entered Prudence's box.

When the play was over, we went down and got an ordinary cab which took us to 7 rue d'Antin. When we reached her door, Prudence invited us up to view her business premises, which we had never seen before, and of which she seemed very proud. You can imagine how eagerly I accepted.

I felt that I was imperceptibly drawing closer to Marguerite. It was not long before I had turned the conversation round to her.

'Is the old Duke with your neighbour?' I asked Prudence.

'No, no; she's most likely on her own.'

'But she'll be terribly bored,' said Gaston.

'We usually spend our evenings together or, when she gets home, she calls down to me. She never goes to bed before two in the morning. She can't get to sleep before then.'

'Why not?'

'Because she's got consumption, and she's almost always feverish.'

'Doesn't she have any lovers?' I asked.

'I never see anybody staying behind when I leave, but I don't say there's nobody comes after I've gone. When I'm there of an evening, I often come across a certain Count de N**** who thinks he can get somewhere with her by paying calls at eleven o'clock and sending her all the jewels she could possibly want; but she can't stand the sight of him. She's wrong, he's a very rich young man. I tell her from time to time, not that it does a bit of good: "My dear child, he's just the man for you!" She listens to me well enough ordinarily, but then she turns her back on me and answers that he is too stupid. He may be stupid, I grant you, but he'd set her up on a good footing, whereas that old Duke could die from one day to the next. Old men are selfish; his family are always on at him about his affection for Marguerite: that makes two reasons why he'll not leave her a penny. I'm forever going on at her about it, but she says that there'll still be time enough to say yes to the Count when the Duke's dead.

'It's not always much fun,' Prudence continued, 'living the way she does. I can tell you it wouldn't do for me. I'd send the old relic packing. He's a dull old thing: he calls her his daughter, looks after her like a little child, and is forever hovering round her. I'm pretty sure that even at this time of night one of his servants is hanging about in the street to see who comes out and especially who goes in.'

'Oh, poor Marguerite!' said Gaston, sitting down at the piano and playing a waltz, 'I had no idea. Still, I have noticed that she hasn't seemed as jolly for some time now.'

'Hush!' said Prudence, pricking up her ears.

Gaston stopped.

'She's calling me, I think.'

We listened.

And indeed, a voice was calling Prudence.

'Come along, gentlemen, off with you,' Madame Duvernoy told us.

'So that's what you mean by hospitality,' Gaston said laughingly, 'we'll be off when it suits us.'

'Why should we go?'

'I'm going to Marguerite's.'

'We'll wait here.'

'I won't have it.'

'In that case, we'll come with you.'

'That's even more out of the question.'

'I know Marguerite,' said Gaston, 'it's perfectly all right for me to drop in to pay my respects.'

'But Armand doesn't know her.'

'I shall introduce him.'

'Impossible.'

Once more we heard Marguerite's voice still calling Prudence.

Prudence ran into her dressing-room. I followed with Gaston. She opened the window.

We hid ourselves so that we could not be seen from outside.

'I've been calling you for ten minutes,' said Marguerite from her window in a tone that verged on the peremptory.

'What do you want with me?'

'I want you to come at once.'

'Why?'

'Because Count de N*** is still here, and he's boring me to death.'

'I can't just now.'

'What's stopping you?'

'I've got two young men here who won't go away.'

'Tell them you've got to go out.'

'I have told them.'

'Well, they can stay there; when they see you've gone, they'll leave.'

'After turning the place upside down?'

'But what do they want?'

'They want to see you.'

'What are their names?'

'You know one of them, Monsieur Gaston R***.'

'Ah, yes, I know him; and the other?'

'Monsieur Armand Duval. Don't you know him?'

'No; but bring them all the same. Anything would be better than the Count. I shall be waiting for you, so hurry.'

Marguerite shut her window, and Prudence shut hers.

Marguerite, who had for an instant recalled my face, did not remember my name. I would have been better pleased to be remembered in an unflattering light than forgotten altogether like this.

'I knew it,' said Gaston, 'I knew she'd be delighted to see us.'

'Delighted isn't the word,' answered Prudence, putting on her hat and shawl, 'she'll see you to make the Count go away. Try to be more agreeable than him, or otherwise—I know Marguerite—she'll take it out on me.'

We followed Prudence down the stairs.

I was shaking; I had a feeling that this visit would have a great influence on my life.

I was even more apprehensive than the evening I had been introduced in the box at the Opéra-Comique.

When we arrived at the door of the apartment with which you are acquainted, my heart was beating so loud that I could not think.

A few chords from a piano reached our ears.

Prudence rang the bell.

The piano stopped.

A woman, who looked rather more like a lady's companion than a maid, opened the door to us.

We passed through the drawing-room, and from the drawing-room into the parlour, which was at that time exactly as you have seen it since.

A young man was leaning against the mantelpiece.

Marguerite, seated at the piano, was letting her fingers run over the keys, starting more pieces than she finished.

Everything about the scene exuded boredom which stemmed, on the man's side, from an embarrassing awareness of his own dullness and, on the woman's, from the visit of this lugubrious personage.

Hearing Prudence's voice, Marguerite rose to her feet and, coming up to us after first exchanging a look of gratitude with Madame Duvernoy, she said to us:

'Do come in, gentlemen, you are most welcome.'

IX

'GOOD evening, my dear Gaston,' Marguerite said to my companion, 'I'm so glad to see you. Why didn't you come to my box at the Variétés?'

'I was afraid of being indiscreet.'

'Friends,' and Marguerite stressed the word, as though she wish to let it be known to all who were present that, despite the familiar way in which she greeted him, Gaston was not and had never been anything other than a friend, 'friends can never be indiscreet.'

'In that case, allow me to present Monsieur Armand Duval!'

'I've already given Prudence leave to do so.'

'I should perhaps say, madame,' I said, bowing and managing to make more or less intelligible sounds, 'I have already had the honour of being introduced to you.'

Marguerite's delightful eyes seemed to be searching among her memories, but she did not remember, or appeared not to remember.

'Madame,' I went on, 'I am grateful that you have forgotten that first meeting, for I behaved quite ridiculously and must surely have seemed very tiresome to you. It was two years ago, at the Opéra-Comique; I was with Ernest de ***.'

'Ah! Now I remember!' Marguerite went on with a smile. 'It wasn't that you were ridiculous, but I who was a tease. As I still am rather, though less so nowadays. Have you forgiven me?'

And she held out her hand which I kissed.

'It's true,' she continued. 'The fact is that I have this awful habit of wanting to embarrass people I see for the first time. It's very silly. My doctor says it's because I am highly-strung and always unwell: you must take my doctor's word for it.'

'But you look extremely well.'

'Oh! I've been very ill.'

'I know.'

'Who told you?'

'Everyone knew. I often used to come to find out how you were, and I was very happy to learn of your convalescence.'

'No one ever brought me your card.'

'I never left one.'

'Are you the young man who called every day to ask after me all the time I was ill, and would never leave his name?'

'I am.'

'Then you are more than kind, you are generous. You, Count, would never have done that,' she added, turning to Monsieur de N*** but not before giving me one of those looks with which women let you know what they think of a man.

'I have known you for only two months,' replied the Count.

'And this gentleman has known me for only five minutes. You always give the silliest answers.'

Women are pitiless with people they dislike.

The Count reddened and bit his lip.

I felt sorry for him, for he seemed just as much in love as I was, and Marguerite's callous frankness must have made him very wretched, especially in the presence of two strangers.

'You were playing something when we arrived,' I then said, to change the subject. 'Won't you give me the pleasure of treating me like an old friend, and continue?'

'Oh!' she said, settling on to the sofa and gesturing to us to sit down beside her, 'Gaston knows exactly what my playing is like. It's all very well when I'm alone with the Count, but I shouldn't wish to put you through such torture.'

'So you do favour me in this respect?' replied Monsieur de N***, with a smile intended to be subtle and ironic.

'You are quite wrong to reproach me for doing so. It's the only time I ever favour you in anything.'

It was clear that the poor fellow could not say anything right. He gave the young woman a truly beseeching look.

'Tell me, Prudence,' she continued, 'did you do what I asked?'

'Yes.'

'Good, you shall tell me all about it later. We have things to talk about, so you mustn't go until I've spoken to you.'

'I think we are intruding,' I said at this point, 'and now that we—or rather I—have managed a second introduction to expunge the memory of the first, Gaston and I will withdraw.'

'I won't hear of it; what I said wasn't intended for you. On the contrary, I'd like you to stay.'

The Count took out an extremely handsome watch which he consulted:

'Time I was going to the club,' he said.

Marguerite did not reply to this.

The Count then moved away from the mantelpiece and, coming up to her:

'Goodbye, madame.'

Marguerite rose to her feet.

'Goodbye, my dear Count, must you go so soon?'

'Yes. I fear I bore you.'

'You do not bore me today more than any other day. When shall we see you again?'

'Whenever you permit.'

'Goodbye, then!'

It was cruel of her, you will agree.

Fortunately, the Count had been brought up very correctly and had an excellent character. He simply kissed the hand which Marguerite rather nonchalantly held out to him and, after taking his leave of us, went out.

As he was stepping through the doorway, he shot a glance at Prudence.

She shrugged her shoulders in a way which said:

'Sorry, but I did all I could.'

'Nanine!' called Marguerite, 'show the Count a light!'

We heard the door open and close.

'At last!' exclaimed Marguerite as she reappeared, 'he's gone; that young man gets terribly on my nerves.'

'My dear girl,' said Prudence, 'you really are too unkind to him, he's so good to you, so thoughtful. On your mantelpiece, there's yet another watch that he's given you, and it will have set him back at least a thousand écus, I'll be bound.'

And Madame Duvernoy, who had been moving towards the mantelpiece, was now playing with the bauble as she spoke, and casting covetous looks at it.

'My dear,' said Marguerite, sitting down at her piano, 'when I weigh in one hand what he gives me and, in the other, the things he says to me, I conclude that I let him have his visits very cheaply.'

'The poor boy is in love with you.'

'If I had to listen to everybody who is in love with me, I wouldn't have the time to eat my dinner.'

And she ran her fingers over the piano, after which she turned and said to us:

'Would you like anything? I'd love a little punch.'

'And I could eat a nice piece of chicken,' said Prudence. 'Shall we have supper?'

'That's it, let's go out for supper,' said Gaston.

'No, we'll have supper here.'

She rang. Nanine appeared.

'Send out for supper.'

'What shall I order?'

'Anything you like, but be quick, as quick as you can.'

Nanine went out.

'How lovely!' said Marguerite, skipping like a child, 'we are going to have supper. How boring that idiotic Count is!'

The more I saw of this woman, the more enchanted I was. She was entrancingly beautiful. Even her thinness became her.

I was lost in contemplation.

I would be hard put to explain what was going on inside me. I was full of indulgence for the life she led, full of admiration for her beauty. Proof of her disinterestedness was provided by the fact that she could turn down a fashionable and wealthy young man who was only too ready to ruin himself for her, and this, in my eyes, acquitted her of all past faults.

There was in this woman something approaching candour. She was visibly still in the virgin stage of vice. Her confident bearing, her supple waist, her pink, flared nostrils, her large eyes faintly ringed with blue, all pointed to one of those passionate natures which give out a bouquet of sensuality, just as flasks from the Orient, however tightly sealed they might be, allow the fragrance of the fluids they contain to escape.

In short, either because it was her nature or else an effect of her state of health, her eyes flickered intermittently with flashes of desires which, if spoken, would have been a heaven-sent relevation to any man she loved. But those who had loved Marguerite were beyond counting, and those whom she had loved had not yet begun to be counted.

In other words, one could detect in this girl a virgin who had been turned into a courtesan by the merest accident of chance, and a courtesan whom the merest accident of chance could have turned into the most loving, the most pure of virgins. Marguerite still had something of a proud spirit and an urge to independence—two sentiments which, when violated, are quite capable of achieving the same results as maidenly modesty. I said nothing. It was as though my soul had flowed completely into my heart, and my heart into my eyes.

'So,' she went on suddenly, 'it was you who came for news of me when I was ill?'

'Yes.'

'You know, that is really quite sublime! And what can I do to thank you?'

'Allow me to come and call on you from time to time.'

'Come as often as you like, between five and six, and from eleven to midnight. I say, Gaston, do play the *Invitation to the Waltz!*'

'Why?'

'Firstly because I should like it, and secondly because I can never manage to play it when I'm by myself.'

'What do you find difficult with it?'

'The third part, the passage with the sharps.'

Gaston got to his feet, sat down at the piano and began to play Weber's* splendid melody, the music of which lay open on the stand.

Marguerite, with one hand resting on the piano, looked at the score, her eyes following each note which she accompanied in a soft singing voice and, when Gaston reached the passage which she had mentioned, she hummed it and played it with her fingers on the back of the piano:

'Re, mi, re, doh, re, fa, mi, re . . . that's the part I can't get. Again.'

Gaston played it again, after which Marguerite said to him:

'Now let me try.'

She took his place and played in turn; but still her stubborn fingers tripped over one or other of the notes which we have just mentioned.

'It's inconceivable,' she said with a quite childlike ring in her voice, 'that I can't manage to play this passage! You won't believe it, but sometimes I sit up working on it until two in the morning! And when I think that fool of a Count can play it without music, and admirably well at that, then I do believe that's why I get so cross with him.'

And she began again, and still with the same result.

'The hell with Weber, music and pianos!' she said, flinging the score to the other end of the room. 'Would anybody believe that I simply can't play eight sharps in a row?'

And she crossed her arms, glaring at us and stamping her foot.

The blood rushed to her cheeks and a small cough parted her lips.

'Come now,' said Prudence, who had removed her hat and was smoothing her hair in a mirror, 'you'll only get angry an make yourself ill. Let's have supper. It's much the best thing: I'm absolutely starving.'

Marguerite rang again, then she turned back to the piano and began quietly crooning a squalid song—without making any mistakes in the accompaniment.

Gaston knew the song, and they turned it into a sort of duet.

'I really wish you wouldn't sing such vulgar rubbish,' I said to Marguerite casually, making it sound like a request.

'Oh, how innocent you are!' she said, smiling and holding out her hand to me.

'It's not for my sake but yours.'

Marguerite made a gesture which meant: 'Oh! it's a long time since I had anything to do with innocence.'

At this juncture, Nanine appeared.

'Is supper ready?' asked Marguerite.

'Yes, madame, in just a moment.'

'By the by,' Prudence said to me, 'you haven't seen round the apartment. Come, I'll show you.'

As you know, the drawing-room was a marvel.

Marguerite came with us for a few steps, then she called Gaston and went with him into the dining-room to see if supper was ready.

'Hullo!' cried Prudence loudly, looking at the contents of a shelf from which she picked up a Dresden figurine, 'I didn't know you had this little chap!'

'Which one?'

'The shepherd boy holding a cage with a bird in it.'

'You can have it if you like it.'

'Oh! but I couldn't deprive you of him.'

'I wanted to give it to my maid, I think it's hideous. But since you like it, take it.'

Prudence saw only the gift and not the manner in which it was given. She put her shepherd boy to one side, and led me into the dressing-room where she showed me two miniatures which made a pair and said:

'That's Count de G*** * who was madly in love with Marguerite. He's the one who made her name. Do you know him?'

'No. And who's this?' I asked, pointing to the other miniature.

'That's the young Vicomte de L***. He had to go away.'

'Why?'

'Because he was just about ruined. Now there was somebody who really loved Marguerite!'

'And I imagine she loved him very much?'

'She's such a funny girl, you never know where you are with her. The evening of the day he went away, she went to the theatre as usual, and yet she had cried when he said goodbye.'

Just then Nanine appeared, and announced that supper was served.

When we went into the dining-room, Marguerite was leaning against one wall and Gaston, who was holding both her hands, was whispering to her.

'You're mad,' Marguerite was saying to him, 'you know perfectly well that I don't want anything to do with you. You can't wait two years after getting to know a woman like me before asking to be her lover. Women like me give ourselves at once or never. Come, gentlemen, let's eat!'

And, slipping out of Gaston's grasp, Marguerite sat him on her right, me on her left, and then said to Nanine:

'Before you sit down, go to the kitchen and tell them they're not to answer the door if anyone rings.'

This order was given at one in the morning.

We laughed, we drank, we ate a great deal at that supper-party. Within minutes, the merriment had sunk to the lowest level, and witticisms of the kind which certain smart circles find so amusing and never fail to defile the lips of those who utter them, erupted periodically to be greeted with loud acclamations by Nanine, Prudence and Marguerite. Gaston was enjoying himself unreservedly: he was a young man whose heart was in the right place, but his mind had been a little warped by the kind of people he had mixed with in his early days. At one point, I had opted to steel myself, to make my heart and my thoughts immune to the spectacle before my eyes, and to contribute my share to the jollity which seemed to be a dish on the menu. But, little by little, I cut myself off from the uproar, my glass had stayed full and I had grown almost sad as I watched this beautiful creature of twenty drink, talk like a stevedore, and laugh all the louder as what was said became more shocking.

But the merriment, this way of talking and drinking, which seemed to me to be in the other guests the effects of dissoluteness, habit and duress, appeared with Marguerite to be a need to forget, a restlessness, a nervous reaction. With each glass of champagne, her cheeks took on a feverish flush, and a cough, which had been nothing at the start of supper, eventually became sufficiently troublesome to force her head against the back of her chair and make her hold her chest with both hands each time the coughing seized her.

I felt the pain which these daily excesses must have inflicted upon so frail a constitution.

At length happened a thing which I had foreseen and dreaded. Towards the end of supper, Marguerite was taken with a fit of coughing much stronger than any she had had while I had been there. It was as though her chest was being torn to pieces from the inside. The poor girl turned purple, closed her eyes with the pain, and put her lips to a serviette which turned red with a splash of blood. Then she got up and ran into her dressing-room.

'What's up with Marguerite?' asked Gaston.

'What's up with her is that she's been laughing too much and is spitting blood,' said Prudence. 'Oh, it won't be anything, it happens every day. She'll come back. Let's just leave her alone. She prefers it that way.'

For my part, I could bear it no longer and, to the great astonishment of Prudence and Nanine who called me back, I went in to join Marguerite.

X

THE room in which she had taken refuge was lit by a single candle on a table. Lying back on a large couch, her dress undone, she held one hand on her heart and allowed the other to hang limply. On the table was a silver basin half full of water. The water was mottled with flecks of blood.

Marguerite, extremely pale and with her mouth half open, was trying to catch her breath. At times, her chest swelled in a long, indrawn sigh which, when released, seemed to afford her some slight relief and left her for a few seconds with a feeling of well-being.

I went to her—she did not stir—sat down and took the hand which was resting on the couch.

'Ah! Is it you?' she said with a smile.

My face must have looked distraught, for she added:

'Aren't you very well either?'

'I'm all right, but how about you? Are you still feeling ill?'

'Not very.' And, with a handkerchief, she wiped away the tears which the coughing had brought to her eyes. 'I'm used to it now.'

'You are killing yourself,' I said, and there was emotion in my voice. 'I wish I could be your friend, a relative, so that I could stop you harming yourself like this.'

'Ah! There's absolutely no need for you to be alarmed,' she replied bitterly. 'You can see how well the others look after me. The truth is they know there's nothing anybody can do about what I've got.'

Thereupon, she got to her feet and, taking the candle, set it on the mantelpiece and looked at herself in the mirror.

'How pale I look!' she said, refastening her dress and running her fingers through her dishevelled hair. 'Oh, who cares! Let's go back into supper. Are you coming?'

But I remained seated and did not move.

She realized just how shaken I had been by this scene, for she came up to me and, holding out her hand, she said:

'Don't be silly. Do come.'

I took her hand which I put to my lips, and despite myself I moistened it with a few pent-up tears.

'Well, now! You really are a child!' she said, as she sat down again beside me. 'There, you're crying! What's the matter?'

'I must seem very stupid to you, but what I've just seen has made me feel quite dreadful.'

'You are really very kind! But what do you expect? I can't sleep, I've got to take my mind off things for a while. And anyhow, with girls like me, if there's one more or fewer of us, what difference does it make? The doctors tell me the blood I cough is really only bronchial; I pretend I believe them, it's all I can do for them.'

'Listen, Marguerite,' I said then, with an effusion which I was unable to check, 'I don't know what sort of influence you might have over my life, but I do know this: at this moment, there is no one, not even my sister, about whom I feel more concerned than you. It's been like that ever since I first saw you. So, in Heaven's name, look after yourself properly, don't go on living as you do.'

'If I looked after myself properly, I'd die. What keeps me going is the pace of the life I lead. In any case, taking care of yourself is all well and good for society ladies who have a family and friends. But women like me are abandoned the moment we're no more use for feeding the vanity or pleasure of our lovers, and then long, empty evenings follow long, empty days. I know, believe me. I was in bed for two months; after the first three weeks, no one came to see me any more.'

'I realize that I mean nothing to you,' I went on, 'but if you wanted, I'd care for you like a brother, I wouldn't leave you and I'd make you better. And then, when you were strong enough, you could go back to the life you lead now, if that's what you wanted; but of this I am sure—you would come to prefer a quiet life which would make you happier and keep you pretty.'

'You may think like that this evening, because the wine has made you sentimental, but you wouldn't have as much patience as you say you have.'

'Let me remind you, Marguerite, that you were ill for two months and during those two months, I called every day to find out how you were.'

'That's true. But why did you never come up?'

'Because I didn't know you then.'

'But whoever observes such niceties with girls like me?'

'One always observes the niceties with any woman; at least, that's what I believe.'

'So you'd look after me?'

'Yes.'

'You'd stay by me every day?'

'Yes.'

'And even every night?'

'For as long as you weren't tired of me.'

'What would you say that was?'

'Devotion.'

'And where does this devotion come from?'

'From an irresistible attraction that draws me to you.'

'In other words you're in love with me? Just say it straight out, it's a great deal simpler.'

'I may be: but if I ever tell you some day that I do, this is not that day.'

'It would be better for you if you never said it.'

'Why?'

'Because there are only two things that can come from such an admission.'

'And they are?'

'Either I turn you down, in which case you will resent me, or I say yes, in which case you won't have much of a mistress; someone who is temperamental, ill, depressed, or gay in a way that is sadder than sorrow itself, someone who coughs blood and spends a hundred thousand francs a year—which is all very well for a rich old man like the Duke, but it's not much of a prospect for a young man like yourself. And, if it's proof you want, the fact is that all the young lovers I have ever had have never stayed around for very long.'

I did not answer: I listened. Her frankness, which seemed to verge on the confessional, and the dismal life which I half-glimpsed beneath the golden veil that covered its stark reality from which the poor girl sought escape in debauchery, drunkenness and sleepless nights, all made such an impression on me that I could not find a thing to say.

'But come,' Marguerite continued, 'we're talking foolish nonsense. Give me your hand and let's go back to the dining-room. The others must be wondering what to make of our absence.'

'Go back, if that's what you want, but please let me stay here.'

'Why?'

'Because I can't bear to see you so bright and cheerful.'

'In that case, I'll be sad.'

'Listen, Marguerite, let me tell you something which other men have no doubt told you often, something which the habit of hearing will perhaps prevent you from believing, though it is nonetheless real, something which I shall never say to you again.'

'And this something . . . ?' she said, with a smile such as young mothers smile when listening to their child being silly.

'. . . is this. From the moment I first saw you, I don't know how or why, you have occupied a place in my life. Though I've tried to drive your image out of my mind, it has always come back. Today, when I met you after two years without seeing you, you took an even stronger hold on my heart and my thoughts. Now you have received me here, now I know you and can see everything that is strange in you, the truth is that you've become indispensable to me, and I shall go out of my mind, not simply if you do not love me, but if you do not let me love you.'

'But, you wretched man, I shall say to you what Madame

D*** used to say: you must be very rich, then! You clearly have no idea that I spend six or seven thousands francs a month, and that spending this much has become necessary for my way of life; can't you see, you poor fool, that I'd ruin you in no time at all? that your family would have you declared unfit to manage your affairs to teach you not to live with creatures like me? Love me, like a good friend, but not otherwise. Come and see me, we'll laugh, we'll talk, but don't go getting ideas about my merits: they are very small. You have a kind heart, you need to be loved, you are too young and too sensitive to live in our world. Find yourself some married woman. You can see I'm a decent sort of girl, and I'm being frank with you.'

'Hello! What on earth are you pair up to?' cried Prudence, whom we had not heard coming, as she appeared at the bedroom door, her hair half undone and her dress open. In her disordered appearance, I recognized Gaston's handiwork.

'We're having a serious talk,' said Marguerite, 'leave us for a while, we'll rejoin you shortly.'

'All right, all right, talk away, my children,' said Prudence, and she left, closing the door as if to reinforce the tone in which she had spoken these last words.

'So it's agreed,' Marguerite went on, when we were alone, 'you will stop loving me.'

'I shall go away.'

'It's as bad as that?'

I had gone too far to turn back, and besides, this girl overwhelmed me. Her mixture of high spirits, sadness, ingenuousness and prostitution, the very illness which as surely heightened her sensitivity to impressions as it did her nervous reactions—everything made me see that if, from the outset, I did not gain some hold over her heedless, fickle nature, then she would be lost to me forever.

'So what you are saying is quite serious?' she said.

'Very serious.'

'But why didn't you tell me all this before?'

'When could I have told you?'

'The day after you were introduced to me at the Opéra-Comique.'

'I think you'd have received me very badly if I had come
to see you.'

'Why?'

'Because I had behaved stupidly the previous evening.'

'Yes, that's true. But all the same, you were already in
love with me then.'

'Yes.'

'None of which prevented you from going home to bed
and sleeping very soundly after the play. We all know about
great loves of that sort.'

'Now that's where you're wrong. Do you know what I did
that evening we met at the Opéra-Comique?'

'No.'

'I waited for you outside the entrance to the Café Anglais.
I followed the carriage which brought you and your friends
back here and, when I saw you get out by yourself and go
up to your apartment alone, I was very happy.'

Marguerite began to laugh.

'What are you laughing at?'

'Nothing.'

'Tell me, I beg you, or I shall think that you're laughing at
me again.'

'You won't be cross?'

'I have no right to be cross.'

'Well, there was a good reason why I should return
alone.'

'What was that?'

'There was someone waiting for me here.'

Had she stabbed me with a knife, she could not have hurt
me more. I stood up and, offering my hand, said:

'Goodbye.'

'I knew you'd be cross,' she said. 'Men have a mania for
wanting to know things that will upset them.'

'But I assure you,' I added coldly, as though I had wanted
to show that I was cured of my passion for ever, 'I assure
you that I am not cross. It was only natural that someone
should have been waiting for you, as natural as it is that
I should leave here at three in the morning.'

'Have you got someone waiting for you at home too?'

'No, but I must go.'

'Goodbye, then.'

'You are sending me away.'

'Not at all.'

'Then why do you say hurtful things?'

'What hurtful things?'

'You told me someone was waiting for you.'

'I couldn't help laughing at the thought of your being so happy to see me coming in by myself, when there was such a good reason for me to do so.'

'People often find happiness in foolish things. It is unkind to destroy their happiness when, simply by allowing it to continue, we can increase the joy of those who have discovered such happiness.'

'But what do you think I am? I am neither a virgin nor a duchess. I'd never met you before today and I don't have to justify my actions to you. Assuming that one day I become your mistress, you must realize that I've had other lovers before you. If you're going to carry on and be jealous now, what's it going to be like after—if there's ever an after! I never met a man like you.'

'That's because no man has ever loved you as I do.'

'Let's be clear about this: are you really in love with me?'

'As much as anyone could possibly love anybody, I believe.'

'And how long has this been going on?'

'Since I saw you one day get out of your barouche and go into Susse's, three years ago.'

'How wonderful, it really is! And what do I have to do to acknowledge this great love?'

'You must love me a little,' I said, with a beating heart which almost prevented me from speaking; for, despite the half-mocking smiles with which she had accompanied the whole of our conversation, it seemed to me that Marguerite was beginning to share my troubled state and that I was approaching the moment which I had been so long awaiting.

'But what about the Duke?'

'What Duke?'

'My old Duke. He's very suspicious.'

'He won't know.'

'And if he does?'

'He'll forgive you.'

'Oh no! He'll leave me and then what'll become of me?'

'You are already running that risk for someone else's sake.'

'How do you know that?'

'From the order you gave that no one should be allowed in tonight.'

'You're right; but he is a good friend.'

'Who you don't much care for, if you can close your door to him at this time of night.'

'You're in no position to criticize me since I did it to receive you and your friend.'

Imperceptibly, I had drawn closer to Marguerite, I had put my arms around her waist and could feel her supple body pressing lightly against my clasped hands.

'If you only knew how much I love you!' I whispered.

'Do you really mean it?'

'I swear it.'

'Well, if you promise to do everything I say without arguing, without finding fault or asking questions, I will love you, perhaps.'

'Whatever you ask!'

'But I warn you, I want to be free to do whatever I choose, without having to tell you anything about the life I lead. For a long time now, I've been looking for a young, easy-going lover, someone who would love me without asking questions, someone I could love without his feeling that he has any rights over me. I have never found one yet. Men, instead of being content with being freely given for long periods what they hardly dared hope to get once, are forever asking their mistresses for an account of the present, the past and even the future. As they get used to a mistress, they try to dominate her, and they become all the more demanding the more they are given. If I decide to take a new lover now, I want him to have three very rare qualities: he must be trusting, submissive and discreet.'

'Very well, I shall be everything you desire.'

'We'll see.'

'And when will we see?'

'Later.'

'Why?'

'Because,' said Marguerite, slipping out of my arms and taking a single bloom from a large bunch of red camellias which had been delivered that morning and putting it in my buttonhole, 'because you can't always implement treaties the day they are signed.'

The meaning is plain.

'And when shall I see you again?' I said, taking her in my arms.

'When this camellia is a different colour.'

'And when will it be a different colour.'

'Tomorrow, between eleven and midnight. Are you happy?'

'How can you ask?'

'Not a word of any of this to your friend, nor to Prudence, nor anyone.'

'I promise.'

'Now kiss me, and let's go back to the dining-room.'

She proffered her lips, smoothed her hair again and then she, singing as she went, and I, who was madly elated, left the room together.

In the drawing-room, she stopped and said softly:

'It must seem strange to you that I should appear ready to accept you straightaway like this: do you know the reason?'

'The reason,' she went on, taking my hand and pressing it to her heart which I could feel beating violently and insistently, 'the reason is that since I shall not live as long as the others, I have promised myself that I shall live my life faster.'

'Don't talk to me like this, I implore you.'

'Oh, cheer up!' she went on, laughing. 'However little time I have to live, I'll live long enough to see your love out.'

And, singing, she went into the dining-room.

'Where's Nanine?' she said, seeing Gaston and Prudence alone.

'Asleep in your bedroom, waiting for you to go to bed,' answered Prudence.

'Poor girl, I'm wearing her out! Come, gentlemen, be off with you, it's high time.'

Ten minutes later, Gaston and I were on our way out. Marguerite squeezed my hand as she said goodbye and remained with Prudence.

'Well?' asked Gaston, when we were outside, 'what do you make of Marguerite?'

'She's an angel and I'm mad about her.'

'I thought so. Did you tell her?'

'Yes.'

'And did she promise to believe you?'

'No.'

'She's not like Prudence, then.'

'Did she promise to believe you?'

'She did more than that, old man! You wouldn't think so, but that Duvernoy woman is still a bit of all right, even if she is on the large side!'

XI

AT this point in his story, Armand paused.

'Would you close the window?' he said to me, 'I'm beginning to feel cold. While you're doing that, I shall go to bed.'

I closed the window. Armand, who was still very weak, took off his dressing-gown and got into bed, allowing his head to rest on the pillow for a few moments, like a man wearied by a long march or troubled by painful memories.

'Perhaps you have talked too much,' I said. 'Would you like me to go and leave you to sleep? You can tell me the end of the story some other day.'

'Do you find it tedious?'

'On the contrary.'

'In that case, I shall go on with it; if you were to leave me on my own, I shouldn't sleep.'

*

When I reached home, he went on (without having to gather his thoughts together, so fresh in his mind were all these particulars), I did not go to bed. I began to reflect on the day's happenings. The meeting, the introduction, Marguerite's pledge to me, had all been so sudden, so unexpected, that there were moments when I thought I had been dreaming. However, it was not the first time a girl like Marguerite had promised herself to a man, with her promise to take effect on the very day after she was asked to give it.

But though I tried to keep this thought uppermost in my mind, that first impression produced in me by my future mistress had been so powerful that it lingered still. Stubbornly, I continued to refuse to think of her as a rather loose girl like all the others and, with the vanity so commonly found in all men, I was ready to believe that she was as unshakeably attracted to me as I was to her.

However, I was personally acquainted with examples which showed the exact opposite, and I had often heard it said that Marguerite's love had sunk to the level of a commodity, the price of which fluctuates according to the season.

But, yet again, how was such a reputation to be reconciled with the repeated refusals given to the young Count we had found in her apartment? You will say that she did not like him and that, since she was already being kept in some splendour by the Duke, then if she was prepared to go to the length of taking another lover, she would naturally prefer to have a man she did like. But if that were so, why did she not want Gaston, who was charming, witty and rich, and why did she appear to want me, whom she had found so ridiculous the first time she saw me?

It is true that events lasting only a moment may achieve more than courtships which last a year.

Among those who had been present at the supper, I was the only one to have been anxious on seeing her leave the table. I had followed her. I had been so affected that I had been unable to hide my feelings. I had wept as I kissed her hand. These circumstances, together with my daily calls during the two months of her illness, had perhaps led her to

regard me as a man quite different from those she had hitherto known, and she may have told herself that she could very
well grant to such devoted love what she had granted on so
many other occasions, and it could well have been that
none of it meant much more to her than that.

All these suppositions, as you can see, were plausible
enough. But whatever the reason for her consenting, one
thing was sure: she had consented.

Now, I was in love with Marguerite, I was going to have
her: I could not ask any more of her. Yet, I repeat, though
she was a kept woman, I had in my mind turned my love—
to poeticize her, perhaps—into such a hopeless passion, that
the closer the moment came when I would have no further
need for hope, the more uncertain I became.

I did not close my eyes that night.

I did not know what to think. I was half mad. At some
moments, I could not believe I was handsome enough nor
rich enough nor sufficiently fashionable to possess a woman
like her; at others, I felt swollen with vanity at the thought
that she was to be mine. Then I would start fearing that
Marguerite had no more than a passing fancy for me which
would last only a few days and, scenting disaster for me
if the affair ended abruptly, I told myself that I would do
better not to call on her that evening but go away and tell
her my fears in a letter. From thinking this, I moved to limit-
less hopes and boundless optimism. I dreamed impossible
dreams for the future; I told myself that this girl would
have me to thank for her spiritual and physical salvation,
that I would spend the whole of my life by her side, and that
her love would make me happier than all the most virginal
of loves in creation.

In short, I should be quite incapable of repeating to you
the countless thoughts which rose from my heart to my head
and faded slowly into the sleep which overpowered me when
it grew light.

When I woke, it was two o'clock. The weather was
magnificent. I cannot recall that life has ever seemed to me
as exquisite or as full. Memories of the previous evening
came back into my mind, untainted, unimpeded and gaily

escorted by my hopes for the night to come. I dressed quickly. I felt contented and capable of the finest deeds. From time to time, my heart fluttered in my chest with joy and love. A pleasant feverishness quickened my blood. I had stopped worrying about the arguments which had filled my mind before I had fallen asleep. I saw only the result. I thought only of the moment when I should see Marguerite again.

Staying at home was out of the question. My bedroom seemed too small to contain my happiness; I needed the whole of nature to give vent to my feelings.

I went out.

I walked by the rue d'Antin. Marguerite's brougham was waiting at her door; I headed in the direction of the Champs-Élysées. I loved all the people I met, even though I had never seen any of them before.

Love brings out the best in us!

After an hour of walking from the Marly Horses to the Rond-Point and from the Rond-Point to the Marly Horses, I saw Marguerite's carriage in the distance: I did not recognize it, I just knew it was hers.

As it was turning the corner into the Champs-Élysées, she ordered it to stop, and a tall young man broke away from a group where he had been chatting in order to speak to her.

They talked together for a few moments; the young man rejoined his friends, the horses set off again, and as I approached the group, I now recognized the man who had spoken to Marguerite as the same Count de G*** whose portrait I had seen and whom Prudence had pointed out as the person to whom Marguerite owed her notoriety.

It was he who had been forbidden her door the previous night. I assumed that she had ordered her carriage to stop to explain the reasons for his exclusion and, at the same time, I hoped that she had found some new excuse for not receiving him the next night either.

How the rest of the day passed, I do not know. I walked, I smoked, I talked, but by ten in the evening, I had no recollection of what I had said or the people I had met.

All I remember is that I returned to my rooms, spent three

hours getting ready, and looked a hundred times at my clock and my watch which, unfortunately, both continued to tell the same time.

When ten thirty struck, I said to myself that it was time to leave.

In those days, I lived in the rue de Provence:* I walked down the rue du Mont Blanc, crossed the Boulevard, went along the rue Louis-le-Grand, the rue de Port-Mahon and the rue d'Antin. I looked up at Marguerite's windows.

There was light in them.

I rang.

I asked the porter if Mademoiselle Gautier was at home.

He replied that she never came home before eleven or a quarter past.

I looked at my watch.

I thought that I had come at leisurely stroll, but I had taken just five minutes to come from the rue de Provence to Marguerite's.

So I walked up and down her shopless street which was deserted at that time of night.

At the end of half an hour, Marguerite arrived. She stepped down from her brougham and looked around as though she were watching out for someone.

The carriage set off at a trot, for the stables and coach-house were not located on the premises. Marguerite was about to ring when I went up to her and said:

'Good evening.'

'Oh! it's you, is it?' she said, in a tone which did little to reassure me that she was pleased to see me.

'Didn't you say I could come and call on you today?'

'So I did. I'd forgotten.'

These words overturned everything I had thought that morning, everything I had been hoping for all day. However, I was beginning to get used to her ways and did not storm off—which I should of course have done at once.

We went in together.

Nanine had opened the door ahead of us.

'Is Prudence back?' asked Marguerite.

'No, Madame.'

'Go and say that she is to come the minute she gets in. But first, turn out the lamp in the drawing-room, and if anyone comes, say I'm not back and won't be coming back.'

She was quite clearly a woman with something on her mind, and was perhaps irritated by the presence of an unwanted guest. I did not know how to react nor what to say. Marguerite walked towards her bedroom; I remained where I was.

'Come,' she said.

She took off her hat and her velvet cloak, and tossed them on to her bed, then sank into a large arm-chair in front of the fire, which she always kept lit until the beginning of each summer and, playing with her watch-chain, said:

'Well then, and what news have you got to tell me?'

'No news—except that I was wrong to come here this evening.'

'Why?'

'Because you seem cross, and because I expect I'm boring you.'

'You're not boring me. Only I'm ill, I've not been well all day, I haven't slept and I have a terrible headache.'

'Do you want me to leave so that you can go to bed?'

'Oh! you can stay. If I want to go to bed, I can go to bed with you here.'

At that moment, there was a ring at the door.

'Who can that be now?' she said, with a gesture of impatience.

A few instants later, the bell rang again.

'There can't be anybody to answer it; I'll have to go myself.'

And so saying, she got up.

'Wait here,' she said.

She walked through the apartment and I heard the front door open. I listened.

The person she had admitted halted in the dining-room. By his first words, I recognized the voice of young Count de N***.

'How are you this evening?' he was saying.

'Ill,' replied Marguerite curtly.

'Am I disturbing you?'

'Perhaps.'

'You're not very welcoming! What have I done to upset you, my dear Marguerite?'

'My dear friend, you haven't done anything. I am ill, I must go to bed, so you will be so kind as to go away. I am sick and tired of not being able to come home each evening without seeing you show your face five minutes later. What do you want? You want me to be your mistress? Haven't I said no a hundred times? And haven't I told you that I find you dreadfully irritating and that you can go and look elsewhere? Let me say it again today for the last time: I don't want anything to do with you, that's final. Goodbye. There, that's Nanine just coming back. She'll show you a light. Goodnight.'

And without another word, without heeding the young man's stammered replies, Marguerite came back into her bedroom, violently slamming the door through which Nanine duly appeared almost immediately.

'Do you hear,' Marguerite told her, 'you are always to say to that oaf that I'm not in, or that I don't want to see him. I'm so tired of seeing people forever coming and asking for the same thing, paying me for it and thinking that they've wiped the slate clean. If girls who start in this shameful trade of ours only knew what it's like, they'd sooner be chamber-maids. But oh no! vanity, and the idea of having gowns, carriages, and diamonds lure us on; we believe what we hear, for prostitution has its own articles of faith, and little by little we use up our hearts, our bodies, our beauty. We are feared like wild beasts, scorned like outcasts, surrounded only by people who always take more than they give, and then, one fine day, we crawl away to die like dogs, having ruined the others and ruined ourselves.'

'There, Madame, calm yourself,' said Nanine, 'your nerves are bad tonight.'

'This dress is too tight,' Marguerite went on, tearing open the fasteners of her bodice, 'get me a robe. Well, what about Prudence?'

'She wasn't back, but they'll tell her to come the minute she gets home.'

'There's another one,' Marguerite went on, removing her dress and slipping into a white robe, 'there's another one who knows exactly where to find me when she needs me, and can't ever do me a good turn without wanting something. She knows I'm waiting for that answer tonight, that I must have it, that I'm worried, and I just know that she's gone gallivanting without a thought for me.'

'Perhaps she's been delayed.'

'Get them to bring us some punch.'

'You're going to make yourself ill again,' said Nanine.

'Good. And bring me some fruit, some pâté or a chicken wing, something at once. I'm hungry.'

There is no need to say what impression this scene made on me, for I am sure you can guess.

'You are going to have supper with me,' she said. 'Meantime, read a book. I'm going into my dressing-room for a moment.'

She lit the candles of a candelabra, opened a door facing the end of her bed, and disappeared.

Left to myself, I began to ponder the life this girl led, and my love was swelled by pity.

I was walking up and down in her bedroom, thinking, when Prudence came in.

'Hello, you here?' she said. 'Where's Marguerite?'

'In her dressing-room.'

'I'll wait for her to come out. Well now, she thinks you're nice. Did you know?'

'No.'

'Hasn't she told you? Not even a little bit?'

'Not at all.'

'How do you come to be here?'

'I came to pay a call.'

'At midnight?'

'Why not?'

'That's a good one!'

'As a matter of fact, she didn't give me much of a welcome.'

'She'll make you feel more at home in a while.'

'You think so?'

'I've brought her good news.'

'That's all right then. So she's talked to you about me?'

'Yesterday evening—or rather last night, after you'd gone with your friend . . . By the way, how is your friend? It's Gaston R***, I believe; isn't that what they call him?'

'Yes,' I said, unable to stop myself smiling as I remembered what Gaston had confided to me, and realized that Prudence hardly knew his name.

'He's a very nice boy. What does he do?'

'He has a private income of twenty-five thousand francs.'

'Oh! Really? Well anyhow, coming back to you, Marguerite asked me a lot of questions about you. She asked who you were, what you did, what mistresses you'd had, everything, really, that can be asked about a man of your age. I told her all I know, and said that you were a very nice boy, and that's about it.'

'I'm grateful. Now, tell me what was this errand she sent you on yesterday?'

'There wasn't one. What she said was intended to make the Count go away. But she did ask me to do something for her today, and I've brought her the answer tonight.'

Just then, Marguerite emerged from her dressing-room, daintily wearing a night-cap decorated with bunches of yellow ribbons, known in the trade as cabbage-bows.

She looked ravishing in it.

On her bare feet she was wearing satin slippers, and she was finishing her nails.

'Well?' she said, when she saw Prudence, 'did you see the Duke?'

'Of course!'

'What did he say?'

'He came up with it.'

'How much?'

'Six thousand.'

'Have you got it?'

'Yes.'

'Did he seem cross?'

'No.'

'Poor man!'

The way she said 'Poor man!' is impossible to render. Marguerite took the six one-thousand-franc notes.

'And not before time,' she said. 'My dear Prudence, do you need any money?'

'As you know, my child, it'll be the fifteenth in two days, so if you could lend me three or four hundred francs, you'd be doing me a good turn.'

'Send round for it tomorrow morning, it's too late to get change now.'

'Don't forget.'

'No need to worry. Are you going to have supper with us?'

'No, Charles is waiting in my apartment.'

'So you're still mad about him?'

'Quite crazy, my dear! I'll see you tomorrow. Goodbye, Armand.'

Madame Duvernoy left.

Marguerite opened her china-cabinet and tossed the bank-notes inside.

'You don't mind if I lie down?' she said, smiling and making for her bed.

'Not only do I not mind, I do wish you would.'

She threw the counterpane over the foot of the bed and climbed between the sheets.

'Now,' she said, 'come and sit by me and we'll talk.'

Prudence was right: the answer she had brought Marguerite brightened her mood.

'Will you forgive me for being bad-tempered this evening?' she said, taking my hand.

'I am ready to forgive you much more.'

'And you love me?'

'To distraction.'

'In spite of my awful temper?'

'In spite of everything.'

'Do you swear it?'

'Yes,' I whispered to her.

Nanine came in then, carrying plates, a cold chicken, a

bottle of bordeaux, strawberries and cutlery and glasses for two.

'I didn't get any punch made up,' Nanine said, 'the bordeaux will do you better. Isn't that right, sir?'

'Quite right,' I answered, still deeply moved by Marguerite's last words, and with my eyes fixed ardently on her.

'Good,' she said, 'put it all on the little table, and bring it nearer the bed; we'll serve ourselves. That's three nights you've been up, you'll be wanting some sleep. Go to bed: I shan't be needing anything else.'

'Should I double-lock the door?'

'Yes, you should! And, most important of all, say that no one is to be admitted before noon.'

XII

At five in the morning, when daylight began to appear through the curtains, Marguerite said to me:

'Forgive me if I shoo you away now, but I must. The Duke comes every morning; when he arrives, he'll be told I'm asleep, and he may wait for me to wake.'

I took Marguerite's head in both my two hands, her loosened hair cascading on to her shoulders, and I gave her one last kiss, saying:

'When will I see you again?'

'Listen,' she went on, 'take the little gold key on the mantelpiece there and unlock the door. Then bring me back the key and go. Sometime during the day, you'll receive a letter with my instructions, for you know that you must obey blindly.'

'Yes—but what if I were already to ask you something?'

'What is it?'

'That you leave the key in my keeping.'

'I've never done for anyone what you're asking me to do now.'

'Well, do it for me, for I swear that I do not love you as the others loved you.'

'Very well, keep it. But I warn you that I could at any time see to it that your key served no useful purpose.'

'How?'

'There are bolts on this side of my door.'

'You wicked creature!'

'I'll have them removed.'

'So you do love me a little?'

'I don't know how it is, but it seems I do. And now, go: I'm almost asleep.'

We remained a few moments in each others' arms and then I left.

The streets were deserted, the great city was sleeping still, and a pleasant coolness ran through the neighbourhood which, a few hours later, would be overrun by the noise of men.

I felt as though the sleeping city belonged to me. I ransacked my memory for the names of men whose happiness, up to that moment, I had envied; and I could not recall one without finding that I was happier than he.

To be loved by a chaste young girl, to be the first to show her the strange mystery of love, is a great joy—but it is the easiest thing in the world. To capture a heart unused to attack is like walking into an open, undefended city. Upbringing, the awareness of duty, and the family, are watchful sentries of course, but there are no sentries, however vigilant, that cannot be eluded by a girl of sixteen to whom nature, through the voice of the man she adores, whispers those first counsels of love which are all the more passionate because they seem so pure.

The more sincere a young girl's belief in goodness, the more easily she gives herself, if not to her lover, then at least to love. Because she is unsuspecting, she is powerless, and to be loved by her is a prize which any young man of twenty-five may have whenever he likes. And to see how true this is, simply consider how much supervision and how many ramparts surround young girls! Convents cannot have walls too high, nor mothers locks too strong, nor religion duties too unrelenting to keep all these charming birds safe in cages which no one even tries to disguise with flowers.*

And so, how keenly must they want that world which is kept hidden from them! How tempting must they believe it to be! How eagerly must they listen to the first voice which, through the bars of their cage, tells of its secrets! And how gratefully do they bless the first hand which lifts a corner of its mysterious veil!

But to be truly loved by a courtesan is a much more difficult victory to achieve. In such women, the body has consumed the soul, the senses have burnt out the heart, debauchery has buckled stout armour on to feeling. The words you say to them, they first heard long ago; the tactics you use, they have seen before; the very love they inspire in you, they have sold to others. They love because love is their trade, not because they are swept off their feet. They are better guarded by their calculations than a virgin by her mother and her convent. Which is why they have coined the word 'caprice' to describe those non-commercial affairs in which they indulge from time to time as a relief, an excuse or as a consolation. Such women are like money-lenders who fleece large numbers of people, and think they can make amends by lending twenty francs one day to some poor devil who is starving to death, without asking him to pay interest or requiring him to sign a receipt.

But when God allows a courtesan to fall in love, her love, which at first looks like a pardon for her sins, proves almost invariably to be a punishment on her. There is no absolution without penance. When such a creature, who has all the guilt of her past on her conscience, suddenly feels herself gripped by a deep, sincere, irresistible love such as she had never dreamed herself capable of experiencing; when she finally declares her love—how complete the power of the man she loves! How strong he feels once he has the cruel right to say: 'What you do now for love is no more than you have done for money.'

When this happens, they are at a loss for ways of proving what they feel. A boy in a field who, so the fable goes, persisted in finding it amusing to shout 'Help!' to disturb some workmen, was eaten one fine day by a bear, without it occurring to those he had so often deceived that this time his shouts were real. And so it is with these wretched girls when they genuinely fall in love. They have lied so often that no one believes them any more and, beset by remorse, they are eaten by their love.

Which explains the great self-sacrifices, the austere self-seclusions of which a few such women have afforded examples.

But if a man who inspires such saving love is sufficiently generous of soul to accept it without thought for the past, if he commits himself totally to her, if he really loves as he is loved, then such a man drains in one draught all terrestrial emotions and, after a love like this, his heart is thereafter closed to any other.

It was not then, as I returned home that morning, that these thoughts came to me. They could not in any case have been much more at that point than a presentiment of what was to befall me and, in spite of my love for Marguerite, I did not anticipate any such outcome. But I think these thoughts today: now that it is all irrevocably ended, they emerge naturally from what has been.

But let us return to that first day of our affair. When I reached home, I was wildly exhilarated. Feeling that the barriers which my imagination had erected between Marguerite and me had disappeared, and believing that she was mine, that I had a small place in her thoughts, that I had the key to her apartment in my pocket and permission to use it, I felt pleased with life and pleased with myself, and I praised God who had let it all happen.

One day, a young man walks along a street, comes across a woman, looks at her, turns and looks again, then walks on. This woman, whom he does not know, has pleasures, sorrows, loves in which he has no part. He does not exist for for her, and perhaps, if he spoke to her, she would laugh at him just as Marguerite had laughed at me. Weeks, months, years pass by and then, quite unexpectedly, when both have followed their destiny in their separate ways, the logic of chance brings them face to face. The woman becomes the man's mistress and loves him truly. How? Why? Their two lives are now as one; no sooner is their affection sealed

than they feel as though it has always existed, and everything that has gone before is blotted from the memory of
the two lovers. It really is the oddest thing, you must
admit.

For my own part, I could not recall how I had ever lived
before the previous evening. My whole being cried out for
joy at the memory of the words we had exchanged during
that first night. Either Marguerite was skilled at deceit, or
she truly felt for me one of those sudden passions which
can come with the first kiss but sometimes fade as quickly
as they came.

The more I thought about it, the surer I was that Marguerite could have no reason to feign a love she did not feel
and, furthermore, I told myself that women have two ways
of loving which may derive the one from the other: they
love either with their hearts or with their senses. A woman
will often take a lover merely to do the bidding of her
senses and, without expecting to, acquires knowledge of the
mystery of ethereal love, and henceforth lives only through
her heart; a young girl, seeking in marriage simply the
union of two pure affections, will often acquire the sudden
revelation of physical love, the emphatic culmination of the
purest impressions of the soul.

I fell asleep in the middle of my thoughts. I was woken by
a letter from Marguerite which contained these words:

'These are my orders: This evening at the Vaudeville.*
Come during the third interval.
                            M. G.'

I put her note away in a drawer, so that I would always
have reality to hand should I ever have doubts, as happened
from time to time.

As she did not say that I should go and see her during
the day, I dared not call on her; but so great was my desire
to meet up with her before that evening that I ventured on
to the Champs-Élysées where, like the previous day, I saw
her drive up and then down again.

At seven, I was at the Vaudeville.

I had never arrived at a theatre quite so early.

All the boxes filled one after the other. Just one remained unoccupied: the front box in the stalls.

At the start of the third act, I heard someone opening the door to this box, on which I had kept my eyes more or less permanently fixed, and Marguerite appeared.

She immediately came and stood in the front of her box, scanned the stalls, saw me and thanked me with a glance.

She was radiantly beautiful that evening.

Was I the reason why she had taken such care to look her best? Did she love me enough to think that the more beautiful I found her, the happier I would be? I still could not be sure; but if this was her intention, then she fully succeeded. For when she appeared, there was a ripple of turning heads and even the actor who was speaking at that moment looked in the direction of the woman whose entrance had disturbed the audience.

And I had the key to that woman's apartment, and in three or four hours she would be mine once more!

We decry men who ruin themselves for actresses and kept women; what surprises me is that they do not commit twenty times as many follies for them. You need to have lived that kind of life, as I have, to understand just how strongly all those little gratifications of vanity which a mistress provides each day can weld to a man's heart, for want of a better word, the love which he has for her.

Then Prudence took her seat in the box and a man, who I recognized as Count de G***, sat down at the back.

When I saw him, my heart went cold.

No doubt Marguerite noticed what effect the presence of this man in her box was having on me, for she smiled at me once more and, turning her back on the Count, appeared to be concentrating hard on the play. When the third interval began, she turned round and spoke briefly; the Count left the box, and Marguerite signalled me to come and see her.

'Good evening,' she said as I entered, and she held out her hand.

'Good evening,' I replied, directing the greeting at both Marguerite and Prudence.

'Do sit down.'

'But this is someone's seat. Isn't Count de G*** coming back?'

'Yes. I sent him off to fetch me some sweets so that we could have a moment alone to talk. Madame Duvernoy knows everything.'

'Yes, my children,' said she. 'But don't worry. I shan't tell.'

'What's wrong with you this evening?' said Marguerite, rising and coming into the dark back of the box where she kissed me on the forehead.

'I'm not feeling too well.'

'You should go to bed,' she went on, with that ironic expression which went so well with her fine, quick-witted head.

'Whose?'

'Yours.'

'You know very well that I shan't sleep.'

'In that case, you shouldn't come here sulking just because you saw a man in my box.'

'That's not the reason.'

'Oh yes it is, I know all about such things and you're wrong. Let's not say any more about it. After the play, come to Prudence's and stay there until I call you. Understood?'

'Yes.'

Did I have any choice but to obey?

'Do you still love me?' she went on.

'How can you ask!'

'Have you thought about me?'

'All day long.'

'Do you know something? I'm seriously beginning to be afraid I could fall in love with you. You'd better ask Prudence.'

'Ah!' Prudence cried heartily, 'stop pestering me!'

'Now, you are to go back to your seat in the stalls. The Count will return at any minute and there's nothing to be gained if he finds you here.'

'Why not?'

'Because you don't much like seeing him.'

'It's not that. It's just that if you had told me you wanted to come to the Vaudeville this evening, I could have sent you tickets for a box every bit as well as he could.'

'Unfortunately, he brought them round without my asking him to, and offered to escort me. You know very well I couldn't refuse. The most I could do was to write and let you know where I was going, because then you could see me, and because I wanted to see you sooner rather than later. But if that's the thanks I get, let it be a lesson to me.'

'I was wrong. Do forgive me!'

'Very well. Go back to your seat like a good boy, and for heaven's sake no more jealous scenes!'

She kissed me again, and I left.

In the corridor, I met the Count on his way back.

I returned to my seat.

After all, the presence of Monsier de G*** in Marguerite's box was the most uncomplicated thing. He had been her lover, he brought her tickets for a box, he came to the play with her—it was all very natural, and the moment I took a girl like Marguerite as my mistress, I had no alternative but to accept her ways.

All the same, such considerations did not make me any the less wretched for the rest of the evening, and I felt extremely miserable as I left, having seen Prudence, the Count and Marguerite stepping into the barouche which stood waiting for them at the door.

Even so, a quarter of an hour later I was at Prudence's. She had returned only a moment before.

XIII

'You got here almost as quickly as we did,' said Prudence.

'Yes,' I replied mechanically. 'Where's Marguerite?'

'In her apartment.'

'By herself?'

'With Monsieur de G***.'

I strode up and down in her drawing-room.

'Whatever's the matter with you?'

'Do you imagine I think it's funny waiting around like
this for Monsieur de G*** to come out of Marguerite's?'

'You're being unreasonable too. You must understand
that Marguerite can't show the Count the door. Monsieur
de G*** has been with her a long time now; he's always
given her a lot of money. He still does. Marguerite spends
more than a hundred thousand francs a year; she has huge
debts. The Duke sends her whatever she asks him for, but
she doesn't always dare ask for everything she needs. She
can't afford to fall out with the Count who gives her
around ten thousand francs a year at least. Marguerite really
loves you, my dear, but your affair with her mustn't get
serious both for her sake and yours. Your allowance of seven
or eight thousand francs wouldn't be anything like enough
to pay for her extravagance; it won't even run to the upkeep
of her carriage. Just take Marguerite for what she is—a
good-hearted, lively, pretty girl. Be her lover for a month,
two months. Give her flowers, buy her sweets, pay for boxes
at the theatre. But don't go getting any other ideas, and
don't go in for silly jealous scenes. You know what sort of
girl you're dealing with: Marguerite's no saint. She likes
you, you love her, leave it at that. I think you're foolish
to get so touchy! You have the sweetest mistress in the
whole of Paris! She receives you in a magnificent apartment,
she's covered in diamonds, she needn't cost you a penny
unless you decide otherwise, and you're still not satisfied.
Hang it all, you expect too much!'

'You're quite right, but I can't help it. The thought that
this man is her lover is agony.'

'To begin with,' Prudence went on, 'is he still her lover?
He's just a man that she needs, that's all. For two days now,
she's closed her door to him. He came this morning. She
had no alternative: she had to accept the tickets for the box
and say he could escort her. He brought her home, he came
up for a moment, but won't stay, or otherwise you wouldn't
be waiting here. All very natural, as I see it. Anyhow, you
don't mind the Duke?'

'No, but he's an old man, and I'm sure Marguerite isn't
his mistress. In any case, a man can often put up with one

affair, but not two. Even so, the ease with which he tolerates such an arrangement can look suspiciously calculating. It brings anyone who submits to it, even if he does so out of love, very close to people just one step beneath who make a business out of submitting and a profit out of their business.'

'Ah, dear man! How behind the times you are! How many times have I seen the noblest, the most fashionable, the wealthiest men do what I now advise, and they have done it without fuss or shame or remorse! It happens every day of the week. How do you imagine all the kept women in Paris could carry on living the kind of lives they lead if they didn't have three or four lovers at the same time? There isn't a man around, however much money he had, who'd be rich enough to cover the expenses of a woman like Marguerite by himself. A private income of five hundred thousand francs is a colossal fortune in France; well, dear man, a private income of five hundred thousand francs wouldn't do it, and here's why. A man who has an income like that has an established household, horses, servants, carriages, hunting estates, friends; often he is married, he has children, he keeps a racing stable, he gambles, travels and a lot more besides. All these habits are so firmly rooted that he cannot drop them without appearing to be ruined and becoming the talk of the town. All in all, with five hundred thousand francs a year, he can't give a woman more than forty or fifty thousand in any twelve months, and even that's a great deal. So other lovers must make up the woman's annual expenditure. With Marguerite, it works out even more conveniently. By a miracle of heaven, she's got in with a rich old man worth ten millions whose wife and daughter are both dead and whose surviving relatives are nephews with a lot of money of their own. He gives her everything she wants without asking anything in exchange. But she can't ask him for more than seventy thousand francs a year, and I'm sure that if she did, then in spite of all his money and his affection for her, he would say no.

'All those young men in Paris with incomes of twenty or thirty thousand francs, that is with barely enough to get by in the circles they move in, are all quite aware, when they are the lovers of a woman like Marguerite, that their mistress couldn't even pay the rent or her servants on what they give her. They don't ever say that they know. They just appear not to see anything and, when they've had enough, they move on. If they are vain enough to want to provide for everything, they ruin themselves like idiots, and go off to get themselves killed in Africa, leaving a hundred thousand francs' worth of debts in Paris. And do you imagine that the woman is grateful? Not a bit of it. The very opposite. She'll say that she sacrificed her position for them, and that as long as she was with them she was losing money. Ah! all these dealings strike you as shameful, don't they? But it's all true. You are a nice boy and I couldn't be fonder of you. I've lived among women like these for twenty years, and I know what they're like and what sort of stuff they're made of. I wouldn't want to see you taking to heart a caprice which some pretty girl has for you.

'Anyway, on top of all that,' Prudence continued, 'let's say Margurite loves you enough to give up the Count and even the Duke, if the Duke should find out about your affair and tell her to choose between you and him. If that happened, then the sacrifice which she'd be making for you would be enormous, no question about it. What sacrifice could you make to match hers? When you'd had enough of her and didn't want to have anything more to do with her, what would you do to compensate her for what you'd made her lose? Nothing. You would have cut her off from the world in which her fortune and her future lay, she would have given you her best years, and she would be forgotten. Then you'd either turn out to be the usual sort and throw her past in her face, telling her as you walked out that you were only behaving like all her other lovers, and you'd abandon her to certain poverty. Or else you would behave correctly and, believing you had an obligation to keep her by you, you'd land yourself inevitably in trouble, for an affair such as this, forgiveable in a young man, is inexcusable in older men. It becomes an obstacle to everything. It stands in the way of family and ambition which are a man's second and last loves. So believe me, my friend, take things for what they are worth and women as they are, and never give a kept woman any right to say that you owe her anything whatsoever.'

All this was sensibly argued, and it had a logic of which I would not have thought Prudence capable. I could think of nothing to say in reply, except that she was right; I gave her my hand and thanked her for her advice.

'Come, come,' she said, 'now just forget all this gloomy theorizing and laugh. Life is delightful, my dear, it all depends on the prism you look at it through. Listen, ask your friend Gaston. Now there's someone who strikes me as understanding love as I understand it. What you've got to realize—and you'll be a dull lad if you don't—is that not far from here there's a beautiful girl who is waiting impatiently to see the back of the man she's with, who is thinking about you, who is keeping tonight for you and who I'm sure loves you. Now come and stand by the window with me, and we'll watch the Count leave: it won't be long now before he leaves the field clear for us.'

Prudence opened a window and we leaned on our elbows side by side on the balcony.

She watched the occasional passers-by. I stood musing.

Everything she had said reverberated inside my head, and I could not help admitting that she was right. But the true love I felt for Marguerite was not easily reconciled with her arguments. Consequently, I heaved intermittent sighs which made Prudence turn round and shrug her shoulders, like a doctor who has lost all hope of a patient.

'How clearly we see how brief life is,' I said to myself, 'in the fleeting passage of our sensations! I have known Marguerite for only two days, she has been my mistress since just yesterday, and yet she has so overrun my thoughts, my heart and my life that a visit from this Count de G*** can make me wretched.'

Finally, the Count emerged, got into his carriage and drove off. Prudence closed her window.

At the same instant, Marguerite was already calling us.

'Come quickly, the table is being set,' she said, 'and we'll have supper.'

When I entered her apartment, Marguerite ran towards me, threw her arms around my neck and kissed me with all her might.

'Are we still grumpy, then?' she said to me.

'No, that's all finished with,' answered Prudence, 'I've been telling him a few home-truths, and he's promised to be good.'

'Wonderful!'

Despite myself, I cast a glance in the direction of the bed. It had not been disturbed: as for Marguerite, she had already changed into a white dressing-gown.

We sat down at table.

Charm, sweetness, high-spirits—Marguerite had everything, and from time to time I had to admit that I had no right to ask anything else of her, that many a man would be happy to be in my shoes and that, like Virgil's shepherd, I had only to partake of the easy times which a god, or rather a goddess, held out to me.

I tried to put Prudence's theories into practice and be as gay as my two companions. But what came naturally to them was an effort for me, and my excited laughter, which they misunderstood, was very close to tears.

At length, supper ended and I remained alone with Marguerite. As was her habit, she went and sat on her rug in front of the fire and looked sadly into the flames in the hearth.

She was thinking! Of what? I cannot say. But I looked at her with love and almost with dread at the thought of what I was prepared to suffer for her sake.

'Do you know what I was thinking?'

'No.'

'About this scheme I've hit on.'

'And what is this scheme?'

'I can't tell you yet, but I can tell you what'll happen if it works. What would happen is that in a month from now I'd be free, I wouldn't have any more debts, and we'd go and spend the summer in the country together.'

'And can't you tell me how this is to be managed?'

'No. All it needs is for you to love me as I love you, and everything will come out right.'

'And did you hit on this scheme all by yourself?'

'Yes.'

'And you will see it through alone?'

'I'll have all the worry myself,' Marguerite said with a smile which I shall never forget, 'but we will both share the profits.'

I could not help colouring at the mention of the word profits: I recalled Manon Lescaut running through M. de B***'s money with Des Grieux.

I answered a little roughly as I got to my feet:

'You will be good enough, my dear Marguerite, to allow me to share the profits of only those enterprises which I myself contrive and execute.'

'And what does that mean?'

'It means that I strongly suspect that Count de G*** is your associate in this splendid scheme, of which I accept neither the costs nor the profits.'

'Don't be childish. I thought you loved me, but I was wrong. As you wish.'

And, so saying, she got up, opened her piano and once more began playing The Invitation to the Waltz as far as the famous passage in the major key which always got the better of her.

Was this done out of habit, or was it to remind me of the day we first met? All I know is that with this tune, the memories came flooding back and, drawing close to her, I took her head in my hands and kissed her.

'Do you forgive me?' I said.

'Can't you tell?' she answered. 'But note that this is just our second day, and already I've got something to forgive you for. You're not very good at keeping your promises of blind obedience.'

'I'm sorry, Marguerite, I love you too much, and I just have to know everything you think. What you suggested just now should make me jump for joy, but your mysteriousness about what happens before the plan is carried out makes my heart sink.'

'Oh come now, let's talk about this seriously for a moment,' she went on, taking my two hands and looking at me with a bewitching smile which I was quite incapable of resisting. 'You love me, do you not, and you'd be happy to spend three or four months alone with me in the country? I too would be happy for us to be alone together, not just happy to go away with you but I need to for my health. I can't leave Paris for so long without putting my affairs in order, and the affairs of a woman like me are invariably very tangled. Well, I've found a way of bringing it all together—my affairs and my love for you, yes, you, don't laugh, I'm mad enough to be in love with you! And then you get all hoity-toity and start coming out with fine words. Silly boy! Silly, silly boy! Just remember that I love you and don't worry your head about a thing. Well, is it agreed?'

'Everything you want is agreed, as you know very well.'

'In that case, a month from now we'll be in some village or other, strolling by the river and drinking milk. It must sound odd to you hearing me, Marguerite Gautier, talk like this. The fact is, my dear, that when life in Paris, which ostensibly makes me so happy, is not burning me out, it bores me. When that happens, I get sudden yearnings to lead a quieter life which would remind me of my childhood. Everybody, whatever has become of them since, has had a childhood. Oh! don't worry, I'm not about to tell you that I'm the daughter of a retired colonel and that I was raised at Saint-Denis.* I'm just a poor girl from the country who couldn't even write her name six years ago. I expect you're relieved, aren't you! Why is it that you should be the first man I've ever approached to share the joy of the desire which has come upon me? I suppose it's because I sensed that you loved me for my sake and not for yours, whereas the others never loved me except for themselves.

'I've been to the country many times, but never the way I should have liked. I'm counting on you to provide the simple happiness I want. Don't be unkind: indulge me. Tell yourself this: "She's not likely to live to be old, and some day

I should be sorry I didn't do the very first thing she ever asked me, for it was such a simple thing." '

What answer could I give to such words, especially with the memory of a first night of love behind me and with the prospect of a second to come?

An hour later, I was holding Marguerite in my arms, and if she had asked me to commit a crime for her, I would have obeyed.

I left her at six in the morning. Before I went, I said:

'Shall I see you this evening?'

She kissed me harder, but did not reply.

During the day, I received a letter containing these words:

'Darling boy, I'm not very well and the doctor has told me to rest. I shall go to bed early tonight and so shall not see you. But, as a reward, I shall expect you tomorrow at noon. I love you.'

My first thought was: 'She's deceiving me!'

An icy sweat broke out on my forehead, for I was already too much in love with her not to be aghast at the thought.

And yet I was going to have to expect it to happen almost daily with Marguerite; it had often happened with my other mistresses without it ever bothering me too much. How was it then that this woman had such power over my life?

Then, since I had the key to her apartment, I thought I might call and see her as usual. In this way, I should know the truth soon enough, and if I found a man there, I would offer to give him satisfaction.

To while away the time, I went to the Champs-Élysées. I stayed there for four hours. She did not make an appearance. In the evening, I looked in at all the theatres where she usually went. She was not in any of them.

At eleven o'clock, I made my way to the rue d'Antin.

There was no light in any of Marguerite's windows. Even so, I rang.

The porter asked me where I wanted to go.

'To Mademoiselle Gautier's,' I said.

'She's not back.'

'I'll go up and wait.'

'There's nobody in.'

Of course, he had his orders which I could have circumvented since I had a key, but I was afraid of an embarrassing scene and went away.

But I did not go home. I could not leave the street and did not take my eyes off Marguerite's house for a moment. I felt that I still had something to learn, or at least that my suspicions were about to be confirmed.

About midnight, a brougham, which was all too familiar, pulled up near number 9.

Count de G*** got out and went into the house after dismissing his coach.

For a moment, I hoped that he was about to be told, as I had been, that Marguerite was not at home, and that I should see him come out again. But I was still waiting at four in the morning.

These last three weeks, I have suffered a great deal. But it has been nothing compared with what I suffered that night.

XIV

WHEN I reached home, I began to weep like a child. There is not a man alive who has not been deceived at least once but does not know what it is to suffer so.

Weighed down by the kind of fervent resolution which we always think we shall be strong enough to keep, I told myself that I had to put an end to this affair at once, and impatiently waited for morning to come so that I could go and buy a ticket and return to my father and my sister—twin loves on which I could count and which would never let me down.

However, I did not want to go away without ensuring that Marguerite knew exactly why I was going. Only a man who is quite out of love with his mistress will leave her without writing.

I wrote and rewrote a score of letters in my head.

I had been dealing with a woman who was like all other kept women; I had poeticized her far too much. She had treated me like a school-boy and, to deceive me, had resorted to an insultingly simple ruse—that much was clear. My pride then took over. I had to leave this woman without giving her the satisfaction of knowing how much our parting made me suffer, and this is what I wrote to her, in my most elegant hand and with tears of rage and pain in my eyes:*

'My dear Marguerite,

I trust that yesterday's indisposition has not proved too troublesome. I called, at eleven last evening, to ask after you, and was told you had not yet returned. Monsieur de G*** was altogether more fortunate, for he arrived a few moments later and was still with you at four o'clock this morning.

Forgive me the tiresome few hours which I inflicted on you, and rest assured that I shall never forget the happy moments which I owe you.

I would certainly have called to ask after you today, but I propose to return and join my father.

Farewell, my dear Marguerite. I am neither rich enough to love you as I should wish, nor poor enough to love you as you would like. Let us both forget: you, a name which must mean very little to you, and I, happiness which has become impossible for me to bear.

I am returning your key which I have never used and which you may find will answer some useful purpose, if you are often ill the way you were yesterday.'

As you see, I did not have the strength to end my letter without a touch of supercilious irony, which only went to prove how much in love I still was.

I read and reread my letter ten times over, and the thought of the pain it would cause Marguerite calmed me a little. I tried to live up to the bold note it had struck, and when, at eight o'clock, my servant answered my summons, I handed it to him to deliver at once.

'Must I wait for an answer?' Joseph asked. (My manservant was called Joseph. All manservants are called Joseph.)

'If you are asked whether a reply is expected, you will say that you don't know, and you will wait.'

I clung to hope that she would answer.

Poor, weak creatures that we are!

The whole of the time my servant was out, I remained in a state of extreme agitation. At some moments, recalling how completely Marguerite had given herself to me, I asked myself by what right had I written her an impertinent letter when she could quite well reply that it was not Monsieur de G*** who was deceiving me but I who was deceiving Monsieur de G***—which is an argument which allows many a woman to have more than one lover. At other moments, recalling the hussy's solemn oaths, I tried to convince myself that my letter had been far too mild and that there were no words strong enough to scourge a woman who could laugh at love as sincere as mine. Then again, I told myself that it would have been better not to write at all, but to have called on her during the day: in this way, I would have been there to enjoy the tears I made her weep.

In the end, I came round to wondering what she would say in her answer, and I was already prepared to believe whatever excuse she gave me.

Joseph returned.

'Well?' I said.

'Sir,' he answered, 'Madame had not risen and was still asleep, but the moment she rings, the letter will be given to her and if there is a reply, it will be brought.'

Asleep!

A score of times I was on the point of sending round to get the letter back, but I persisted in telling myself:

'Perhaps someone has already given it to her, in which case I would look as though I was sorry I'd sent it.'

The nearer it got to the time when it seemed most likely that she would give me an answer, the more I regretted having written.

Ten o'clock, eleven o'clock, midday struck.

At noon, I was on the point of setting off for our rendez-vous, as though nothing had happened. I was at a complete loss for a way of breaking out of the iron ring that held me fast.

Then, with the superstition of those who wait, I thought that if I went out for a while, I should find an answer when I got back. Replies which we await with impatience always come when we are not at home.

I went out, ostensibly to lunch.

Instead of lunching at the Café Foy, on the corner of the Boulevard, as was my custom, I thought I would have lunch in the Palais-Royal and go via the rue d'Antin. Every time I saw a woman in the distance, I thought it was Nanine bringing me a reply. I walked the length of the rue d'Antin without coming across any sort of messenger. I arrived at the Palais-Royal and went into Véry's.* The waiter gave me something to eat, or, more accurately, served me whatever he wished, for I ate nothing.

Despite myself, my eyes remained fixed on the clock.

I returned home, convinced that I would find a letter from Marguerite.

The porter had received nothing for me. I still had hopes of my servant. He had seen no one since the time I went out.

If Marguerite was going to give me an answer, she would have done so long before.

I began to regret the terms of my letter; I should have remained totally silent, since this would doubtless have made her uneasy, and spurred her to make a move; for, seeing that I had not kept our appointment the previous day, she would have asked the reason for my absence and only then should I have given it. In this way, she would have had no alternative but to establish her innocence, and I wanted her to establish her innocence. I already sensed that whatever the excuses she gave me, I would have believed her, and I knew that I should have preferred anything than never to see her again.

In the end, I fell to thinking that she would come herself, but the hours ticked by, and she did not come.

Marguerite was clearly quite unlike other women, for there are not many who, on receiving a letter like the one I had just written, do not send some sort of reply.

At five, I hurried to the Champs-Élysées.

'If I meet her,' I thought, 'I shall appear unconcerned, and she will see that I have stopped thinking about her already.'

On the corner of the rue Royale, I saw her drive past in her carriage. The encounter happened so suddenly that I felt myself grow pale. I have no idea if she noticed my reaction, for I was so taken aback that I saw only her carriage.

I did not continue with my stroll to the Champs-Élysées. I looked at the theatre bills, for I still had one chance left of seeing her.

There was a first night at the Palais-Royal. Marguerite would obviously be there.

I was in the theatre at seven o'clock.

All the boxes filled up, but Marguerite did not appear.

After a while, I left the Palais-Royal and did the rounds of all the theatres where she went most often—to the Vaudeville, the Variétés and the Opéra-Comique.

She was not at any of them.

Either my letter had hurt her too much for her to be able to think of going to the theatre, or she was afraid of coming across me and wanted to avoid having things out.

This is what my vanity was whispering in my ear on the Boulevard when I ran into Gaston who asked me where I had been.

'To the Palais-Royal.'

'I've been to the Opéra,' he said. 'I rather thought I'd see you there.'

'Why?'

'Because Marguerite was there.'

'Oh! Was she?'

'Yes.'

'On her own?'

'No, with one of her women friends.'

'Anyone else?'

'Count de G*** showed up in her box for a moment or two, but she went off with the Duke. I thought I'd see you appear any minute. I had a seat next to me which stayed empty the whole evening, and I was sure it had been paid for by you.'

'But why should I go wherever Marguerite goes?'

'Because, dammit, you're her lover!'

'And who told you that?'

'Prudence. I met her yesterday. I congratulate you, old boy. She's a pretty mistress to have, and it's not everybody that can have her. Hang on to her, she'll be a credit to you.'

This straightforward observation of Gaston's showed me how ridiculously touchy I was being.

If I had met him the previous evening and he had talked to me like this, I would never have written the stupid letter I had sent that morning.

I was on the point of going round to Prudence's and sending word to Marguerite that I had to talk to her. But I was afraid that, to get back at me, she would send word that she could not see me, and I returned home after walking by the rue d'Antin.

Once again I asked my porter if he had a letter for me. Nothing!

'She'll have wanted to see whether I'd try some new move and retract my letter today,' I told myself as I got into bed, 'but when she sees I haven't written to her, she'll write to me tomorrow.'

That night especially did I regret what I had done. I was alone in my apartment, unable to sleep, fretting with worry and jealousy whereas, by letting things take their true course, I should have been at Marguerite's side hearing her say those sweet words which I had heard on only two occasions, and which now made my ears burn in my loneliness.

The most dreadful part of my predicament was that logic put me in the wrong. Indeed, all the indications were that Marguerite loved me. In the first place, there was her scheme for spending a whole summer alone with me in the country. Then there was the plain fact that there was nothing that obliged her to be my mistress, for the money I had was insufficient for her needs or even her whims. So there was nothing more to it, on her part, than the hope of finding sincere affection through me which would be a relief from the mercenary loves which beset her life. And now, on the second day, I was in the process of blighting that hope and repaying with high-handed irony the two nights of love which I had accepted! What I was doing was therefore worse than ridiculous: it was dishonest. Had I simply paid the woman back in order to have the right to pass judgment on her way of life? And did not withdrawing on the second day make me look like some parasite of love who is afraid he is about to be presented with the bill for his dinner? It was extraordinary! I had known Marguerite for thirty-six hours, I had been her lover for twenty-four of them, and was acting like some easily injured party. Far from being only too delighted that she should divide her affections to include me, I wanted to have her all to myself, I wanted to force her, at a stroke, to put an end to the affairs of her past which, of course, represented the income of her future. What cause had I to reproach her? None. She had written to tell me she was unwell when she could easily have said bluntly, with the appalling frankness of some women, that she was expecting a lover; and instead of going along with her letter, instead of taking a walk in any street in Paris except the rue d'Antin, instead of spending the evening with my friends and presenting myself the next day at the time she had indicated, I was behaving like Othello, spying on her, thinking I was punishing her by not seeing her any more. But quite the reverse: she was probably delighted by this separation and must have thought me supremely inane. Her silence was nothing so grand as rancour: it was contempt.

At this point, I should have given Marguerite some present or other which would have left her in no doubt about my liberality and also allowed me, because I had treated her like any other kept woman, to believe that I had no further obligations towards her. But I felt that with the least hint of trade, I should degrade, if not the love she had for me, then at least the love I had for her; and since this love of mine was so pure that it refused to be shared with others, it was incapable of offering a present, however fine, as payment in full for the happiness, however brief, I had been given.

This is what I kept telling myself over and over that night. I was ready at any moment to go and say it all to Marguerite.

When morning came, I was still awake and feverish. I could not think of anything but Marguerite.

As you will appreciate, I had to decide one way or the other: to have done either with the woman or my scruples—always assuming, of course, that she would still agree to go on seeing me.

But, as you know, one always puts off taking crucial decisions: as a result, neither able to stay in my rooms nor daring to wait upon Marguerite, I embarked on a course of action that might lead to a reconciliation which, should it succeed, my pride could always blame on chance.

It was nine o'clock. I hurried round to Prudence's. She asked me to what she owed this early call.

I did not dare say openly what brought me. I replied that I had gone out early to book a seat on the coach for C***, where my father lived.

'You are very lucky,' she said, 'to be able to get out of Paris in such marvellous weather.'

I looked hard at Prudence, wondering whether she was laughing at me.

But her face was serious.

'Are you going to say goodbye to Marguerite?' she went on, with the same seriousness.

'No.'

'Very wise.'

'You think so?'

'Of course. Since you've finished with her, what's the point of seeing her again?'

'So you know it's all over?'

'She showed me your letter.'

'And what did she say?'

'She said: "My dear Prudence, your protégé has no manners. People compose letters like this in their heads, but no one actually writes them down."'

'And how did she say it?'

'She was laughing. And she also said: "He came to supper twice and now won't even make his party call."'

So this was all the effect my letter and jealous torments had produced! I was cruelly humiliated in my pride of love.

'And what did she do yesterday evening?'

'She went to the Opera.'

'I know. But afterwards?'

'She had supper at home.'

'Alone?'

'With Count de G***, I believe.'

So the break I had made had altered nothing in Marguerite's habits.

It is because of moments like this that some people will tell you: "You shouldn't have given the woman another moment's thought. She clearly didn't love you."

'Ah well, I'm very pleased to see that Marguerite isn't pining for me,' I went on, with a forced smile.

'And she's absolutely right. You did what you had to. You've been much more sensible than her, for she really loved you. All she did was talk about you, and she might have ended up doing something silly.'

'If she loves me, why didn't she reply?'

'Because she realized that she was wrong to love you. And besides, women will sometimes allow a man to take advantage of their love but not to injure their pride, and a man always injures a woman's pride when two days after becoming her lover, he leaves her, whatever reason he gives for doing so. I know Marguerite; she'd sooner die than give you an answer.'

'What should I do, then?'

'Nothing. She will forget you, you will forget her and neither of you will have anything to reproach each other for.'

'What if I wrote asking her to forgive me?'

'Don't. She would.'

I nearly flung my arms around Prudence.

A quarter of an hour later, I was back in my rooms and writing to Marguerite.

'Someone who repents of a letter which he wrote yesterday, someone who will go away tomorrow if you do not

forgive him, wishes to know at what time he may call and
lay his repentance at your feet.

When will he find you alone? For, as you know,
confessions should always be made without witnesses.'

I folded this kind of madrigal in prose and sent Joseph
with it. He handed it to Marguerite herself, and she told him
that she would reply later.

I went out only for a moment, to dine, and at eleven in
the evening still had no reply.

I resolved that I should suffer no more and leave the next
day.

Having made up my mind, knowing that I would not
sleep if I went to bed, I began to pack my trunks.

XV

JOSEPH and I had been getting everything ready for my
departure for about an hour, when there was a violent ringing at my door.

'Should I answer it?' said Joseph.

'Yes,' I told him, wondering who could be calling so late,
and not daring to hope it was Marguerite.

'Sir,' said Joseph when he returned, 'there are two
ladies...'

'It's us, Armand,' cried a voice which I recognized as
belonging to Prudence.

I emerged from my bedroom.

Prudence was standing and gazing about her at the few
curios dotted around my drawing-room; Marguerite was sitting on the sofa, occupied by her thoughts.

When I entered, I went to her, knelt before her, took both
her hands and, in a voice touched with emotion, I said:

'Forgive me.'

She kissed me on the brow and said:

'That's the third time I've forgiven you.'

'I was going to go away tomorrow.'

'How can my visit change your mind? I haven't come
here to stop you leaving Paris. I came because I haven't had

time all day to reply to your letter, and I didn't want to leave you with the impression that I was cross with you. Even so, Prudence didn't want me to come: she said I might be in your way.'

'You! In my way, Marguerite! But how?'

'Why, you could have had a woman here,' answered Prudence, 'and it wouldn't have been very funny for her to see another two turning up.'

While Prudence was making this remark, Marguerite watched me closely.

'My dear Prudence,' I replied, 'you're talking nonsense.'

'You've got a very nice apartment,' answered Prudence. 'Mind if I take a look at the bedroom?'

'Not at all.'

'Prudence went off into my bedroom, not so much to see inside as to cover up her unfortunate remark and to leave Marguerite and me alone together.

'Why did you bring Prudence with you?' I said.

'Because she was with me at the theatre, and because I wanted to have someone to see me home when I left here.'

'Couldn't I have done it?'

'Yes. But apart from the fact that I didn't want to disturb you, I was quite certain that when you got to my door you would ask if you could come up and, since I couldn't let you, I didn't want you to go away feeling you had any right to blame me for refusing you anything.'

'And why couldn't you let me come up?'

'Because I'm being watched very closely, and because the least hint of suspicion could do me a great deal of harm.'

'Is that the only reason?'

'If there was another, I would tell you what it was; we've got past the stage of having secrets from each other.'

'Listen, Marguerite, I'm not going to make any bones about what I want to say to you. Tell me, do you love me a little?'

'A great deal.'

'Then why did you deceive me?'

'My dear, if I were the Duchess of This or That, if I had two hundred thousand livres a year, if I were your mistress and had another lover besides you, then you'd have every right to ask why I deceive you. But I am Mademoiselle Marguerite Gautier, I have debts of forty thousand and not a penny behind me, and I spend a hundred thousand francs a year: your question is out of order and my answer irrelevant.'

'You're quite right,' I said, letting my head fall on to Marguerite's knees, 'but I do love you, to distraction.'

'Well, my dear, you should have loved me a little less or understood me a little better. Your letter hurt me very deeply. If I'd been free to choose, then in the first place I would never have seen the Count the day before yesterday, or, if I had, I would have come to beg you for the forgiveness which you asked of me a few moments ago and, from that moment on, I would have had no other lover but you. There was a moment when I thought I could indulge myself and be really happy for those six months. You would have none of it; you just had to know how I was going to manage it— good heavens! it was easy enough to guess. The sacrifice I was going to have to make if it was to be possible, was much greater than you think. I could have told you: "I need twenty thousand francs." You were in love with me, you would have raised it somehow, though there was a risk that one day you'd be sorry you'd done so and blame me. I chose to owe you nothing; you didn't understand my delicacy, for delicacy it is. Girls of my sort, at least those of us who still have some feelings left, take words and things further and deeper than other women. I repeat: coming from Marguerite Gautier, the means which she found of repaying her debts without asking you for the money it took, was an act of great delicacy of which you should now take advantage without another word. If you met me today for the first time, you'd be only too delighted with the promises I'd make you, and you wouldn't ask questions about what I did the day before yesterday. Sometimes, we have no choice but to buy gratifications for the soul at some cost to the body, and it hurts all the more when those gratifications subsequently elude us.'

I heard and saw Marguerite with admiration. When I reflected that this marvellous creature, whose feet I once had longed to kiss, should consent to give me a place in her thoughts and a role in her life, and when I thought that I was still not content with what she was giving me, I asked myself whether man's desire has any limits at all if, though satisfied as promptly as mine had been, it can still aspire to something more.

'It's true,' she went on, 'we creatures of chance have weird desires and unimaginable passions. Sometimes we give ourselves for one thing, sometimes for another. There are men who could ruin themselves and get nowhere with us; there are others who can have us for a bunch of flowers. Our hearts are capricious: it's their only diversion and their only excuse. I gave myself to you more quickly than I ever did to another man, I swear. Why? Because when you saw me coughing blood, you took me by the hand, because you wept, because you are the only human being who ever felt sorry for me. I'm now going to tell you something silly. Once I had a little dog who used to look at me with sad eyes when I coughed: he was the only living creature I have ever loved.

'When he died, I cried more than after my mother's death. Mind you, she did spend twelve years of her life beating me. Well, from the start, I loved you as much as my dog. If men only knew what can be had with just one tear, they would be better loved and we should ruin fewer of them.

'Your letter gave you away: it showed me that you didn't understand the workings of the heart, and it injured you more in the love I had for you than anything else you could have done. It was jealousy, of course, but a sarcastic, haughty kind of jealousy. I was feeling miserable when I got the letter. I was counting on seeing you at midday, on having lunch with you, hoping the sight of you would chase away a thought I kept having which, before I knew you, never bothered me in the least.

'Then again,' continued Marguerite, 'you were the only person with whom I'd sensed from the first I could think and speak freely. People who congregate around girls like me can gain a great deal by paying close attention to the slightest words we say, and by drawing conclusions from our most insignificant actions. Naturally, we have no friends,

We have egotistical lovers who spend their fortunes not on us, as they claim, but on their vanity.

'For men like these, we have to be cheerful when they are happy, hale and hearty when they decide they want supper, and as cynical as they are. We are not allowed to have feelings, for fear of being jeered at and losing our credibility.

'Our lives are no longer our own. We aren't human beings, but things. We rank first in their pride, and last in their good opinion. We have women friends, but they are friends like Prudence—yesterday's kept women who still have expensive tastes which their age prevents them from indulging. So they become our friends, or rather associates. Their friendship may verge on the servile, but it is never disinterested. They'll never give you a piece of advice unless there's money in it. They don't care if we've got ten lovers extra as long as they get a few dresses or a bracelet out of them and can drive about every now and then in our carriages and sit in our boxes at the theatre. They end up with the flowers we were given the night before, and they borrow our Indian shawls. They never do us a good turn, however trifling, without making sure they get paid twice what their trouble was worth. You saw as much yourself the evening Prudence brought me the six thousand francs which I'd asked her to go and beg from the Duke; she borrowed five hundred francs which she'll never give back, or else she'll pay it off in hats that will never get taken out of their boxes.

'So we can have, or rather I had, only one hope of happiness: and this was, sad as I sometimes am and ill as I am always, to find a man of sufficiently rare qualities who would never ask me to account for my actions, and be the lover of my wilder fancies more than the lover of my body. I found this man in the Duke, but the Duke is old and old age neither shields nor consoles. I'd thought I could settle for the life he made for me. But it was no use. I was dying of boredom, and I felt that if I was going to be destroyed, then I might as well jump into the flames as choke on the fumes.

'Then I met you. You were young, passionate, happy, and I tried to turn you into the man I had cried out for in my crowded but empty life. What I loved in you was not the man you were but the man you could be. You refuse to accept the part; you reject it as unworthy of you; you are a commonplace lover. Just do what the others do: pay me and let's not talk about it any more.'

Marguerite, tired by this long confession, settled back into the sofa and, to check a mild fit of coughing, put her hand-kerchief to her lips and even wiped her eyes.

'Forgive me, forgive me,' I murmured, 'I knew all this, but I wanted to hear you say it, my darling Marguerite. Let's forget the rest. Let's just remember one thing: we belong to one another, we are young and we are in love.

'Marguerite, do with me what you will. I am your slave, your dog. But, in the name of God, tear up the letter I wrote you and don't let me go away tomorrow. It would kill me.'

Marguerite withdrew the letter from the bodice of her dress and, as she handed it back to me, said with a smile of infinite sweetness:

'Here, I was bringing it back to you.'

I tore up the letter and, with tears in my eyes, kissed the hand which held it.

At this juncture, Prudence reappeared.

'Oh, Prudence, can you guess what he wants me to do?' said Marguerite.

'To forgive him.'

'That's right.'

'And have you?'

'I can't do otherwise. But there's something else he wants.'

'What's that?'

'He wants to come and have supper with us.'

'And are you going to say yes?'

'What do you think?'

'I think you're a couple of children without an ounce of common sense between you. But I also think that I'm ravenous, and the sooner you do say yes, the sooner we'll have supper.'

'Come on, then,' said Marguerite, 'we can all fit into my carriage. By the way,' she added, turning to me, 'Nanine will have gone to bed, so you'll have to open the door. Take my key, and try not to lose it again.'

I kissed Marguerite until she had no breath left.

Thereupon, Joseph came in.

'Sir,' he said with the air of a man terribly pleased with himself, 'the trunks are packed.'

'All of them?'

'Yes, sir.'

'Well, unpack them. I'm not leaving.'

XVI

I COULD have told you the start of the affair in a few lines (Armand said to me), but I wanted you to see for yourself the events and stages by which we reached the point where I agreed to everything Marguerite wanted, and Marguerite conceded that she could live only with me.

It was on the day following the evening when she had come seeking me out that I sent her *Manon Lescaut*.

From that moment on, since I could not alter my mistress's way of life, I altered mine. More than anything, I wanted to leave my mind with no time to dwell on the role I had just accepted, for, despite myself, I should have been very unhappy with it. And thus my life, normally so calm, suddenly took on an air of riot and chaos. You must not imagine that the love of a kept woman, however disinterested, costs nothing. Nothing costs more than the constant capricious requests for flowers, boxes at the theatre, supper parties, outings to the country which can never be denied a mistress.

As I have told you, I had no real money of my own. My father was, and still is, the District Collector of Taxes for C***. He has a wide reputation for loyal service, thanks to which he was able to raise the money for the surety he had to find before taking up the post. The Collectorship brings in forty thousand francs a year and, during the ten years he has held it, he has paid off his bond and set about putting a dowry for my sister to one side. My father is the most honourable man you could hope to meet. When my mother died, she left an income of six thousand francs which he divided between my sister and myself the day he acquired the appointment for which he had canvassed; then, when I was twenty-one, he added to this small income an annual allowance of five thousand francs, and assured me that I could be very happy in Paris on eight thousand francs if, beside this income, I could establish myself in a position at the bar or in medicine. Accordingly, I came to Paris, read law, was called to the bar and, like any number of young men, put my diploma in my pocket and rather let myself drift along on the carefree life of Paris. My expenses were very modest. However, I regularly got through my year's income in eight months, and spent the four summer months at my father's place, which in all gave me twelve thousand a year and a reputation as a good son. And, moreover, I didn't owe anyone a penny.

That was how things stood with me when I met Marguerite.

You will appreciate that, in spite of my wishes, my level of expenditure rose. Marguerite's was a most capricious nature, and she was one of those women who never consider that the countless amusements of which their life is made can be a serious financial drain. As a result, since she wanted to spend as much time with me as possible, she would write me a note in the morning to say that she would have dinner with me, not in her apartment, but in some restaurant either in Paris or in the country. I would collect her, we would dine, go on to the theatre, and often have supper together, and I would spend four or five *louis* on the evening. Which came to two thousand five hundred or three thousand francs a month. Which shortened my year to three and a half months, and put me in the position of either having to run up debts or to leave Marguerite.

Now I was prepared to agree to anything, except the latter possibility.

Forgive me for telling you all this in such detail, but, as you shall see, these circumstances were the cause of the events which follow. The story I tell is true and simple, and I have allowed the unvarnished facts to stand and the onward march of events to emerge unobstructed.

I realized therefore that, since nothing in the world could weigh heavily enough with me to make me forget my mistress, I should have to find a way of meeting the expense which she forced me to incur. Furthermore, love had run such riot in me that every moment I spent away from Marguerite seemed like a year, and I felt the need to pass those moments through the flame of some passion or other, and to live them so fast that I would not notice that I was living them at all.

I set about borrowing five or six thousand francs against my small capital and began to play the tables, for since the gambling houses were shut down, people have been gambling everywhere. Time was, when you went to Frascati,* you stood a chance of winning a fortune: you played against a bank and, if you lost, you had the consolation of telling yourself you might have won. Whereas nowadays, except in the gaming clubs where you still find they are pretty strict about paying up, you can be fairly sure that if you win a large sum you won't see a penny of if. You will readily understand the reasons why.

Gambling is only for young men who have expensive tastes and not enough money to keep up the kind of lives they lead. So they gamble and, in the natural way of things, this is the result: they may win, and then the losers are expected to foot the bill for these gentlemen's horses and mistresses, which is thoroughly disagreeable. Debts are contracted, and friendships begun around the gaming table end in quarrels from which honour and lives invariably emerge somewhat tattered. And if you are a gentleman, you may find you have been ruined by very gentlemanly young men whose only fault was that they did not have two hundred thousand francs a year.

There is no need for me to tell you about the ones who cheat. One day, you learn that they have had to go away and that—too late—judgement has been passed on them.

*

I accordingly threw myself into the fast-moving, bustling, volcanic life which once upon a time had frightened me when I thought of it, and which had now come to be in my eyes the inescapable corollary of my love for Marguerite. What else could I have done?

During the nights I did not spend in the rue d'Antin, I should not have slept if I had spent them alone in my apartment. Jealousy would have kept me awake and heated my thoughts and blood. On the other hand, gambling temporarily beguiled the fever which would otherwise have overrun my heart which was, thereby, diverted towards a passion fascinating enough to absorb me despite myself until the time came for me to go to my mistress. When that hour struck—and this was how I became aware of how violent my love was—then, whether I was winning or losing, I would abandon the table without compunction, feeling pity for those I left there who, unlike me, would not find happiness when they came to take their leave.

For most of them, gambling was a necessity; for me, it was a kind of antidote.

When I was cured of Marguerite, I would be cured of gambling.

And so, in the middle of it all, I was able to keep a fairly cool head. I lost only what I could afford, and won only what I could have afforded to lose.

Moreover, luck was on my side. I did not run up debts, and spent three times as much as before I started playing the tables. It was not easy to resist the allurements of a way of life which enabled me to cater for Marguerite's innumerable whims without feeling the pinch. For her part, she still loved me as much, and even more.

As I have told you, I began at first by being allowed to stay only between midnight and six in the morning. Then I was allowed into her box at various theatres from time to time. Next, she came and dined with me occasionally. One morning, I did not leave until eight, and there was a day when I did not go until noon.

Pending her moral transformation, a physical transformation had come over Marguerite. I had undertaken to cure her, and the poor girl, guessing what I was about, did everything I told her as a way of showing her gratitude. Without too much trouble or persuasion, I managed to cut her off almost totally from her old habits. My doctor, whom I had arranged for her to meet, had told me that only rest and quiet could keep her in good health, and consequently, for the supper parties and late nights, I succeeded in substituting a healthy diet and regular sleep. Reluctantly at first, Marguerite took to her new life, the beneficial effects of which she could feel. And soon she began to spend odd evenings at home or, if the weather were fine, she would wrap up well in an Indian shawl, cover her face with a veil, and we would set off on foot, like a couple of children, to roam the evening away along the dusky avenues of the Champs-Élysées. She would return weary, take a light supper and retire to bed after playing a little music or reading a few pages, something which had never happened to her before. The coughing fits, which I had found heartrending whenever I heard her racked by them, had almost completely gone.

Within six weeks, there was no further mention of the Count who had been permanently sacrificed. There remained only the Duke to compel me to hide my affair with Marguerite, and even he had often been sent away in my presence on the pretext that Madame was asleep and had left orders that she was not to be disturbed.

As a direct result of the habit of seeing me—or rather the need to see me—which Marguerite had contracted, I abandoned gambling at the precise moment when an experienced gambler would also have given up. All in all, with what I had won, I found myself in possession of twelve thousand francs which seemed an inexhaustible capital to me.

The time of year had come round when I normally went off to join my father and my sister, and still I did not go. As a result, I received frequent letters from both of them asking me to come and stay with them.

To all their entreaties, I answered as best I could, repeating that I was well and that I was not short of money, two considerations which, I believed, would go some way to consoling my father for delaying the start of my annual visit.

Meantime, it came about one morning that Marguerite, who had been woken up by bright sunshine, leaped out of bed and asked me if I would like to take her out to the country for the day.

Prudence was sent for and the three of us set out, after Marguerite had left orders with Nanine to tell the Duke that she had wanted to make the most of the weather and had gone to the country with Madame Duvernoy.

Apart from the fact that the presence of la Duvernoy was necessary to set the old Duke's mind at rest, Prudence was the sort of woman who seems expressly cut out for country outings. With her unquenchable high spirits and insatiable appetite, she was quite incapable of allowing anyone she was with to be bored for an instant, and was more than likely to be an old hand at ordering the eggs, cherries, milk, sautéd rabbit and all the usual ingredients of the traditional lunch for which the countryside around Paris is known.

All that remained was to decide where we should go.

Once again, it was Prudence who got us out of this difficulty.

'Is it the real country you want to go to?' she asked.

'Yes.'

'Well, let's go to Bougival,* to the *Point du Jour*. It's run by a widow named Arnould. Armand, go and hire a barouche.'

An hour and half later we were in the establishment run by the widow Arnould.

Perhaps you know the inn I mean: it is a hotel during the week and pleasure garden on Sundays. From the garden, which is raised and stands as high as an ordinary first floor, you get a magnificent view. On the left, the Marly aqueduct commands the horizon; on the right, the view unfolds across a never-ending succession of hills; the river, which at this point hardly moves at all, stretches away like a wide ribbon of shimmering white silk between the plain of Les Gabillons and the Île de Croissy, and is rocked ceaselessly by the whisper of its tall poplars and the soughing of its willows.

Far off, picked out in a wide swathe of sunlight, rise small white houses with red roofs, and factories which, shorn by

LA DAME AUX CAMÉLIAS

distance of their grim, commercial character, complete the landscape in the most admirable way.

And, far off, Paris shrouded in smoke!

As Prudence had told us, it was really the country and, I must say, it was a real lunch we had.

It is not out of gratitude for the happiness I have to thank the place for that I'm saying all this. Bougival, in spite of its unattractive name, is one of the prettiest spots you could possibly imagine. I have travelled a great deal and seen great sights, but none more charming than this tiny village cheerfully nestling at the foot of the hill which shelters it.

Madame Arnould offered to arrange for us to take a boat out on the river, and Marguerite and Prudence accepted with alacrity.

The countryside has always been associated with love, and rightly so. Nothing creates a more fitting backdrop to the woman you love than the blue sky, the fragrances, the flowers, the breezes, the solitary splendour of fields and woods. However much you love a woman, however much you trust her, however sure of the future her past life makes you, you are always jealous to some degree. If you have ever been in love, really in love, you must have experienced this need to shut out the world and isolate the person through whom you wished to live your whole life. It is as though the woman you love, however indifferent she may be to her surroundings, loses something of her savour and consistency when she comes into contact with men and things. Now I experienced this more intensely than any other man. Mine was no ordinary love; I was as much in love as mortal creature can be. But I loved Marguerite Gautier, which is to say that in Paris, at every turn, I might stumble across some man who had already been her lover, or would be the next day. Whereas, in the country, sur-rounded by people we had never seen before who paid no attention to us, surrounded by nature in all her springtime finery, which is her annual gesture of forgiveness, and far from the bustle of the city, I could shelter my love from prying eyes, and love without shame or fear.

There, the courtesan faded imperceptibly. At my side, I

had a young and beautiful woman whom I loved, by whom I was loved and whose name was Marguerite: the shapes of the past dissolved and the future was free of clouds. The sun shone on my mistress as brightly as it would have shone on the purest fiancée. Together we strolled through delightful glades which seemed as though they were deliberately designed to remind you of lines by Lamartine and make you hum tunes by Scudo.* Marguerite was wearing a white dress. She leaned on my arm. Beneath the starry evening sky, she repeated the words she had said to me the previous night, and in the distance the world went on turning without casting its staining shadow over the happy picture of our youth and love.

Such was the dream which that day's burning sun brought me through the leafy trees and I, lying full-length in the grass of the island where we had landed, free of all human ties which had hitherto bound me, allowed my mind to run free and gather up all the hopes it met with.

Add to this that, from the spot where I lay, I could see, on the bank, a charming little two-storied house which crouched behind a railing in the shape of a semi-circle. Beyond the railing, in front of the house, was a green lawn as smooth as velvet, and, behind the building, a small wood full of mysterious hideaways, where each morning all traces of the previous evening's passage would surely be all mossed over.

Climbing flowers hid the steps leading up to the door of this empty house, and hugged it as far up as the first floor.

Gazing long and hard at the house, I convinced myself in the end that it belonged to me, so completely did it enshrine the dream I was dreaming. I could picture Marguerite and me there together, by day walking in the wood which clothed the hill and, in the evenings, sitting on the lawn, and I wondered to myself if earthly creatures could ever be as happy as we two should be.

'What a pretty house!' said Marguerite, who had been following the direction of my eyes and perhaps my thoughts.

'Where?' said Prudence.

'Over there.' And Marguerite pointed to the house in question.

'Oh, it's lovely,' replied Prudence. 'Do you like it?'

'Very much.'

'Well, then, tell the Duke to rent it for you. He'll rent it for you all right, I'm sure of it. You can leave it all to me if you want.'

Marguerite looked at me, as though to ask what I thought of the suggestion.

My dream had been shattered with these last words of Prudence, and its going had brought me back to reality with such a jolt that I was still dazed by the shock.

'Why, it's an excellent idea,' I stammered, not knowing what I was saying.

'In that case, I'll arrange it,' said Marguerite, squeezing my hand and interpreting my words according to her desires. 'Let's go this minute and see if it's to let.'

The house was empty, and to let for two thousand francs.

'Will you be happy here?' she said to me.

'Can I be sure of ever being here?'

'Who would I choose to bury myself here for, if not for you?'

'Listen, Marguerite, let me rent the house myself.'

'You must be mad! It's not only unnecessary, it would be dangerous. You know perfectly well that I can only take money from one man. So don't be difficult, silly boy, and don't say another word.'

'This way, when I've got a couple of days free, I can come down and spend them with you,' said Prudence.

We left the house and set off back to Paris talking of this latest decision. I held Marguerite in my arms and, by the time we stepped out of the carriage, I was beginning to view my mistress's scheme with a less scrupulous eye.

XVII

THE next day, Marguerite sent me away punctually, saying that the Duke was expected early that morning, and promising to write the moment he left to let me know where we should meet in the evening.

Accordingly, during the day, I received this note:

'Am going to Bougival with the Duke. Be at Prudence's this evening at eight.'

At the appointed time, Marguerite was back and she came to meet me at Madame Duvernoy's.

'Well, it's all arranged,' she said as she came in.

'The house is taken?' asked Prudence.

'Yes. He agreed at once.'

I did not know the Duke, but I was ashamed to be deceiving him like this.

'But that's not all,' Marguerite went on.

'There's more?'

'I was worried about where Armand could stay.'

'Not in the same house?' asked Prudence with a laugh.

'No, at the *Point du Jour*, where the Duke and I had lunch. While he was looking at the view, I asked Madame Arnould—she is called Madame Arnould, isn't she?—I asked her if she had any suitable apartments. And she has one, with a drawing-room, a reception room and a bedroom. That's all we need, I'd say. Sixty francs a month. The whole place furnished in a manner that would take a hypochondriac's mind off his ailments. I took it. Did I do well?'

I flung my arms around Marguerite's neck.

'It'll be lovely,' she went on. 'You'll have a key to the side door, and I promised the Duke that he shall have a key to the main gate which he won't take since he'll only ever come during the day when he comes at all. Between ourselves, I think he's delighted by this whim of mine, for it'll get me out of Paris for a while and help to shut his family up. Even so, he did ask how it was that I, who love Paris so much, could make up my mind to bury myself in the country. I told him I wasn't well and this way I could rest. He didn't seem to believe me altogether. The poor old thing always seems to have his back against a wall. So we will be very careful, dear Armand, because he'll have me watched there. And he's not done with just renting a house for me: he's also going to have to pay my debts and, unfortunately, I've a few of those. Is all this all right with you?'

'Yes,' I replied, trying to silence the scruples which this kind of life awakened from time to time.

'We went over the house from top to bottom, and it will be just perfect for us. The Duke fussed over everything. Ah, my dear,' she added, kissing me like a mad thing, 'you can't complain, you've got a millionaire to make your bed for you.'

'And when are you thinking of moving down there?' asked Prudence.

'As soon as possible.'

'Will you be taking your carriage and the horses?'

'I shall be taking everything. You can look after the apartment while I'm away.'

A week later, Marguerite had taken possession of the house in the country and I was installed at the *Point du Jour*.

And so began a life which I could hardly attempt to describe to you.

In the early days of her stay at Bougival, Marguerite was unable to make a complete break with her old ways and, since the house was always in a party mood, all her girl-friends came down to see her. A month went by without a single day when Marguerite did not have eight or ten people sitting round her table. For her part, Prudence invited along everybody she knew and did all the honours of the house, as though the place belonged to her.

The Duke's money paid for it all, as you will have gathered, yet even so Prudence was apt to ask me, from time to time, for the odd thousand-franc note, saying that it was for Marguerite. As you know, I had won some money at the gaming table. So I promptly handed over to Prudence what Marguerite, through her, had asked me for, and, fearing that she might need more than I had, I travelled up to Paris where I borrowed the equivalent of the sum of money which I had borrowed before and had repaid in full.

I thus found myself rich once more to the tune of ten thousand francs or so, in addition to my allowance.

However, the pleasure Marguerite derived from playing host to her women friends slackened off somewhat in view of the expense it involved, and especially in view of the fact that she was on occasion forced to ask me for money. The Duke, who had leased the house so that Marguerite could rest, stopped coming altogether, fearing as always that he would run into a large and high-spirited gathering of people by whom he had no wish to be seen. The reason largely for this was that, turning up one day for a private dinner with Marguerite, he had wandered into the middle of a luncheon party for fifteen which was still going on at a time when he had imagined he would be sitting down to his dinner. When, all unsuspecting, he had opened the dining-room door, his entrance had been greeted by a burst of laughter, and he had been obliged to withdraw hurriedly in the face of the withering glee of the girls who were there.

Marguerite had left the table, caught up with the Duke in the next room and had done everything she could to make him overlook the incident. But the old man's pride had been wounded, and he had taken umbrage: he had told the poor girl quite cruelly that he was tired of footing the bill for the follies of a woman who could not even ensure that he was respected under her roof, and he had left very angry.

From that day on, we heard nothing more of him. Marguerite sent her guests away and changed her ways, but it did no good: the Duke did not contact her thereafter. I had gained thereby, for my mistress now belonged to me more completely, and my dream was at last coming true. Marguerite could no longer live without me. Without worrying her head about the consequence, she flaunted our affair publicly, and I reached the point where I never left her house. The servants called me 'sir' and regarded me officially as their master.

Of course, Prudence had lectured Marguerite about her new life very sternly, but Marguerite had replied that she loved me, could not live without me and, however it all turned out, would not forgo the joy of having me constantly at her side. And she added that anyone who did not like it was perfectly free to stay away.

I had heard this for myself one day when Prudence told Marguerite that she had something very important to say to her, and I had listened at the door of the bedroom in which they had closeted themselves.

Some days later, Prudence came down to see us again.

I was at the bottom of the garden when she arrived. She did not see me. Judging by the way Marguerite had gone to meet her, I suspected that another conversation like the one I had already overheard was about to take place, and I was no less anxious to hear what was said.

The two women shut themselves in a parlour and I took up my position.

'Well?' asked Marguerite.

'Well now, I saw the Duke.'

'What did he say?'

'He said he was quite ready to forgive that first scene, but he'd found out that you were living openly with Monsieur Armand Duval. He couldn't forgive that. "If Marguerite leaves this young man," he told me, "I'll give her anything she wants, as in the past. If she doesn't, she can stop asking me for anything." '

'What did you say to that?'

'I said I'd pass on his decision, and I promised I'd make you see sense. Just think, dear girl, of the niche you'll be losing. Armand will never be able to make it up to you. He loves you with all his soul, but he doesn't have the money to pay for everything you need, and some day he's bound to leave you—when it'll be too late, and the Duke won't want to lend any more helping hands. Do you want me to speak to Armand?'

Marguerite seemed to be thinking, for she did not reply. My heart beat violently as I waited for her answer.

'No,' she resumed, 'I shall not leave Armand, and I shan't hide myself away so that I can go on living with him. Madness it may be, but I love him, there it is! And anyway, he's got into the habit of loving me without anything standing in his way. It would be much too painful for him to have to leave me for even an hour a day. Besides, I haven't got so much time to live that I can afford to make myself miserable just to please an old man: the very sight of him makes me feel old. Let him keep his money. I'll manage without.'

'But what will you do?'

'I have no idea.'

Prudence was probably about to reply to this, but I burst in, ran across to Marguerite and threw myself at her feet, covering her hands with the tears which the joy of being loved made me shed.

'My life is yours, Marguerite. You don't need this man: am I not here? How could I ever desert you? How could I ever repay the happiness you give me? Away with all constraints, dearest Marguerite! We love each other! What does the rest matter?'

'Oh yes! I do love you, my Armand!' she murmured, circling my neck with both arms, 'I love you as I never believed I could love anybody. We will be happy, we'll live in peace, and I'll say goodbye forever to the old life I'm so ashamed of now. You'll never hold my past against me, will you?'

The tears dimmed my voice. The only answer I could give was to clasp Marguerite to my heart.

'Come,' she said, turning to Prudence, her voice tinged with emotion, 'you can go and report this scene to the Duke and, while you're at it, tell him we don't need him.'

From that day on, the Duke was never mentioned again. Marguerite was no longer the girl I had met. She avoided anything which might have reminded me of the life she had been leading when I first made her acquaintance. Never did wife or sister show husband or brother such love, such consideration as she showed me. Her state of health left her open to sensation, and made her vulnerable to her feelings. She had broken with her women friends just as she had broken with her old ways; she controlled her language just as she curbed the old extravagance. Had you observed us leave the house for an outing in a delightful little boat I had bought, you would never have thought that this woman in a white dress, wearing a large straw hat and carrying on her arm a simple fur-lined silk coat which would protect her against the chill of the water, was the same

Marguerite Gautier who, four months before, had attracted such attention with her extravagant ways and scandalous conduct.

Alas! we made haste to be happy, as though we had sensed that we should not be happy for long.

We had not set foot in Paris for two months. No one had come down to see us, except Prudence and the same Julie Duprat whom I have already mentioned as the person in whose keeping Marguerite would later place the moving story now in my possession.

I spent whole days at my mistress's feet. We would open the windows overlooking the garden and, as we watched the bright summer swoop down and open the flowers and settle under the trees, we would sit side by side and drink in this real, live world which neither Marguerite nor I had understood before.

She reacted with childish wonder to the most trivial things. There were days when she ran round the garden, like a girl of ten, chasing a butterfly or a dragonfly. This courtesan, who had made men spend more on flowers than would be needed to enable a whole family to live without a care, would sometimes sit on the lawn for an hour on end, examining the simple flower whose name she bore.

It was at this time that she read *Manon Lescaut* so frequently. Many a time, I caught her writing in the margin of the book. And she always said that if a woman is truly in love, then that woman could never do what Manon did.

The Duke wrote to her two or three times. She recognized his writing and gave me his letters unread.

On occasions, the wording of his letters brought tears to my eyes.

He had thought that, by closing his purse to Marguerite, he could make her go back to him. But when he saw how ineffective his stratagem was, he was unable to carry it through. He had written, again asking her, as he had asked in the past, to allow him back to the fold, whatever conditions she chose to set for his return.

I thus had read his pressing, repeated letters and had torn them up, without telling Marguerite what they said or

advising her to see the old man again—though a feeling of
pity for the poor man's unhappiness did tempt me to do so.
But I was afraid that she would see in my urging no more
than a wish on my part to see the Duke resume his old
visits, and thereby to see him assume responsibility once
more for the household expenses. And above all, I feared
that she would conclude that her love for me might lead
to situations in which I would be capable of repudiating my
responsibilities for her existence.

The outcome was that the Duke, continuing to receive
no answer, eventually stopped writing, and Marguerite and
I continued our life together without a thought for the
future.

XVIII

To tell you of our new life in any detail would be no easy
matter. It was made up of a series of frivolous diversions
which, though delightful to us, would be quite meaningless
to anyone who heard me recount them. You know what it
is to love a woman. You know how short the days seem and
how loving the ease with which you let yourself drift
towards the morrow. You are acquainted with that general
neglect of things which is bred of violent, trusting, requited
love. Any mortal being who is not the woman you love
seems superfluous to creation. You regret having tossed
pieces of your heart to other women, and you cannot
imagine the prospect of ever holding a hand which is not
the hand that you now hold clasped in yours. Your brain
will entertain neither work nor memories, nor anything
which might divert it from the one thought with which it
is endlessly regaled. Each day you discover some new attraction in your mistress, some unknown sensual delight.

Life is no more than the repeated fulfilling of a permanent
desire. The soul is merely the vestal handmaid whose task is
to keep the sacred flame of love burning.

Often, after dark, we would go and sit in the little wood
which overlooked the house. There we listened to the happy

song of evening as we both thought of the approaching moment which would leave us in each other's arms till morning. At other times, we would stay in bed all day and not let even the sun into our bedroom. The curtains would be tightly drawn, and for us the world outside momentarily stopped turning. Nanine alone was authorized to open our door, but only to bring us our meals—and even so we ate them without getting up, and interrupted them constantly with laughter and all kinds of foolishness. And then would follow a few moments of sleep, for, retreating completely into our love, we were like two persistent divers who return to the surface only to take breath.

However, I would catch Marguerite looking sad, and sometimes there were tears in her eyes. I would ask what was the reason for her sudden dejection and she would answer:

'This love of ours, my dearest Armand, is no ordinary love. You love me as though I'd never belonged to anyone else, and I tremble for fear that with time, regretting that you ever loved me and turning my past into a crime to hold against me, you might force me to resume the life from which you took me. Remember this: now that I've tasted a new kind of life, I should die if I had to take up the old one. So tell me you'll never leave me.'

'I swear it!'

At this, she would stare at me, as though she could read in my eyes whether my oath was sincere. Then she would throw herself into my arms and, burying her head in my chest, say:

'It's just that you have no idea how much I love you!'

One evening, we were leaning over the balcony outside our window. We gazed at the moon struggling to rise from its bed of clouds. We listened to the noise of the wind as it shook the trees. We held hands, and had not spoken for a good quarter of an hour when Marguerite said:

'Winter's coming. Would you like us to go away?'

'Where would we go?'

'Italy.'

'Are you bored here?'

'I'm afraid of winter. And I'm even more afraid of our going back to Paris.'

'Why?'

'Lots of reasons.'

And she went on quickly, without explaining the reasons for her fears:

'Do you want to leave this place? I'll sell everything I have. We'll go and live far away. There'll be nothing left of the person I used to be. No one will know who I am. Would you like that?'

'We'll go, if that's what you want, Marguerite. Let's travel,' I said, 'but why the need to sell things you'll be glad to have when we get back? I haven't got enough money to accept a sacrifice like that, but I do have enough for us to travel in style for five or six months, if you fancy the idea at all.'

'If that's the way of it, no,' she continued, leaving the window and moving to the sofa in the dark shadow of the bedroom. 'What's the point of going all that way to spend money? I cost you enough here as it is.'

'That sounds like a reproach, Marguerite. You're being ungracious.'

'Forgive me, my dear,' she said, holding out her hand to me, 'this stormy weather makes me irritable. I'm not saying what I mean.'

And, after kissing me, she sat for a long time, lost in thought.

Scenes like this occurred on several occasions and, though I remained ignorant as to their cause, I nevertheless sensed in Marguerite a feeling of anxiety for the future. It was not that she could have any doubts about my love for her, for it grew deeper with each passing day. And yet I often saw that she was sad, though she never explained why she was sad other than by alleging some physical reason.

Fearing that she would weary of too monotonous a life, I suggested that we might return to Paris, but she invariably rejected the suggestion, and assured me that she could not be as happy anywhere as she was in the country.

Prudence made only rare visits now. On the other hand,

she wrote a number of letters which I never asked to see, although each one left Marguerite deeply preoccupied. I did not know what to make of it.

One day, Marguerite remained in her room. I entered. She was writing.

'Who are you writing to?' I asked her.

'Prudence. Do you want me to read out what I've written?'

I had a profound distaste for anything that could seem like suspiciousness. So I answered Marguerite saying that there was no need for me to know what she was writing. And yet, I was sure of it, that letter would have acquainted me with the real reason for her fits of sadness.

The next day, the weather was superb. Marguerite suggested that we might take a boat out on the river and visit the Île de Croissy. She seemed in the best of spirits. It was five o'clock by the time we got back.

'Madame Duvernoy came,' said Nanine as soon as she saw us come in.

'Did she go away again?' asked Marguerite.

'Yes, in Madame's carriage. She said it was all right to take it.'

'Very good,' said Marguerite quickly. 'Let dinner be served at once.'

Two days later, there was a letter from Prudence, and for the next fortnight Marguerite seemed to have done with her mysterious sad moods, for which she never stopped asking me to forgive her now that they had ceased.

However, the carriage did not come back.

'How is it that Prudence hasn't returned your brougham?' I asked one day.

'One of the horses is sick, and the carriage needs some repairs. It's better for all that to be done while we are still here where we don't need a carriage, than to wait until we get back to Paris.'

Prudence came down to see us a few days after this and confirmed what Marguerite had told me.

The two women went for a stroll by themselves in the garden, and when I joined them they changed the subject they had been discussing.

That evening, as she was going, Prudence complained of the cold and asked Marguerite to lend her an Indian shawl.

And so a month went by during which Marguerite was gayer and more loving than she had ever been.

However, the carriage had not come back, and the Indian shawl had not been returned. All this puzzled me in spite of myself and, since I knew in which drawer Marguerite kept Prudence's letters, I took advantage of a moment when she was at the bottom of the garden, hurried to the drawer and tried to open it. But it was no use: it was double-locked.

I then searched through the drawers where her trinkets and diamonds were normally kept. They opened without difficulty, but the jewel-cases had disappeared—along with their contents, naturally.

A pang of fear shot through my heart.

I was about to go and ask Marguerite to tell me exactly why these items were missing. But I knew for certain that she would not admit the truth.

So I said: 'My dear Marguerite, I want to ask if it's all right for me to go up to town. No one where I live knows where I am, and there must have been letters from my father. I expect he's worried. I must write to him.'

'Go, my dear,' she said. 'But be back soon.'

I left.

I hurried round to Prudence's at once.

'Look here,' I said, without preamble of any sort, 'answer me frankly: where are Marguerite's horses?'

'Sold.'

'Her shawl?'

'Sold.'

'The diamonds?'

'Pawned.'

'And who did the selling and the pawning?'

'I did.'

'Why didn't you tell me about all this?'

'Because Marguerite ordered me not to.'

'And why didn't you ask me for money?'

'Because she wouldn't let me.'

'And what's the money been spent on?'

'Paying debts.'

'So she owes a great deal?'

'There's thirty thousand francs or so outstanding. I told you, dear, didn't I? You just wouldn't believe me. Well then, are you convinced now? The upholsterer, who had the Duke as her guarantor, was shown the door when he went to see the Duke who wrote him a letter the next day saying that he wouldn't lift a finger for Mademoiselle Gautier. The man wanted money. He was given something on account— the few thousand francs I asked you for. Then some kind souls let him know that his non-paying customer had been dropped by the Duke and was living with some young man who had no money. The other creditors were likewise told. They demanded money, and repossessed some of their goods. Marguerite wanted to sell everything, but it was too late and, besides, I should have been against it. She had to pay of course, and to avoid asking you for money, she sold her horses and her Indian shawls and pawned her jewels. Do you want the buyers' receipts and the pawn tickets?'

And, pulling out a drawer, Prudence showed me the papers.

'Do you imagine,' she continued, as persistent as any woman who is entitled to say: 'I was right!', 'do you imagine that it's enough to love each other and go off to the country and live some dreamy, rustic life? Oh no, my dear. Alongside the ideal life, there's the necessities to think of, and the purest designs are earthbound, secured by threads which, ludicrous though they may be, are made of steel and cannot be easily snapped. If Marguerite hasn't deceived you twenty times and more it's because she has an exceptional nature. It's not her fault if I advised her to do so, because it grieved me to see the poor girl strip herself of everything. And she wouldn't have anything to do with it! She told me she loved you and wouldn't deceive you for anything. All that's very nice, very poetic, but it's not coin you can pay off creditors with. And now she's reached the stage where she won't get away with it unless she comes up with, let me say it again, thirty thousand francs.'

'It's all right. I'll find the money.'

'You'll borrow it?'

'But of course.'

'Now that would be really clever. You'll fall out with your father, tie up your allowance and, anyway, you can't just come up with thirty thousand francs from one day to the next. Take it from me, my dear Armand, I know women better than you do. Don't do it: it would be sheer folly and you'd regret it some day. Be reasonable. I don't say you should leave Marguerite; just live with her on the same footing as at the start of the summer. Let her find ways out of this mess. The Duke will come round gradually. Count de N***, if she takes him on, he was telling me just yesterday, will pay all her debts and give her four or five thousand francs a month. He's got two hundred thousand livres a year. She'll be set up, whereas you're going to have to leave her in any case: don't wait until you're ruined, especially since this Count de N*** is a fool and there'll be nothing to stop you being Marguerite's lover. She'll cry a little to start with, but she'll get used to it in the end, and she'll thank you one day for what you did. Tell yourself that Marguerite's married, and then deceive her husband. That's all there's to it.

'I've already told you all this once. But then I was just giving you advice. Today, you've got very little option.'

Prudence was right, cruelly right.

'That's how it is,' she continued, shutting away the papers she had just shown me. 'Kept women always expect that there'll be men around who'll love them, but they never imagine that they themselves will fall in love. Otherwise, they'd put a bit to one side and, by the time they're thirty, they'd be able to afford the luxury of taking a lover who pays nothing. If only I'd known once what I know now! But that's by the by. Don't say anything to Marguerite; just bring her back to Paris. You've had four or five months alone with her, which isn't bad. Turn a blind eye, that's all you're asked to do. Within a fortnight, she'll take on Count de N***, she'll put some money by this winter, and then next summer you can pick up where you left off. That's how it's done, my dear!'

Prudence seemed delighted with her advice, which I rejected indignantly.

Not only did love and self-respect make it impossible for me to act along these lines, but I was further convinced that, having got to the stage she had now reached, Marguerite would rather die than accept such an arrangement.

'Enough of this nonsense,' I told Prudence. 'How much exactly does Marguerite need?'

'I told you. Around thirty thousand francs.'

'And when must she have it?'

'Within two months.'

'She'll have it.'

Prudence shrugged her shoulders.

'I'll get it to you,' I continued. 'But you must swear you'll never tell Marguerite that I gave it to you.'

'Don't worry, I won't.'

'And if she sends you anything else to sell or pawn, let me know.'

'There's no danger of that. She's got nothing left.'

From there, I went to my apartment to see if there were any letters from my father.

There were four.

XIX

In the first three letters, my father expressed his concern for my silence and asked the reason for it. In the last, he made it clear that he had been informed of my changed way of life, and announced his arrival in the very near future.

I have always felt great respect and a genuine affection for my father. So I wrote back saying that the reason for my silence was that I had been away travelling for a while, and I asked him to let me know on which day he proposed to arrive so that I could be there to meet him.

I gave my servant my country address and left orders that he was to bring the first letter that came postmarked C***. Then I set off again immediately for Bougival.

Marguerite was waiting for me at the garden gate.

Her look was anxious. She threw her arms around my neck and could not stop herself asking:

'Did you see Prudence?'

'No.'

'Why did you stay so long in Paris?'

'I found some letters from my father which I had to answer.'

A few moments after this, Nanine came in. She was out of breath. Marguerite stood up, went over and spoke to her softly.

When Nanine had gone, Marguerite sat down beside me once more and, taking my hand, said:

'Why did you deceive me? You went to Prudence's, didn't you?'

'Who told you?'

'Nanine.'

'And who told her?'

'She followed you.'

'So you told her to follow me?'

'Yes. I thought there must have been a very good reason to make you go up to Paris like that. You've not left my side for four months. I was afraid that something awful had happened or that perhaps you were going to see another woman.'

'Silly girl!'

'My mind's easy now. I know what you did, but I still don't know what you were told.'

I showed Marguerite my father's letters.

'That's not what I asked. What I'd like to know is why you called on Prudence.'

'To see her.'

'You're lying, my dear.'

'All right then. I went to ask her if the horse was better, and if she'd finished with your shawl and your jewels.'

Marguerite flushed, but said nothing.

'And,' I continued, 'I found out to what use you'd put the horses, shawls and diamonds.'

'And you're angry with me?'

'I'm angry with you for not thinking of asking me for whatever you needed.'

'In affairs like ours, as long as the woman has something of her self-respect left, she must shoulder any number of sacrifices herself rather than ask her lover for money and in so doing taint her love with mercenary motives. You love me, I know you do, but you have no idea just how weak are the ties that bind the love men have for girls like me. Who knows? Perhaps one day, when you were short of money or feeling annoyed, you'd have come round to thinking that our affair was a carefully worked-out plot! Prudence talks too much. I didn't need those horses! I've saved myself money by selling them: I can manage without, and now I don't have to spend anything on them. As long as you love me, that's all I ask. And you can love me just as much without horses and shawls and diamonds.'

She said all this in so natural a tone of voice that there were tears in my eyes as I listened.

'But, my sweet Marguerite,' I answered, lovingly pressing my mistress's hands in mine, 'you must have known that some day I'd find out about your sacrifice, and that the day I did find out, I'd never have allowed it.'

'And why not?'

'Because, dearest girl, I do not intend that the affection you truly feel for me should leave you the poorer by even a single piece of jewelry. Like you, I don't ever want you to think, when things are hard or you're feeling angry, that such bad times would never have happened if you'd lived with somebody else. Nor can I stand the thought that you should ever regret living with me, even for a moment. A few days from now, your horses, your diamonds and your shawls will be returned to you. You need them as much as life needs air. It may be ridiculous, but I'd rather have you lavish than frugal.'

'Which is to say you don't love me any more.'

'Don't be silly!'

'If you really loved me, you'd let me love you in my own way. But you persist in thinking of me as though I'm some girl who can't live without all this luxury, someone you still think you have to pay. You are ashamed to accept proof that I love you. In your heart, you're thinking of leaving me some day, and you're being very careful to put your scruples beyond suspicion. You're quite right, my dear, but I had expected better.'

And Marguerite stirred, as though she were about to get up. I held her back a moment, saying:

'I want you to be happy. I don't want there to be anything that you can reproach me for. That's all.'

'Even so, we shall go our separate ways!'

'Why, Marguerite? Who can separate us?' I exclaimed.

'You. You won't take me into your confidence by saying exactly where you stand, and you're vain enough to want to keep me in my place. You want to keep me in the luxury to which I was accustomed, but you also want to maintain the moral distance between us. You're the one. You don't consider that my feelings are sufficiently disinterested to want to share what money you have with me so that we could live happily together. No, you'd sooner ruin yourself. A slave to a stupid prejudice, that's what you are. Do you really think I compare a carriage and bits of jewelry with your love? Do you imagine I think happiness consists of those empty pleasures which people make do with when they've got nothing to love, but which seem so unimportant when they have? You'll pay my debts, you'll sign away all you have and you'll be my keeper! And how long will that last? Two or three months—and then it'll be too late to start the life I'm offering you, for then you'd be kept by me, and that's something which no self-respecting man could accept. Whereas at the moment, you've got eight or ten thousand francs a year on which we can manage. I'll sell everything I don't need, and by investing the proceeds I'd have a steady two thousand a year. We'll rent a nice little apartment and live there together. In summer, we'll come down to the country, not to a house like this, but to something smaller, just big enough for two. You've no ties, I'm free, and we're young. For heaven's sake, Armand, don't make me go back to the life I had to lead once!'

I could not answer. My eyes brimmed over with tears of

gratitude and love, and I threw myself into Marguerite's arms.

'I wanted,' she went on, 'to arrange everything without telling you. I wanted to pay my debts and get my new apartment ready. In October, we would have reeturned to Paris and it would have been too late to say no. But since Prudence has told you everything, you'll have to agree before and not after. Do you love me enough to say yes?'

I could not hold out against such devotion. I kissed Marguerite's hands with great feeling and told her:

'I shall do whatever you want.'

And so what she had decided was agreed between us.

Then she became wildly exhilarated. She danced, she sang, she went into raptures about how homely her new apartment would be, and was already asking me in what part of Paris it should be and how it should be laid out.

I could see she was happy and very proud of this arrangement which seemed as though it would bring us together for good.

Which was why I had no wish to be any less keen than she was.

In a moment, I decided what course my life was to take. I worked out how I stood financially, and made over to Marguerite the income from my mother's estate, though it did not seem anything like an adequate return for the sacrifice which I was accepting.

There remained the allowance of five thousand francs which my father made me and, however things turned out, this annual allowance would always be enough to live on.

I did not tell Marguerite what I had decided, for I was quite convinced that she would refuse to accept my deed of gift.

The money in question derived from a mortgage of sixty thousand francs on a house which I had never even seen. All I knew was that each quarter, my father's solicitor, an old family friend, handed over seven hundred and fifty francs against my signature.

The day Marguerite and I came to Paris to look at apartments, I called at his office and asked him how I should set about transferring this income to another party.

The good man thought that I was ruined, and asked me questions about why I had decided to take such a step. Now, since I was going to have to tell him sooner or later in whose favour I was making the deed of gift, I decided to confess the truth there and then.

He did not raise any of the objections which his position as solicitor and friend entitled him to make, and he assured me that he would see that everything was arranged for the best.

Of course, I urged him to the greatest discretion with regard to my father, and left him to join Marguerite who was waiting for me at Julie Duprat's, where she had preferred to stay rather than go and be lectured by Prudence.

We started looking for apartments. Marguerite found all the ones we saw too expensive, and I thought them too ordinary. Even so, we did agree in the end, and, in one of the quietest parts of Paris, decided on a modest lodge which was situated at a good distance from the main house.

Behind this small lodge there was a delightful garden which was part of the property. It was enclosed by walls high enough to separate us from our neighbours, but not so high that they restricted the view.

It was better than we had hoped for.

While I went back to my apartment to arrange to vacate the premises, Marguerite went to see a dealer who, she said, had already done for one of her friends what she was now going to ask him to do for her.

She came for me in the rue de Provence, quite delighted. The man had promised to pay all her debts, give her a receipt in full, and let her have around twenty thousand francs in exchange for relinquishing all her furniture.

You can see from the sum realized by the auction that this good man of business stood to make upwards of thirty thousand francs out of his client.

We set off back to Bougival in high spirits. As we went, we continued telling each other about our plans for the future which, with the help of our thoughtlessness but especially our love, we saw in the rosiest of lights.

A week later, we were having lunch when Nanine came in and told me that my servant was asking for me.

I told her to show him in.

'Sir,' he said, 'your father has arrived in Paris, and asks you to return to your apartment at once. He's waiting for you there.'

The news was the simplest thing imaginable, and yet, as we took it in, Marguerite and I exchanged looks.

We scented trouble in this turn of events.

Which was why, though she did not intimate to me anything of her reaction which I shared, I responded by holding out my hand to her:

'There's nothing to be afraid of.'

'Come back as soon as you can,' murmured Marguerite as she kissed me. 'I'll be waiting by the window.'

I sent Joseph on ahead to let my father know I was on my way.

And two hours later, I was in my apartment in the rue de Provence.

XX

My father was sitting in my drawing-room in his dressing-gown. He was writing.

I knew at once, from the way he looked up at me as I entered, that serious matters were about to be broached.

I went up to him, however, as though I had no inkling of anything from his expression, and I embraced him.

'When did you arrive, father?'

'Last night.'

'And you're putting up here, as usual?'

'Yes.'

'I'm so sorry I wasn't here to welcome you.'

I expected that these words would unleash the lecture which my father's cool expression clearly promised. But he did not answer, sealed the letter he had just written, and gave it to Joseph to post.

When we were alone, my father stood up and, leaning against the mantelpiece, said:

'The two of us, my dear Armand, have serious matters to discuss.'

'I'm listening, father.'

'Will you promise to be frank with me?'

'I'm never anything else.'

'Is it true that you are living with a woman named Marguerite Gautier?'

'Yes.'

'Do you know what sort of woman she was?'

'She was a kept woman.'

'Was it on her account that you neglected to come down to see your sister and me this year?'

'Yes, father, I admit it.'

'So you love this woman very much?'

'You can see I do, father, since she made me forget a sacred duty, for which I now humbly ask your pardon.'

Clearly, my father had not been expecting such plain answers, for he appeared to reflect for a moment before saying:

'You must have known, of course, that you couldn't go on living like this forever?'

'I was afraid it might be so, father, but I knew no such thing.'

'But you must have known,' my father continued in a slightly sharper tone of voice, 'that I would never allow it.'

'I told myself that, as long as I did nothing to prejudice the respect which I owe to your name and the time-honoured probity of the family, then I could behave as I have—and this went some way to reassuring me about the fears I had.'

Passion arms us against sentiment. I was ready to fight any battle, even against my father, to keep Marguerite.

'Well, the time has come to behave differently.'

'But why, father?'

'Because you are on the point of committing actions which undermine the respect which you say you have for your family.'

'I don't understand what you're saying.'

'Then I'll explain what I said. If you have a mistress, all well and good. If you pay her like any gentleman pays to be loved by a kept woman, even better. But when you neglect your most sacred obligations on her account; when you allow rumours of your scandalous conduct to travel all the way down to my part of the world and cast the shadow of a stain on the honourable name I have given you, then that is something which cannot continue, nor shall it continue.'

'Allow me to say, father, that whoever told you all this about me was badly informed. I am Marguerite Gautier's lover, I live with her: it's really quite simple. I have not given Mademoiselle Gautier the name I received from you. I spend on her no more than my means permit, I haven't run up any debts and I haven't got myself into any of the predicaments which entitle a father to say to his son what you have just said to me.'

'A father is always entitled to turn his son from the ill-considered path on which he sees him set his foot. You have not done anything wrong as yet, but you will.'

'Really, father!'

'Sir, I know life better than you do. Wholly pure sentiments are to be found only in women who are wholly chaste. Every Manon can turn a man into a Des Grieux, and times and manners have changed. It would be pointless if the world grew older without growing wiser. You will leave your mistress.'

'It distresses me to disobey you, father, but that is out of the question.'

'I shall compel you.'

'Unfortunately, father, there aren't any St-Margaret's Islands* nowadays where courtesans can be transported, and, even if there were, I should follow Mademoiselle Gautier there if you managed to have her sent away. I'm sorry, it may be wrong of me, but I can be happy only on the condition that I remain her lover.'

'Come, Armand, open your eyes and see your father who has always loved you and who wants only your happiness. Is it honourable for you to live as man and wife with a woman who's been had by everybody?'

'What does it matter, father, if no one else shall have her

again? What does it matter if she loves me, if she has been transformed by the love she has for me and the love I feel for her? What can it possibly matter if there has been a spiritual change in her?'

'And do you think, sir, that the mission of a gentleman is to bring about spiritual changes in courtesans?? Do you imagine that God has given life so grotesque a purpose, and that a man's heart must have no other zeal than this? How will this miraculous cure end? And what will you make of what you're saying now, when you're forty? You'll laugh at this affair, if you are still able to laugh, if, that is, it hasn't left an indelible mark on your past. Where would you be now if your father had thought as you do, if he'd surrendered his life to the enticements of love instead of setting it unshakeably upon a belief in honour and integrity? Think, Armand, and stop talking nonsense. Come, you shall leave this woman. Your father begs you to.'

I made no reply.

'Armand,' continued my father, 'in the name of your saintly mother, listen to me: give up this way of life. You will forget it far more quickly than you think and, in any case, you are kept chained to it by a philosophy which is quite absurd. You are twenty-four: think of the future. You won't always be in love with this woman, nor will she love you forever. You have both exaggerated what you feel for each other. You're shutting all the doors to a career. Take one more step, and you'll never be able to get off the path you're on, and you'll regret your misspent youth for the rest of your life. Leave now. Come and stay for a month or two with your sister. Rest and devoted family love will soon cure you of this infatuation, for it is nothing else.

'Meanwhile, your mistress will get over it. She'll take another lover and then, when you see what kind of person almost made you quarrel with your father and forfeit his affection, you will say I was quite right to come and fetch you, and you will bless me for having done so.

'So you will come away, won't you, Armand?'

I felt that my father was right about women in general, but I was convinced that he was wrong about Marguerite.

However, he spoke these last words so gently, so beseechingly, that I dared not answer.

'Well?' he said, in a voice heavy with emotion.

'Look, father, I can't promise anything,' I said at length. 'What you are asking is more than I can do. Please believe me,' I continued, seeing him stir impatiently, 'you're making too much of the consequences of this affair. Marguerite isn't the kind of girl you think she is. Far from setting me on the wrong road, this love of ours, on the contrary, has the power to nurture the finest sentiments in me. True love always makes a man finer, whatever sort of woman inspires it. If you knew Marguerite, you'd see that there's no risk to me. She is as noble as the noblest women. She is as disinterested as the others are grasping.'

'Though that hasn't stopped her pocketing all your money, for the sixty thousand francs your mother left you, which you want to give her, represents—and take note of what I'm saying—all the money you have.'

In all likelihood, my father had kept this peroration as a threat intended to undermine my last defences.

I felt stronger against his threats than against his entreaties.

'Who told you that I was to make the money over to her?' I went on.

'My solicitor. Would any honourable man have drawn up a deed of that kind without letting me know first? Well, it was to prevent you beggaring yourself for the benefit of some loose woman that brought me to Paris. When your mother died, she left you enough to live on decently, but not enough for you to go giving it away to your mistresses.'

'I swear to you, father, Marguerite knew nothing of this deed of gift.'

'Why did you have it drawn up, then?'

'Because Marguerite, the woman you've slandered and want me to give up, has sacrificed everything she owns to live with me.'

'And you have accepted this sacrifice? What sort of man are you, sir, that you will allow a Mademoiselle Marguerite Gautier to make sacrifices for you? But, enough. You will leave this woman. A little while ago, I asked you to; now, I order you to. I will not have such obscenities in my family. Pack your trunks and get ready to come with me.'

'Forgive me, father,' I said, 'but I shall not leave here.'

'Why not?'

'Because I am now at an age when I don't have to obey orders any more.'

At this, my father turned pale.

'Very well, sir,' he went on, 'I am clear in my mind what remains to be done.'

He rang.

Joseph appeared.

'Have my trunks sent round to the Hôtel de Paris,'* he told my servant. And with these words, he went into his bedroom where he finished dressing.

When he emerged, I went up to him.

'Will you promise me, father,' I said, 'that you won't do anything to distress Marguerite?'

My father paused, gave me a look of contempt, and merely said:

'I do believe you've taken leave of your senses.'

Thereupon, he stormed out, slamming the door violently behind him.

Then I too left, took a cab and set off for Bougival.

Marguerite was waiting for me at the window.

XXI

'At last!' she cried, throwing her arms around my neck. 'You're back! You look so pale!'

Then I told her about the scene with my father.

'Oh my God! I was expecting something like this,' she said. 'When Joseph came and told us your father had arrived, my heart stopped as though he'd brought bad news. Poor dear! And I'm to blame for all your troubles. Perhaps it would be better for you to leave me than quarrel with your father. Still, I never did him any harm. We live very quietly and we'll live more quietly still. Of course, he realizes that you must have a mistress, and he should be pleased it's me, because I love you and won't ask you for anything more than your circumstances warrant. Did you tell him what we've worked out for the future?'

'Yes, and that's what upset him most, because he took the fact that our minds were made up as a sure sign of our love for each other.'

'What do we do now?'

'Stay together, sweet Marguerite, and let the storm blow over.'

'And will it blow over?'

'Storms always do.'

'But your father won't leave it at that, will he?'

'What can he do?'

'How should I know? Everything a father can do to force his son to obey him. He'll remind you of my past life, and may even credit me with some new treachery invented for the purpose of persuading you to give me up.'

'You know how I love you.'

'Yes, but there's something else I know: sooner or later you'll have to obey your father, and in the end you may let yourself be convinced.'

'No, Marguerite, I'll do the convincing. He's furious because of the stories some of his friends have been putting about. But he's good and he's fair-minded, and he'll get over his first impressions. Anyway, even if he doesn't, it won't make any difference to me!'

'You mustn't say that, Armand. I'd rather anything than give people the idea that I've come between you and your family. Leave it for today, and return to Paris tomorrow. Your father will have thought things over and so will you, and perhaps you'll understand each other better. Don't offend his principles. Try to appear as though you're making some concessions to what he wants. Make it look as if you're not all that attached to me, and he'll leave matters as they are. Keep hoping, my dear, and be sure of one thing: whatever happens, your Marguerite will still be yours.'

'You swear it?'

'Do I need to?'

How sweet it is to let yourself be won round by a voice you love! Marguerite and I spent all day going over our plans as though we somehow knew we had to hurry them through. We were expecting something to happen at any minute but, happily, the day passed without further event.

The following morning, I set off at ten o'clock and reached the hotel around noon.

My father had already gone out.

I went to my apartment hoping that he might be there. No one had called. I went round to my solicitor's. There was no one there either!

I returned to the hotel and waited until six. Monsieur Duval did not return.

I set off back to Bougival.

I found Marguerite not waiting for me, as on the previous evening, but sitting by the fire which the season already required.

She was deep enough in her thoughts for me to come right up to her chair without her hearing me or turning round. When my lips touched her forehead, she started as though the kiss had woken her suddenly.

'You gave me a fright,' she said. 'What did your father say?'

'I didn't see him. I can't make it out. I couldn't find him at his hotel nor in any of the places where he was likely to be.'

'Well, you'll have to try again tomorrow.'

'I've a good mind to wait for him to ask to see me. I think I've done everything that could be expected of me.'

'No, my dear, it's not enough. You must go and see your father again, and do it tomorrow.'

'Why tomorrow rather than any other day?'

'Because,' said Marguerite, who, I thought, flushed slightly at my question, 'because then your determination will seem all the greater and consequently we shall be forgiven more quickly.'

For the remainder of that day, Marguerite seemed pre-occupied, listless, downcast. I had to say everything twice to get an answer. She attributed her inattentiveness to the fears for the future which the events of the past two days had prompted.

I spent the night trying to reassure her, and she sent me off the next morning displaying a distinct uneasiness which I could not fathom.

As on the previous day, my father was out. But, before going, he had left me this letter:

'If you return to see me today, wait until four. If I'm not back by four, come back and dine with me tomorrow. I must speak with you.'

I waited until the appointed time. My father did not put in an appearance. So I left.

The evening before, I had found Marguerite downcast; now I found her feverish and agitated. When she saw me come in, she threw her arms around my neck, but she remained weeping in my arms for some time.

I questioned her about her sudden dejection which, as it worsened, alarmed me. She gave me no specific reason for it, and merely fell back on the excuses a woman falls back on when she does not want to give truthful answers.

When she was a little more herself again, I told her the outcome of my journey to town. I showed her my father's letter, and observed that some good might very well come of it.

When she saw the letter and heard my view of it, her tears began coming so fast that I called Nanine and, fearing some sort of nervous attack, we put her to bed. The poor girl wept without uttering a word, but she kept my hands clasped in hers and kissed them continually.

I asked Nanine if, during my absence, her mistress had received a letter or a visit which could account for the state she was in, but Nanine replied that no one had come and nothing had been delivered.

And yet something had been going on since the previous evening which was all the more worrying because Marguerite was hiding it from me.

She seemed to be a little calmer during the evening and, motioning me to sit at the foot of her bed, she gave me lengthy, renewed assurances that she loved me. Then she smiled, though it was an effort for her to do so, for despite herself her eyes were masked with tears.

I used every means to make her reveal the real cause of her sorrows, but she stubbornly continued to give me the same vague excuses which I have already mentioned.

In the end, she fell asleep in my arms, but her sleep was the kind which wearies the body instead of giving it rest. From time to time, she would cry out, wake with a start and, after reassuring herself that I was really by her side, would make me swear I would love her always.

I could make nothing of these fits of distress which continued until morning. Then Marguerite lapsed into a sort of torpor. She had not slept now for two nights.

Her rest was short-lived.

About eleven o'clock, Marguerite woke and, seeing that I was up and about, looked around her and exclaimed:

'Are you going already?'

'No,' I said, taking her hands in mine, 'but I wanted to let you sleep. It's still early.'

'What time are you going to Paris?'

'Four o'clock.'

'So soon? You'll stay with me till then, won't you?'

'Of course. Don't I always?'

'I'm so glad!'

Then she went on listlessly: 'Are we going to have lunch?'

'If you want.'

'And then you'll hold me right up to the moment you go?'

'Yes, and I'll come back as soon as I can.'

'Come back?' she said, staring wild-eyed at me.

'Of course.'

'That's right, you'll come back tonight and I'll be waiting for you, as usual, and you'll love me, and we'll be happy just as we've been since we met.'

These words were said so falteringly, and seemed to hide some painful notion that was so persistent, that I feared for her reason.

'Listen,' I told her, 'you're ill, I can't leave you like this. I'll write to my father and say he's not to expect me.'

'No! no!' she exclaimed vehemently, 'you mustn't do that. Your father would only accuse me of preventing you from going to him when he wants to see you. No! no! you must go, you must! Besides, I'm not ill, I couldn't be better. I had a bad dream, that's all, I wasn't properly awake.'

From then on, Marguerite tried to appear more cheerful. There were no more tears.

When it was time for me to leave, I kissed her and asked her if she wanted to come with me as far as the station: I hoped that the ride would take her mind off things, and that the air might do her good.

But most of all, I wanted to remain with her as long as possible.

She agreed, put her cloak on and came with me, bringing Nanine so that she would not have to return alone.

A score of times I was on the point of not goiing. But the hope of returning soon and fear of further antagonizing my father kept my purpose firm, and the train bore me away.

'Until tonight,' I said to Marguerite as I said good-bye.

She did not answer.

Once before she had not answered when I had said those selfsame words, and Count de G***, as you will recall, had spent the night with her. But that time was so far off that it seemed to have been erased from my memory. If I had anything to fear, it was assuredly not that Marguerite was deceiving me.

When I reached Paris, I hurried round to Prudence's to ask her to go down and see Marguerite. I hoped that her zest and good spirits would cheer her up.

I entered without waiting to be announced, and found Prudence getting dressed.

'Ah!' she said anxiously, 'is Marguerite with you?'

'No.'

'How is she?'

'She's not well.'

'So she's not coming?'

'Was she supposed to?'

Madame Duvernoy reddened and, somewhat embarrassed, answered:

'What I meant was, now you've come to Paris, isn't she going to come and join you?'

'No.'

I stared at Prudence. She lowered her eyes, and from the way she looked, I had the feeling that she was afraid of seeing me stay much longer.

'As a matter of fact, my dear Prudence, I came to ask you, if you've nothing else to do, to go down and see Marguerite this evening. You could keep her company and stay the night. I've never seen her the way she was today, and I'm terrified she's going to be ill.'

'I'm dining in town,' Prudence replied, 'and I can't see Marguerite this evening. But I will tomorrow.'

I said goodbye to Madame Duvernoy, who seemed to me as though she was almost as preoccupied as Marguerite, and went to call on my father who, from the start, gave me studied, searching looks.

He held out his hand.

'You called twice to see me. That pleases me, Armand,' he said. 'It's given me hope that you've reflected on your position, as I have on mine.'

'May I ask, father, what the outcome of your reflections has been?'

'The outcome, my boy, is that I realize I attached too much importance to the reports I was given, and I have made up my mind not to be quite so hard on you.'

'Do you mean it, father!' I exclaimed, overjoyed.

'What I mean, my dear boy, is that a young man needs a mistress and, after further enquiries, I would prefer to know that you were the lover of Mademoiselle Gautier than of some other woman.'

'Oh, thank you, father! You've made me so happy!'

We talked in this vein for a short while, and then sat down to dine. My father remained most affable throughout the meal.

I was very anxious to get back to Bougival to tell Marguerite all about this auspicious development. I glanced continually at the clock.

'You've got your eye on the time,' said my father, 'you can't wait to get away. Oh, you young people! always sacrificing genuine feelings for suspect attachments!'

'Don't say that, father! Marguerite loves me. I know she does.'

My father did not answer. His manner suggested that he neither believed nor disbelieved me.

He was very insistent that I should spend the entire evening with him so that I would not have to set off again until the following day. But I had left Marguerite feeling ill, said so, and asked his leave to go and join her soon, promising to return the following day.

It was a fine evening. He decided he would accompany me on to the platform. I had never been so happy. The future looked exactly as I had wanted it to look for so long.

I loved my father more than I had ever loved him.

As I was on the point of taking my leave, he pressed me one last time to stay. I refused.

'So you really love her?' he asked.

'To distraction.'

'In that case, go!' and he put his hand to his brow as though to drive a thought away, and then opened his mouth as if to tell me something. But he simply shook my hand and turned away abruptly, shouting after me:

'I shall see you tomorrow, then!'

XXII

I FELT that the train was hardly moving.

I reached Bougival at eleven.

Not one window in the house was lit. I rang, but no one answered.

It was the first time anything like this had happened. At length, the gardener appeared. I entered the house.

Nanine met me with a light. I reached Marguerite's room.
'Where is your mistress?'
'Madame has gone to Paris,' Nanine answered.
'Paris!'
'Yes, sir.'
'When?'
'An hour after you.'
'Did she leave anything for you to give me?'
'Nothing.'
Nanine left me.

'It's quite likely she was afraid,' I thought, 'and went to Paris to see for herself whether the visit I'd said I was going to make to my father's wasn't just an excuse for having a day away from her.

'Perhaps Prudence wrote to her about something important,' I said to myself when I was alone. 'But I saw Prudence as soon as I got there, and she didn't say anything to make me suppose that she'd written to Marguerite.'

Suddenly, I recalled the question Madame Duvernoy had asked me: 'So she's not coming today?', when I had told her Marguerite was ill. Simultaneously, I remembered Prudence's embarrassed reaction when I'd stared at her after hearing her words, which had seemed to hint at a secret rendezvous. To this was added my recollection of the tears Marguerite had wept all that day which had been pushed into the back of my mind by my father's warm welcome.

From this moment on, all of the day's events began to congregate around my original suspicion and rooted it so firmly in my thoughts that everything seemed to confirm it, even my father's leniency.

Marguerite had virtually insisted that I should go to Paris. She had pretended to be calm when I suggested I should stay by her side. Had I fallen into a trap? Was Marguerite deceiving me? Had she counted on getting back in sufficiently good time for me to remain unaware of her absence, and had some chance occurrence detained her? Why had she not said anything to Nanine, or why had she not left me a note? What was the meaning of the tears, her absence, this whole mystery?

Such were the questions which, with some trepidation, I put to myself as I stood in that empty bedroom, with my eyes fixed on the clock which, striking midnight, seemed to be telling me that it was too late now for me to hope to see my mistress return.

And yet, after the plans we had made, after the sacrifice which had been offered and accepted, was it likely she should be unfaithful? No. I made a conscious effort to dismiss my initial assumptions.

'The poor girl has probably found a buyer for her furniture and has gone to Paris to finalize the details. She didn't want to tell me beforehand because she knows that, though I may have agreed to her selling everything, for our future happiness depends on it, I don't like the idea at all. She was afraid she'd wound my pride and my scruples if she mentioned it. She'd much prefer to turn up again when everything is settled. It's obvious that Prudence was expecting her in connection with all this, and she gave herself away to me. Marguerite won't have been able to conclude her business today and is spending the night in her apartment, or perhaps she'll be here any minute, for she must have some idea of how anxious I am and certainly won't want to leave me to worry.

'But if that's the way of it, why the tears? She loves me of course, but I expect the poor girl couldn't help crying at the thought of giving up the luxury she's lived in up to now, for it made her happy and envied.'

I readily forgave Marguerite her regrets. I waited impatiently for her to come so that I could tell her, as I smothered her in kisses, that I had guessed the reason for her mysterious absence.

But the night wore on and still Marguerite did not come.

Imperceptibly, my anxiety tightened its hold, and gripped both my mind and my heart. Perhaps something had happened to her! Perhaps she was lying injured or ill or dead! Perhaps I would see a messenger arrive with news of some terrible accident! Perhaps the new day would find me still plunged in the same uncertainties, the same fears!

The thought that Marguerite was being unfaithful to me even as I waited in the midst of the terrors unleashed by her absence, no longer entered my head. There had to be some good reason, independent of her will, to keep her far from me, and the more I thought about it, the more convinced I was that this reason could only be some misfortune or other. Oh, the pride of man assumes protean shapes!

It had just struck one. I told myself I would wait another hour and then, if Marguerite were not back by two o'clock, I would leave for Paris.

To while away the time, I looked for a book, for I dared not let myself think.

Manon Lescaut lay open on the table. It appeared to me that here and there the pages were damp, as though tears had been shed over them. After skimming through the volume, I closed it: the print made no sense through the veil of my doubts.

Time passed slowly. The sky was overcast. Autumn rain lashed the windows. At times, the empty bed seemed, I thought, to resemble a grave. I felt afraid.

I opened the door. I listened, but heard nothing save the sound of the wind in the trees. No carriage rattled by on the road outside. Half past struck lugubriously from the church tower.

I had reached the point where I was afraid that someone would come. I felt that only misfortune would come seeking me out at such an hour and in such dismal weather.

It struck two. I waited a little longer. Only the regular, rhythmic ticking of the clock disturbed the silence.

At length, I left the room. Even the most trivial object in it had assumed that air of gloom which an anxious and lonely heart lends to everything around it.

In the next room, I found Nanine asleep over her needle-work. The creaking of the door woke her, and she asked me if her mistress had returned.

'No, but if she does, you will say that I couldn't stand the worry and that I've gone to Paris.'

'At this time of night?'

'Yes.'

'But how will you get there? You won't find a carriage now.'

'I'll walk.'

'But it's raining.'

'So?'

'Madame will be back, or if she's not, there'll still be time in the morning to go and see what's kept her. You'll get yourself murdered on the way.'

'There's no danger of that, my dear Nanine. I'll see you tomorrow.'

She was a good girl and went to get my coat. She helped me on with it, offered to run round and wake the widow Arnould to enquire whether it would be possible to order a carriage. But I said no. I was certain that her efforts, which might in any case come to nothing, would waste more time than it would take for me to get half way there.

Besides, I needed air, needed to tire myself physically as a way of working off the agitation which gripped me.

I took the key to the apartment in the rue d'Antin and, saying goodbye to Nanine who came with me as far as the gates, I left.

At first, I set off at a run, but the ground was wet with the recent rain, and I tired quickly. After running for half an hour, I was forced to stop. I was bathed in perspiration. I recovered my breath and went on. The night was so dark that I went in constant fear of colliding with one of the trees lining the road which, as they loomed up unexpectedly, looked like enormous ghosts bearing down on me.

I encountered one or two waggoner's carts, but soon left them behind.

A barouche passed making for Bougival at a fast trot. As it drew level with me, my hopes rose that Marguerite was inside.

I stopped and shouted: 'Marguerite! Marguerite!'

But no one answered and the barouche continued on its way. I watched it go, and then set off again.

It took me two hours to get to the Barrière de l'Étoile.*

The sight of Paris revived me, and I ran down the long avenue which I had walked along so often.

That night, no one was walking along it.

It was like an avenue in a dead city.

Day was just beginning to break.

When I reached the rue d'Antin, the great city was already beginning to stir before waking.

The clock of the church of Saint-Roch* was striking five when I entered the building where Marguerite lived.

I flung my name at the porter, who had got enough twenty-franc tips out of me to know I was quite entitled to call on Mademoiselle Gautier at five in the morning.

In this way, I got past him unimpeded.

I could have asked him if Marguerite was at home. But he might have replied that she wasn't, and I preferred to keep my doubts for another two minutes. While there was doubt there was hope.

I listened at her door, trying to detect a sound or a movement.

But there was nothing. The silence of the country seemed to extend as far as here.

I unlocked the door and went inside.

All the curtains were tightly closed.

I drew back those in the dining-room and made for the bedroom. I pushed the door open.

I leaped on the curtain cord and pulled it savagely.

The curtains opened. A faint glimmer of light pierced the gloom and I ran over to the bed.

It was empty!

I opened all the doors one after another. I looked in all the rooms.

There was no one there.

I thought I would go out of my mind.

I went into the dressing-room, opened the window and called several times to Prudence.

Madame Duvernoy's window remained shut.

Then I went down to the porter's lodge and asked him if Mademoiselle Gautier had been to her apartment the previous day.

'Yes,' the man said, 'with Madame Duvernoy.'

'She left no word for me?'

'No.'

'Do you know what they did afterwards?'

'They got into a carriage.'

'What sort of carriage?'

'A gentleman's brougham.'

What could it all mean?

I rang at the house next door.

'Who are you wanting, sir?' the porter asked as he opened the door to me.

'Madame Duvernoy.'

'She's not back.'

'Are you sure?'

'Yes, sir. There's even a letter that was delivered yesterday evening that I haven't had chance to give her.'

And the man showed me a letter at which I glanced mechanically.

I recognized Marguerite's handwriting.

I took the letter.

It was addressed like this: 'To Madame Duvernoy, to be given to Monsieur Duval'.

'This letter is for me,' I told the porter, and I showed him the address.

'Are you Monsieur Duval?' the man answered.

'Yes.'

'Now I recognize you. You often come here to see Madame Duvernoy.'

As soon as I was in the street, I broke open the seal on the letter.

Had lightning struck at my feet, I would not have been more appalled than by what I read.

'By the time you read this, Armand, I shall be another man's mistress. Consequently, all is finished between us.

Go back to your father, my dear. Go and see your sister. She's a pure young woman who knows nothing of all our miseries. With her, you will very quickly forget what you have suffered at the hands of a fallen creature named Marguerite Gautier who, for an instant, you truly loved and who stands in your debt for the only happy moments in her life which, she hopes, will not last much longer.'

When I reached the end, I thought I was going out of my mind.

For a moment, I was genuinely afraid that I would collapse on to the cobbles of the street. My eyes clouded over and the blood pulsated in my temples.

After a while, I recovered something of my composure and looked around me in astonishment as I saw other people going about their lives without pausing over my unhappiness.

I was not strong enough by myself to bear the blow which Marguerite had dealt me.

Then I recalled that my father was there in the same city as myself, that I could be with him in ten minutes and that, whatever the reason for my sorrows, he would share them.

I ran like a madman, like a thief, all the way to the Hôtel de Paris. The key was in the door of my father's apartment. I let myself in.

He was reading.

Judging by the small show of surprise which he displayed when he saw me, you might have thought that he had been expecting me.

I flung myself into his arms without a word, gave him Marguerite's letter and, sliding to the floor at his bedside, wept long, bitter tears.

XXIII

WHEN I was something like myself once more, I could not believe that the new day which was dawning would not be exactly like all the days that had gone before. There were moments when I felt that some circumstance or other, which I could not remember, had obliged me to spend the night away from Marguerite, and that, if I returned to Bougival, I should find her waiting anxiously, just as I had waited, and she would ask me what had kept me from her.

When your life has become so dependent on a habit as strong as our habit of loving, it hardly seems possible that the habit can be broken without also demolishing everything else which buttresses your life.

And so, from time to time, I was driven to reread Marguerite's letter, to convince myself that I had not been dreaming.

My body, giving way under the nervous shock, was incapable of any kind of movement. The worry, my walk through the night and the morning's revelations had exhausted me. My father took advantage of my state of total collapse to ask me for my strict promise that I would go away with him.

I promised everything he asked. I was incapable of arguing, and stood in need of sincere affection to help me over what had happened.

I was very glad that my father felt able to comfort me in my great sorrow.

All I remember is that the same day, at about five o'clock, he put us both into a post-chaise. Without telling me, he had arranged for my trunks to be got ready and had them strapped along with his to the back of the carriage, and then he took me away with him.

I became aware of what I was doing only when the city had dropped behind us, when the empty road reminded me of the emptiness in my heart.

Then the tears got the better of me once more.

My father had sensed that words alone, even his words, could not comfort me, and he let me cry without saying anything, content to pat my hand from time to time, as though to remind me that I had a friend at my side.

That night, I slept a little. I dreamed of Marguerite.

I woke with a start. I could not understand what I was doing in a carriage.

Then reality returned, and I let my head fall on to my chest.

I dared not talk to my father, for I was still afraid that he would say: 'You do see I was right when I told you that woman didn't love you!'

But he took no unfair advantage of the situation, and we reached C*** without his having spoken save of matters completely foreign to the events which had led to my departure.

When I embraced my sister, I was reminded of the words in Marguerite's letter concerning her. But I saw at once that, however fine and good she was, my sister could never make me forget my mistress.

The hunting season had begun, and my father thought that a spot of shooting might take my mind off things. So he organized hunting parties with neighbours and friends. I went along as unprotesting as I was unenthusiastic, in the mood of apathy which had characterized all my actions since my departure.

We went out with beaters. I would be installed in my butt. Then I would put my unloaded gun beside me and let my mind wander.

I watched the clouds pass over. I let my thoughts run wild over the deserted plains and, from time to time, would hear one of the hunters signalling that there was a hare not ten paces in front of me.

None of this escaped my father's notice, and he refused to allow himself to be taken in by my outward calm. He was quite aware that, however unmanned my heart was now, it could provoke a terrible, perhaps even dangerous reaction at any time, and, going out of his way to avoid giving the impression that he was consoling me, he did his utmost to occupy my mind with other things.

Of course, my sister had been told nothing of the events which had occurred. She thus found it difficult to understand why I, who had always been so carefree, should suddenly have become so preoccupied and melancholy.

Sometimes in my sadness, catching my father's anxious eye, I would reach out to him and grasp his hand as though to ask a silent pardon for the unhappiness which, despite myself, I was causing him.

A month went by in this manner, but a month was all I could bear.

The memory of Marguerite pursued me wherever I went. I had loved that woman—still loved her—too much for her suddenly to cease to mean anything to me. Whatever feelings I might have for her now, I had to see her again. At once.

The longing to do so crept into my mind and took root there with all the force which the will displays when finally it reasserts itself in a body that has long remained inert.

I needed Marguerite, not at some time in the future, not in a month nor a week from the moment the idea first entered my head, but before another day passed. I immediately went to my father and told him that I proposed to take my leave to attend to some matters which had called me back to Paris, but added that I would return promptly.

He probably guessed the real reasons for my departure, because he insisted that I should stay. But, seeing that if my desires were thwarted, then in my present excitable state, the consequences might prove fatal to me, he embraced me and begged me, almost tearfully, to come back to him soon.

I did not sleep all the way to Paris.

What would I do when I got there? I had no idea. But the first thing was to attend to Marguerite.

I went to my apartment to change and, as it was fine and still not too late in the day, I went to the Champs-Élysées.

A half an hour later, in the distance, coming from the Rond-Point down to the Place de la Concorde, I saw Marguerite's carriage approaching.

She had bought back her horses, for the carriage was just as it used to be. Only she was not in it.

I had only just noticed that she was not inside when, looking round me, I saw Marguerite walking towards me in the company of a woman I had never seen before.

As she passed quite close to me, she turned pale and her lips contracted into an uneasy smile. As for me, my heart beat so violently that it took my breath away. But I managed to give a cold expression to my face and a cold greeting to my former mistress, who went back to her carriage almost at once and got into it with her friend.

I knew Marguerite. Meeting me so unexpectedly must have thrown her into a state of great confusion. In all likelihood, she had got to hear of my departure which had set her mind at rest as to the consequences of our sudden parting. But, seeing me back and coming face to face with me, pale as I was, she had sensed that my return had a purpose, and must have wondered what was going to happen.

If, when I saw her again, Marguerite had been unhappy; if, in taking my revenge, there had also been some way of helping her—then I might well have forgiven her, and would certainly never have dreamed of doing her any harm. But when I saw her again, she was happy, at least on the surface. Another man had restored her to the luxury in which I had been unable to keep her. Our estrangement, which she had initiated, accordingly acquired the stamp of the basest self-interest. I was humiliated both in my pride and my love: she was going to have to pay for what I had suffered.

I could not remain indifferent to what she did now. It followed that the thing that would hurt her most would be precisely for me to show indifference. Indifference, therefore, was the sentiment which I now needed to feign, not only in her presence but in the eyes of others.

I tried to put a smile on my face, and I went to call on Prudence.

Her maid went in to announce me, and kept me waiting briefly in the drawing-room.

Madame Duvernoy appeared at length and showed me into her parlour. As I was about to sit down, I heard the drawing-room door open and a light footfall made a floor-board creak. Then the door to the landing slammed shut.

'I'm not disturbing you?' I asked Prudence.

'Not in the least. Marguerite was with me. When she heard you being announced, she ran away. That was her just leaving.'

'So now I scare her?'

'No, but she's afraid you wouldn't relish seeing her again.'

'Why ever not?' I said, making an effort to breathe freely, for my emotions were choking me. 'The poor creature left me so that she could get her carriage and furniture and diamonds back. She was quite right, and it's not for me to bear grudges. I ran into her earlier on,' I went on nonchalantly.

'Where?' said Prudence, who was staring at me and

evidently wondering if this was the same man she had known so much in love.

'On the Champs-Élysées. She was with another, very attractive woman. Who would that be?'

'What's she look like?'

'A blonde girl, slim. Had her hair in ringlets. Blue eyes, very fashionably dressed.'

'Ah! That's Olympe. Yes, she's a very pretty girl.'

'Who's she living with?'

'Nobody. Everybody.'

'And her address?'

'In the rue Tronchet,* number . . . Well, I declare! You want to take up with her?'

'You never know what can happen.'

'And Marguerite?'

'I'd be lying if I told you that I never think of her any more. But I'm one of those men who set great store by the way an affair is ended. Now Marguerite gave me my marching orders in such an offhand sort of way, that I was left feeling I'd been rather silly to have fallen in love with her the way I did—for I really was in love with her.'

You can guess in what tone of voice I tried to say all this: the perspiration was pouring off my forehead.

'She loved you too, you know, and still does. You want proof? Well, after she met you today, she came straight round here to tell me all about it. When she got here, she was all of a tremble, almost ill she was.'

'And what did she tell you?'

'She said: "I expect he'll come to see you," and she begged me to ask you to forgive her.'

'I've forgiven her, you can tell her. She's a good girl, but she's a good-time girl, and I should have expected what she did to me. I'm grateful to her for making the break, because I wonder now where my idea that I could live exclusively with her would have got us. It was very silly.'

'She'll be very happy when she learns you took it like that when you saw she had no alternative. It was high time she left you, my dear. The rogue of a dealer she'd offered to sell her furniture to, had been to see her creditors to ask how much she owed them. They'd got cold feet and were planning to sell everything in another two days.'

'And now, it's all paid back?'

'Almost.'

'And who provided the money?'

'Count de N***. Listen, dear, there are men who were put in this world for paying up. To cut a long story short, he came up with twenty thousand francs—but he's got what he wanted. He knows Marguerite doesn't love him, but that doesn't prevent him being very nice to her. You saw for yourself that he's bought back her horses and redeemed her jewels, and he gives her as much money as the Duke used to. If she's prepared to settle for a quiet life, then this is one man who'll stay with her for a long time.'

'And what does she do with herself? Does she stay in Paris all the time?'

'She's never once wanted to go back to Bougival since the day you left. It was me that went down to fetch all her things, and yours too: I've made a bundle of them that you can send round for. It's all there except for a little pocket-book with your monogram on it. Marguerite wanted to have it, and she's got it with her in the apartment. If you want it particularly, I could ask for it back.'

'She can keep it,' I stammered, for I could feel tears welling up from my heart into my eyes at the memory of the village where I had been so happy, and at the thought that Marguerite should want to keep something that had been mine and reminded her of me.

If she had come into the room at that moment, all my plans for revenge would have collapsed, and I would have fallen at her feet.

'Mind you,' Prudence went on, 'I've never seen her the way she is at the minute. She hardly sleeps at all, goes to every ball, eats late suppers and even has too much to drink. Just recently, after a supper party, she was in bed for a week. And when the doctor allowed her up, she started where she'd left off, though she knows it could kill her. Are you going to see her?'

'What's the point? It was you I came to see, because

you've always been extremely nice to me, and I knew you before I met Marguerite. It's you I have to thank for having been her lover, just as it's you I must thank for not being her lover any more. Am I right?'

'Well, yes. I did everything I could to make her give you up, and I do believe that, in time, you won't think too badly of me.'

'I owe you a double debt of gratitude,' I added, getting to my feet, 'because I was getting sick of her when I saw how seriously she took everything I said.'

'Are you going?'

'Yes.'

I had heard enough.

'When shall we see you again?'

'Soon. Goodbye.'

'Goodbye.'

Prudence saw me to the door, and I returned to my apartment with tears of rage in my eyes and a thirst for revenge in my heart.

So Marguerite was really a whore like the rest of them. So this fathomless love she felt for me had not held out for long against her wish to revert to her old life, and her need to have a carriage and indulge her taste for orgies.

This is what I kept telling myself when I could not sleep, whereas, if I had thought about it as coolly as I made out, I would have seen Marguerite's new, wild behaviour as her hope of silencing persistent thoughts and burying recurring memories.

But, alas, I was ruled by sour resentments, and thought only of finding a way of tormenting the poor creature.

Oh, how small, how vile is man when one of his petty passions is wounded!

Olympe, the girl I had seen with Marguerite, was, if not a close friend, then at least the friend she had seen most of since returning to Paris. She was to throw a ball and, since I assumed Marguerite would be there, I set about getting myself an invitation, and got one.

When I arrived, overflowing with painful emotions, the ball was already in full swing. People were dancing, there was a great deal of shouting and, during one of the quadrilles, I saw Marguerite dancing with Count de N*** who looked inordinately proud to be showing her off, as though he were declaring to the assembled company: 'This woman belongs to me!'

I went and leaned against the mantelpiece, just across from Marguerite, and watched her dance. She grew flustered almost the moment she noticed me. I indicated that I had seen her, and acknowledged her perfunctorily with a wave of the hand and a look of recognition.

When I thought that, after the ball, she would be leaving, not with me, but with that wealthy oaf, when I pictured what would very likely happen after they got back to her apartment, the blood rushed to my face and I felt a need to upset the course of true love.

When the quadrille was over, I went over and said good evening to the hostess who, for the benefit of her guests, was displaying a dazzling pair of shoulders and much of her magnificent breasts.

She was a beautiful girl, more beautiful, in terms of her figure, than Marguerite. This was brought home to me even more forcibly by certain glances which Marguerite cast towards Olympe as I was speaking to her. The man who became this woman's lover could be every bit as pleased with himself as Monsieur de N***, and she was beautiful enough to start a passion the equal of the one which Marguerite had inspired in me.

At that time, she had no lover. It would not be difficult to remedy that. The trick was having enough gold to fling about in order to get oneself noticed.

My mind was made up. This woman would be my mistress.

I took the first steps in my initiation by dancing with Olympe.

Half an hour later, Marguerite, pale as death, put on her fur-lined cape and left the ball.

XXIV

IT was something, but it was not enough. I knew what power I had over her, and took cowardly advantage of it.

When I reflect that she is dead now, I wonder if God will ever forgive me for the hurt I caused her.

After supper, which was very rowdy, people began to gamble.

I sat next to Olympe, and bet my money so boldly that she could hardly fail to notice. In a trice, I won a hundred and fifty or two hundred louis which I spread out in front of me; she stared at them with eager eyes.

I was the only person there who was not totally absorbed by the play, and I alone paid her any attention. For the rest of the night, I went on winning, and it was I who gave her money to gamble with, for she had lost everything she had on the table in front of her, and most probably all the money she had in the house.

People started to leave at five in the morning.

I had won three hundred louis.

All the gamblers had gone downstairs. Only I had stayed behind. No one noticed, for none of the other gentlemen were friends of mine.

Olympe herself was lighting them down the staircase, and I was about to go down like everyone else, when, turning back to her, I said:

'I must speak to you.'

'Tomorrow,' she said.

'No. Now.'

'What is it you want to say?'

'You'll see.'

And I went back into her apartment.

'You lost,' I said.

'Yes.'

'Everything you had here?'

She hesitated.

'Speak frankly.'

'Oh very well, you're right.'

'I won three hundred louis. They're yours, if you let me stay.'

And, as I spoke, I tossed the gold on to the table.

'Why the offer?'

'Because I love you, dammit!'

'No so. Because you're in love with Marguerite and want to have your revenge by becoming my lover. You can't fool a woman like me, you know. Unfortunately, I'm still too young and too beautiful to accept the role you propose.'

'So you refuse?'

'Yes.'

'Would you rather have me for love than money? If so, I should be the one to refuse. Think, my dear Olympe. If I'd sent somebody or other along to offer you these same three hundred louis on my behalf and on the same terms that I have set out, you would have accepted. I preferred to deal with you directly. Say yes, and don't look for motives behind what I'm doing. Keep telling yourself that you're beautiful, that there's nothing surprising in the fact that I'm in love with you.'

Marguerite was a kept woman like Olympe, and yet the first time I saw her, I would never have dared say to her what I had just said to this woman. The difference was that I loved Marguerite, and had sensed instincts in her which were lacking in this other creature who, for all her very great beauty, even as I put the arrangement to her and prepared to agree terms, sickened me.

In the end she consented, of course, and when I walked out of her apartment at noon, I was her lover. But I slipped from her bed carrying away no memory of the caresses and loving words which she had felt obliged to lavish on me in exchange for the six thousand francs which I left for her.

And yet men had ruined themselves for that woman.

Starting from that day, I subjected Marguerite to constant persecution. Olympe and she stopped seeing each other: you can easily understand why. I gave my new mistress a carriage and jewels, I gambled and, in a word, committed all the follies which a man in love with a woman like Olympe normally commits. Rumours of my new passion spread at once.

Even Prudence was taken in by them and ended up believing that I had completely forgotten Marguerite. Marguerite, either because she guessed the motive which drove me or because she was deceived like everyone else, responded with great dignity to the slights I inflicted on her every day. Yet she appeared to be ill, for everywhere I met her I found her looking paler and paler and increasingly sad. My love for her, exalted to the point where it felt as though it had turned to hate, revelled in the spectacle of her daily sufferings. Several times, in situations where I behaved with unspeakable cruelty, Marguerite looked at me with such imploring eyes that I reddened at the role I had chosen to play, and came near to asking for her forgiveness.

But my repentance never lasted longer than a flash of lightning. Besides, Olympe, who in the end had set aside all thought of self-respect and realized that by hurting Marguerite she could get anything she wanted out of me, constantly set me against her and, whenever she had the chance, insulted her with the relentless cowardice of a woman who has the backing of a man.

Finally, Marguerite stopped going either to the ball or the theatre for fear of meeting Olympe and me. Then the direct insults were replaced by anonymous letters: there was nothing too shameful which I did not urge my mistress to put about nor too despicable which I did not myself spread concerning Marguerite.

I must have taken leave of my senses to allow affairs to come to such a pass. I was like a man who has got fighting drunk and falls into an uncontrollable rage in which his hand is quite capable of committing a crime without involving his mind. In the midst of it all, I went through torment. The way Marguerite reacted to all my attacks—with a calmness that was as free of scorn as her dignity was of contempt—made her my superior even in my eyes, but served only to provoke me further.

One evening, Olympe had gone out somewhere and met Marguerite who, on this occasion, did not spare the stupid girl who insulted her, and things reached the point where Olympe was forced to back down. She came back seething. Marguerite, who had fainted, had to be carried home.

As soon as she came in, Olympe told me what had happened. She said that when Marguerite had seen that she was by herself, she had wanted revenge because Olympe was my mistress. She said that I had to write a letter saying that, whether I was with her or not, the woman I loved was to be respected.

I have no need to tell you that I agreed. I put everything bitter, shameful and cruel I could think of into that missive which I sent to her home address that same day.

This time, the cut went too deep for the unhappy girl to be able to bear it in silence.

I was confident that a reply would be delivered. Accordingly, I was determined not to go out all that day.

Around two o'clock, there was a ring at the door and Prudence was shown in.

I tried to appear unconcerned as I asked her to what I owed her visit. But that day Madame Duvernoy was in no mood for laughter and, sounding terribly upset, she pointed out that since my return, that is for the last three weeks or so, I had not missed an opportunity to hurt Marguerite. It was making her ill. The scene the night before, and the letter I'd sent that morning, had forced her to take to her bed.

And so, without framing a single reproach, Marguerite had sent to ask for mercy, informing me that she no longer had either the emotional nor physical strength to endure what I was doing to her.

'If Mademoiselle Gautier,' I told Prudence, 'wishes to close her door to me, then she is perfectly entitled to do so. But that she should insult a woman I love on the ground that the woman is my mistress, is something which I shall never tolerate.'

'My dear,' said Prudence, 'you're being ruled by the influence of a heartless, thoughtless, common girl. You love her, it's true, but that's no reason for tormenting a woman who can't defend herself.'

'Let Mademoiselle Gautier send her Count de N*** to me and the game will be even.'

'You know very well she'll never do that. So let her be, dear Armand. If you saw her, you'd be ashamed of the way you're behaving towards her. She's got no colour, and she's coughing. She's not long for this world now.'

Prudence held out her hand to me and added:

'Come and see her. A visit from you will make her very happy.'

'I have no wish to meet Monsieur de N***.'

'Monsieur de N*** is never there. She can't stand him.'

'If Marguerite really wants to see me, she knows where I live. She can come here. But I shall never set foot in the rue d'Antin.'

'And you'd be nice to her?'

'I'd behave perfectly.'

'Well, I'm sure she'll come.'

'Let her.'

'Are you going out today?'

'I shall be home all evening.'

'I'll go and tell her.'

Prudence left.

I did not even bother to write and let Olympe know that I should not be going to see her. I behaved pretty much as I liked towards her. I hardly spent one night a week with her now. She found consolation with, I believe, an actor from one or other of the Boulevard theatres.

I went out for dinner and came back almost immediately. I had fires lit in every room and told Joseph he would not be needed.

I could not give you any sort of account of the various thoughts which troubled my mind during the hour I waited. But when I heard the doorbell, at around nine o'clock, they all came together in one emotion so powerful that, as I went to open the door, I was obliged to lean against the wall to prevent myself falling.

Fortunately, the hallway was only half-lit, so that the change in my features was less noticeable.

Marguerite came in.

She was dressed entirely in black and wore a veil. I could only just make out her face beneath the lace.

She walked on into the drawing-room and lifted her veil.

She was as pale as marble.

'Here I am, Armand,' she said. 'You wanted to see me. I came.'

And, lowering her head which she took in both hands, she burst into tears.

I went up to her.

'What is it?' I said falteringly.

She pressed my hand without replying, for the tears still dimmed her voice. But a few moments later, having regained something of her composure, she said:

'You have hurt me a great deal, Armand, and I never did anything to you.'

'Never did anything?' I replied, with a bitter smile.

'Nothing, except what circumstances forced me to do to you.'

I do not know if you have ever experienced in your life, or ever will, what I went through as I looked at Marguerite.

The last time she had come to my apartment, she had sat in the same chair where she was now sitting. But since those days, she had been another man's mistress; other kisses than mine had brushed those lips towards which my own were now involuntarily drawn. And yet I felt that I loved her no less, and perhaps even more, than I had ever loved her.

However, it was difficult for me to broach the subject which had brought her. Most likely Marguerite understood this, for she went on:

'My coming here will be tiresome for you, Armand, for I have two requests to make: your forgiveness for what I said to Mademoiselle Olympe yesterday, and your mercy for what you may still be thinking of doing to me. Whether you wanted to or not, you have hurt me so much since your return that I should not now be able to stand a quarter of the emotions which I have borne up to this morning. You will have pity on me, won't you? And you will remember that there are nobler things for a good man to do than to take his revenge against a woman as ill and as wretched as

I am. Come. Take my hand. I am feverish: I left my bed to come here to ask, not for your friendship, but for your indifference.'

As she asked, I took Marguerite's hand. It was hot, and the poor woman was shivering beneath her velvet cloak.

I rolled the armchair in which she was sitting nearer the fire.

'Do you imagine that I didn't suffer,' I resumed, 'that night when, after waiting for you in the country, I came looking for you in Paris where all I found was that letter which almost drove me out of my mind?

'How could you have deceived me, Marguerite? I loved you so much!'

'Let's not speak of that, Armand, I did not come here to speak of that. I wanted to see you other than as an enemy, that's all, and I wanted to hold your hand once more. You have a young, pretty mistress whom you love, so they say: be happy with her and forget me.'

'And what of you? I suppose you're happy?'

'Have I the face of a happy woman, Armand? Don't mock my sorrows, for you should know their cause and extent better than anyone.'

'It was entirely up to you never to be unhappy, if, that is, you are as unhappy as you say.'

'No, my friend, circumstances were too strong for my will. I did not follow my immoral instincts as you seem to be saying, but obeyed a solemn injunction and yielded to arguments which, when some day you know what they were, will make you forgive me.'

'Why not tell me now what these arguments are?'

'Because they would not bring us together again, for we can never be together again, and because they might alienate you from those from whom you must not be alienated.'

'Who are these people?'

'I cannot tell you.'

'Then you're lying.'

Marguerite stood up and walked to the door.

I could not stand by and watch such silent, expressive grief without being moved by it, when in my mind's eye I compared this white-faced, weeping woman with the high-spirited girl who had laughed at me at the Opéra-Comique.

'You shall not go,' I said, thrusting myself against the door.

'Why not?'

'Because in spite of all you've done to me, I still love you and want to keep you here.'

'So that you can throw me out tomorrow, is that it? No, it's out of the question! Our destinies are separate, let's not try to unite them, for then you might despise me, whereas now you have no choice but hate.'

'No, Marguerite,' I exclaimed, feeling all my love, all my desires awaken with her nearness, 'No, I shall forget all that is past, and we will be happy, as we promised we would.'

Marguerite shook her head uncertainly, then said:

'Am I not your slave, your dog? Do with me what you will. Take me, I am yours.'

And removing her coat and her hat which she flung on to the sofa, she began feverishly unloosing the bodice of her dress, for, her condition deteriorating suddenly, as often happened in her illness, and with the blood rushing from her heart to her head, she was having difficulty breathing.

There followed a bout of dry, hoarse coughing.

'Have my coachman told,' she went on, 'to drive my carriage home.'

I went down myself to dismiss the man.

When I returned, Marguerite was lying in front of the fire, and her teeth were chattering with cold.

I took her in my arms, undressed her where she lay without stirring, and carried her icy body to my bed.

Then I sat by her side and tried to warm her with my caresses. She did not speak, but she smiled at me.

Oh! How strange was the night that followed! The whole of Marguerite's life seemed to be concentrated in the kisses she lavished on me. I loved her so intensely that, in the transports of my loving frenzy, I wondered whether I should not kill her so that she would never belong to anyone else.

A month of such loving, body and soul, would be enough to bury most people.

Day found us both awake.

Marguerite was ghastly pale. She did not utter a word. From time to time, large tears flowed from her eyes and halted on her cheeks where they glistened like diamonds. Her weary arms opened now and then to hold me fast to her, and then fell back lifelessly on to the bed.

For a moment, I thought I could forget everything that had happened since the moment I had left Bougival, and I said to Marguerite:

'Would you like us to go away, to leave Paris?'

'No, no!' she said, near to panic, 'we should be too wretched. There's nothing I can do now to make you happy, but as long as I have breath in my body, I will be the slave of your every whim. Whatever time of day or night you want me, come to me: I shall be yours. But you mustn't go on trying to link your future with mine. You'd only be too unhappy, and you would make me very wretched.

'I'll keep my looks for a little while longer. Make the most of them, but don't ask any more of me.'

When she had gone, I felt frightened by the loneliness to which she had abandoned me. Two hours after her departure, I was still sitting on the bed she had just left, staring at the pillow which bore the imprint of her head, and wondering what should become of me, torn as I was between love and jealousy.

At five o'clock, without having any clear idea of what I would do when I got there, I went round to the rue d'Antin.

It was Nanine who opened the door.

'Madame cannot see you now,' she said, with some embarrassment.

'Why not?'

'Because Count de N*** is with her, and he doesn't want me to let anyone in.'

'Oh, of course,' I stammered, 'I'd forgotten.'

I returned home like a man drunk, and do you know what I did in that moment of jealous frenzy which lasted only long enough for the disgraceful action which I was about to commit, can you guess what I did? I told myself that this woman was making a fool of me, I pictured her locked in inviolable intimacies with the Count, repeating to him the same words she had said to me that night, and, taking a five hundred franc note, I sent it to her with this message:

'You left so quickly this morning that I forgot to pay you. The enclosed is your rate for a night.'

Then, when the letter had gone, I went out as though to escape from the instant remorse which followed this unspeakable deed.

I called on Olympe and I found her trying on dresses. When we were alone, she sang obscene songs for my amusement.

She was the archetypal courtesan who has neither shame nor heart nor wit—or at least she appeared so to me, for perhaps another man had shared with her the idyll I had shared with Marguerite.

She asked me for money. I gave it her. Then, free to go, I went home.

Marguerite had not sent a reply.

There is no point in my telling you in what state of agitation I spent the whole of the following day.

At half past six, a messenger brought an envelope containing my letter and the five hundred franc note, but nothing else.

'Who gave you this?' I said to the man.

'A lady who was leaving on the Boulogne mail coach with her maid. She gave me orders not to bring it until the coach was clear of the depot.'

I ran all the way to Marguerite's apartment.

'Madame left for England today at six o'clock,' said the porter in answer to my question.

There was nothing now to keep me in Paris, neither love nor hate. I was exhausted by the turmoil of these events. One of my friends was about to set off on a tour of the Middle East.* I went to see my father and said I wished to go with him. My father gave me bills of exchange and letters of introduction, and a week or ten days later I boarded ship at Marseilles.

It was at Alexandria, through an Embassy attaché whom I had occasionally seen at Marguerite's, that I learnt about the poor girl's illness.

It was then that I sent her the letter to which she wrote the reply you have read for yourself. I got it when I reached Toulon.

I set out immediately and you know the rest.

All that remains now is for you to read the papers which Julie Duprat kept for me. They are the necessary complement of the story I have just told you.

XXV

ARMAND, wearied by the telling of his long tale which had been frequently interrupted by his tears, placed both hands on his forehead and closed his eyes—either to think or to try to sleep—after giving me the pages written in Marguerite's hand.

Moments later, a slight quickening in his breathing told me that Armand had been overcome by sleep, but sleep of that shallow kind which the least sound will scatter.

This is what I read. I transcribe it without adding or deleting a single syllable:

'Today is the 15th December. I have been ill for three or four days. This morning, I took to my bed; the weather is dull and I feel low. There is no one with me here. I think of you, Armand. And you, where are you now as I write these lines? Far from Paris, far away, I've heard, and perhaps you have already forgotten Marguerite. But be happy, for I owe you the only moments of joy I have known in my life.

I could not resist the temptation of wanting to explain why I behaved as I did, and I wrote you a letter. But, coming from a loose woman like me, any such letter may be regarded as a tissue of lies unless it is sanctified by the authority of death, in which case it becomes a confession rather than a letter.

Today I am ill. I may die of my illness, for I always had a feeling that I would die young. My mother died of consumption, and the way I have lived up to now can only have aggravated a complaint which was the only legacy she left me. But I do not want to die without your knowing how you stand with me—if, that is, when you get back, you still feel anything for the sorry creature you loved before you went away.

Here is what was in that letter which I shall be happy to write out again, for in so doing I shall convince myself anew that I am vindicated.

You remember, Armand, how startled we were at Bougival by the news of your father's arrival; you recall the blind terror his coming prompted in me, and the scene that took place between the two of you which you described to me that evening.

The next day, while you were in Paris waiting for your father who never came back, a man came to the house and handed me a letter from Monsieur Duval.

The letter, which I enclose with this, begged me, in the gravest terms, to find an excuse for getting you out of the way the following day, and to agree to a visit from your father. He had something to say to me, and was most particular that I should say nothing to you about the step he had taken.

You recall how insistent I was, when you got back, that you should return to Paris again the next day.

You had been gone an hour when your father arrived to see me. I will spare you an account of what I felt when I saw the stern expression on his face. Your father believed implicitly in the conventional truths according to which every courtesan is a heartless, mindless creature, a kind of gold-grabbing machine always ready, like any other machine, to mangle the hand that feeds it and crush, pitilessly, blindly, the very person who gives it life and movement.

Your father had written me a very proper letter to

persuade me to see him; when he came, his manner was somewhat at variance with the way he had written. There were enough slights, insults and even open threats in his opening words for me to give him to understand that he was in my house, and that the only account of my life I owed him was dictated by the genuine affection I felt for his son.

Monsieur Duval moderated his tone a little, yet even so he began saying that he could no longer permit his son to go on ruining himself for me. He said I was beautiful, there was no denying it, but however beautiful I was, I ought not to use my beauty to destroy the future of a young man by expecting him to foot the bill for my extravagance.

Now there was only one way of answering that, was there not? and that was to prove that all the time I had been your mistress, no sacrifice had been too great for me to make so that I could remain faithful to you without asking for more money than you could afford to let me have. I showed the pawn-tickets, the receipts given me by people to whom I had sold items I could not pawn; I told your father that I had decided to get rid of my furniture to pay my debts, and that I was determined to live with you without being a drain on your purse. I told him how happy we were. I told him how you had shown me a more tranquil, happier kind of life and, in the end, he conceded that he was in the wrong, and he gave me his hand, asking my pardon for the manner in which he had behaved at first.

Then he said:

"In that case, madame, it shall not be with remonstrations and threats, but with humble entreaties that I must try to persuade you to make a sacrifice greater than any you have so far made for my son."

I trembled at these preliminaries.

Your father drew closer to me, took both my hands in his and, in a kindly voice, went on:

"Child, you are not to take amiss what I am about to say to you. Please understand that life sometimes places cruel constraints upon our hearts, but submit we must. You are good, and you have generous qualities of soul unknown to many women who may despise you but are not to be compared with you. But reflect that mistresses are one thing and the family quite another; that beyond love lie duties; that after the age of passion comes the time when a man who wishes to be respected needs to be securely placed in a responsible station in life. My son's means are slender, and yet he is prepared to make over all his mother left him to you. If he accepts the sacrifice which you are about to make, then his honour and dignity require that, in return, he would relinquish his legacy which you would always have to fall back on should things go hard. But he cannot accept your sacrifice, because people, who do not know you, would misinterpret his acceptance which must not be allowed to reflect on the name we bear. People would not bother their heads about whether Armand loved you, whether you loved him or whether the love you have for each other meant happiness for him and rehabilitation for you. They would see only one thing, which is that Armand Duval had allowed a kept woman—forgive me, child, the things I am obliged to say to you—to sell everything she possessed for his sake. Then the day of reproaches and regrets would dawn, you can be sure of it, for you both just as it would for them, and the pair of you would have a chain around your necks which you could never break. What would you do then? Your youth would be gone, and my son's future would have been destroyed. And I, his father, would have received from only one of my children the return to which I look forward from both of them.

"You are young, you are beautiful: life will heal your wounds. You have a noble heart, and the memory of a good deed done will redeem many past actions. During the six months he has known you, Armand has forgotten all about me. Four times I have written letters to him, and not once has he answered. I could have been dead for all he knew!

"However determined you are to lead a different kind of existence, Armand, who loves you, will never agree to the retiring life which his modest means would force you to live, for seclusion is no state for beauty like yours. Who knows what he might do! He has already taken to gambling once, as I discovered, and without saying anything to you, as I further discovered. But in a wild moment, he could easily have lost part of what I have been putting aside this many a year for my daughter's dowry, for him, and for the peace of my old age. What might have happened once might still happen.

"Besides, can you be sure that the life you'd be giving up for him would never attract you again? Are you certain that, having fallen in love with him, you would never fall in love with anyone else? And, not least, will you not suffer when you see what limitations your affair will set upon your lover's life? You may not be able to console him as he grows older if thoughts of ambition follow the dream of love. Reflect on all these matters, madame. You love Armand. Prove to him in the only way now open to you—by sacrificing your love to his future. Nothing untoward has happened thus far, but it will, and it may be much worse than I anticipate. Armand may become jealous of some man who once loved you; he may challenge him to a duel, he may fight, he may even be killed, and consider then what you would suffer as you stood before a father who would hold you accountable for the life of his son.

"Finally, child, you should know the rest, for I have not told you everything: let me explain my reason for coming to Paris. I have a daughter, as I have just said. She is young, beautiful and pure as an angel. She is in love, and she too has made love the dream of her life. I did write and tell Armand all about it, but, having thoughts for no one but you, he never replied. Well, my daughter is about to be married. As the wife of the man she loves, she will enter a respectable family which requires that there should be nothing dishonourable in my house. The family of the man who is to be my son-in-law has discovered how Armand has been living in Paris, and has declared that the arrangement will be cancelled if Armand continues to live as he does at present. The future of a child of mine who has never harmed you and has every right to look forward to life with confidence, is now in your hands.

"Do you have the right to destroy her future? Are you

strong enough to? In the name of your love and your
repentance, Marguerite, give me my daughter's happiness."

I wept in silence, my dear, as I listened to all these
considerations which had already occurred to me many
times, for now, on your father's lips, they seemed even more
pressing and real. I told myself all the things your father
dared not say, though they had often been on the tip of his
tongue: that I was, when all was said and done, nothing but
a kept woman, and whatever I said to justify our affair
would sound calculating; that my past life did not qualify
me to dream of the future; and that I was taking on responsibilities for which my habits and reputation offered absolutely no guarantee. The truth was that I loved you,
Armand. The fatherly way in which Monsieur Duval spoke,
the pure feelings he aroused in me, the good opinion of this
upright old man which I should acquire, and your esteem
which I was certain I would have some day, all these things
awoke noble thoughts in my heart which raised me in my
own estimation and gave a voice to a kind of sacred self-
respect which I had never felt before. When I thought that
this old man, now begging me for his son's future, would
some day tell his daughter to include my name in her
prayers, as that of a mysterious benefactress, I was transformed and looked on myself with pride.

In the heat of the moment, the truth of what I felt may
perhaps have been exaggerated. But that is what I felt, my
dear, and these unaccustomed feelings silence counsels
prompted by the memory of happy times spent with you.

"Very well," I said to your father as I wiped away my
tears. "Do you believe that I love your son?"

"Yes," said Monsieur Duval.

"That money does not come into it?"

"Yes."

"Do you believe that I had made this love of mine the
hope, the dream of my life, and its redemption?"

"Absolutely."

"Well, Monsieur Duval, kiss me once as you would kiss
your daughter, and I will swear to you that your touch, the
only truly chaste embrace I ever received, will make me

stand strong against my love. I swear that within a week, your son will be back with you, unhappy for a time perhaps, but cured for good."

"You are a noble-hearted young woman," your father replied, as he kissed my forehead, "and you are taking upon yourself a task which God will not overlook. Yet I fear that you will not change my son's mind."

"Do not trouble yourself on that score, Monsieur Duval: he will hate me."

A barrier had to be erected between us which neither of us would be able to cross.

I wrote to Prudence saying that I accepted Count de N***'s proposition, and said that she could go and tell him I would have supper with them both.

I sealed the letter and, saying nothing of what it contained, I asked your father to see that it was delivered the moment he got back to Paris.

Even so, he enquired what was in it.

"Your son's happiness," I answered.

Your father embraced me one last time. On my forehead, I felt two tears of gratitude which were, so to speak, the waters of baptism which washed away my former sins and, even as I consented to give myself to another man, I shone with pride at the thought of everything that this new sin would redeem.

It was all quite natural, Armand. You once told me your father was the most upright man anyone could hope to meet.

Monsieur Duval got into his carriage and drove off.

Yet I was a woman, and when I saw you again, I could not help weeping. But I did not weaken.

Was I right? That is the question I ask myself today when illness forces me to take to my bed which I shall perhaps leave only when I am dead.

You yourself witnessed all that I suffered as the time for our inevitable separation drew near. Your father was not there to see me through, and there was a moment when I came very near to telling you everything, so appalling was the idea that you would hate and despise me.

One thing that you will perhaps not believe, Armand, is that I prayed to God to give me strength. The proof that He accepted my sacrifice is that He gave me the strength I begged for.

During the supper party, I still needed His help, for I could not bring myself to face what I was about to do, such was my fear that my courage would fail me!

Who would ever have told me that I, Marguerite Gautier, would be made to suffer such torment by the simple prospect of having a new lover?

I drank to forget, and when I woke next morning, I was in the Count's bed.

This is the whole truth, my dear. Judge now, and forgive me, as I have forgiven all the hurt you have done me since that day.'

XXVI

'WHAT ensued after that fatal night, you know as well as I do. But what you do not know, what you cannot suspect, is what I went through after the moment we parted.

I had heard that your father had taken you away, but felt sure that you would not be able to go on keeping your distance for long, and the day I ran into you on the Champs-Élysées, I was stunned but not really surprised.

And so began the sequence of days, each with some new insult from you which I suffered almost gladly. For not only was each indignity proof that you still loved me: I also felt that the more you persecuted me, the nobler I should appear in your eyes on the day you finally learned the truth.

Do not be surprised that I should have borne my cross gladly, Armand, for the love you felt for me had aroused noble inclinations in my heart.

But I did not have such strength of purpose at the outset. Between the consummation of the sacrifice I had made for you and your return, a fairly long time went by when I needed to fall back on physical means as a way of preserving my sanity and of drowning my unhappiness in the life to which I had reverted. I believe Prudence told you how I never missed a party or a ball or an orgy.

My hope was that I should kill myself quickly with my excesses, and I think that this hope will not now be long in being realized. Of necessity, my health deteriorated steadily, and the day I sent Madame Duvernoy to beg for your mercy, I was close to collapse in both body and soul.

I will not remind you, Armand, of the way you repaid me the last time I proved my love to you, nor of the indignity by which you made Paris unbearable for a woman who, near to dying, could not resist your voice when you asked her for one night of love, and who, taking leave of her senses, believed for an instant that she could build a bridge between what had been and what was now. It was your privilege, Armand, to act as you did: the rate for one of my nights was not always so high!

So I left it all behind me! Olympe replaced me as Monsieur N***'s mistress and took it on herself, so I hear, to explain my reasons for leaving him. Count de G*** was in London. He is one of those men who attach just enough importance to running after girls of my sort for it to be a pleasant diversion, and thus remain on friendly terms with the women they have had: they never hate them, because they have never been jealous. He is one of those noble Lords who show us one side of their feelings but both ends of their wallets. My first thought was of him. I travelled over to join him.* He gave me a marvellous welcome, but he was the lover of a society lady there, and was afraid of compromising himself by being seen with me. He introduced me to his friends, who organized a supper party for me, after which one of them took me home with him.

What did you expect me to do, my dear? Kill myself? To do so would have meant burdening your life, which must be a happy one, with pointless self-recriminations. And in any case, what is the sense of killing yourself when you are already so close to dying?

I turned into a body without a soul, a thing without thought. I continued in this mechanical way for some time, then came back to Paris and made enquiries about you. It was at this point that I learned that you had gone away on a long journey. There was nothing now to save me. My life once more became what it used to be two years before I met you. I tried to get back on terms with the Duke, but I had wounded him too deeply, and old men are short on patience, no doubt because they are aware that they are not going to live forever. My illness grew on me day by day. I had no colour, I felt desolate, I became thinner all the time. Men who buy love always inspect the goods before taking delivery of them. In Paris, there were many women whose health was better, and who had better figures than mine. I began to be overlooked. So much for the past, up to yesterday.

I am now very ill. I have written to the Duke asking for money, for I have none, and my creditors have returned brandishing their accounts with merciless persistence. Will the Duke give me an answer? Armand, why are you not here in Paris? You would come to see me and your visits would be a comfort.

20 December

The weather is dreadful: it's snowing and I am here alone. For the last three days, a fever has laid me so low that I have been unable to write to you. Nothing has changed, my dear. Each day I have vague hopes of a letter from you, but it does not come and probably never will. Only men are strong enough to be unforgiving. The Duke has not replied.

Prudence has started up her visits to the pawn-shops again.

I cough blood all the time. Oh! how you would grieve if you could see me now! You are so lucky to be where the sun is warm and not to have to face, as I do, an icy winter which lies heavy on your chest. Today, I got up for a while and, from behind the curtains at my window, I watched the bustle of life in Paris which I do believe I have put behind me once and for all. A few faces I knew appeared in the street: they passed quickly, cheerfully, without a care. Not one looked up at my window. However, a few young men have called and left their names. I was ill once before and you, who did not know me and had got nothing from me except a pert answer the day I first set eyes on you, you came to ask for news of me every morning. And now I am ill again. We spent six months together. I felt as much love for you as a woman's heart can contain and give, and now you are far away, you curse me and there is no word of comfort from you. But it was chance alone that made you desert me, I am sure, for if you were here in Paris, you would not leave my bedside nor my room.

25 December

My doctor has forbidden me to write every day. He is right, for remembering only makes the fever worse. But yesterday I received a letter which did me good—more for the sentiments behind it than for any material help it brought me. So I am able to write to you today. The letter was from your father and this is what it said:

"Madame,

I have this moment learned that you are ill. If I were in Paris, I should call myself to ask after you, and if my son were here with me, I should send him to find out how you are. But I cannot leave C***, and Armand is six or seven hundred leagues away. Allow me therefore simply to say, Madame, how grieved I am by your illness, and please believe that I hope most sincerely for your prompt recovery.

One of my closest friends, Monsieur H***, will call on you. He has been entrusted by me with an errand the result of which I await with impatience. Please receive him, and oblige

Your humble servant . . ."

This is the letter I have received. Your father is a man of noble heart: love him well, my dear, for there are few men in the world who deserve as much to be loved. This note, signed by him in full, has done me more good than all the prescriptions dispensed by my learned doctor.

Monsieur H*** came this morning. He seemed terribly embarrassed by the delicate mission which Monsieur Duval had entrusted to him. He simply came to hand over a thousand écus from your father. At first, I would not take the money, but Monsieur H*** said that by refusing I should offend Monsieur Duval, who had authorized him to give me this sum in the first instance and to supplement it with anything further I might need. I accepted his good offices which, coming from your father, cannot be regarded as charity. If I am dead when you return, show your father what I have just written about him, and tell him that as she penned these lines, the poor creature to whom he was kind enough to write this comforting letter, wept tears of gratitude and said a prayer for him.

4 January

I have just come through a succession of racking days. I never knew how much pain our bodies can give us. Oh! my past life! I am now paying for it twice over!

I have had someone sitting with me each night. I could not breathe. A wandering mind and bouts of coughing share what remains of my sorry existence.

My dining-room is crammed full of sweets and presents of all kinds which friends have brought me. Among these people, there are no doubt some who hope that I shall be their mistress later on. If they could only see what illness has reduced me to, they would run away in horror.

Prudence is using the presents I have been getting as New Year gifts to tradesmen.

It has turned frosty, and the doctor has said that I can go out in a few days if the fine weather continues.

8 January

Yesterday, I went out for a drive in my carriage. The weather was splendid. There were crowds of people out on the Champs-Élysées. It seemed like the first smile of spring. Everywhere around me there was a carnival atmosphere. I had never before suspected that the sun's rays could contain all the joy, sweetness and consolation that I found in them yesterday.

I ran into almost all the people I know. They were as

high-spirited as ever, and just as busily going about their pleasures. So many happy people, and so unaware that they are happy! Olympe drove by in an elegant carriage which Monsieur de N*** has given her. She tried to cut me with a look. She has no idea how far removed I have grown from such futilities. A nice boy I have known for ages asked me if I would have supper with him and a friend of his who, he said, wanted to meet me.

I gave him a sad smile and held out my hand, which was burning with fever.

I have never seen such surprise on a human face.

I got back at four o'clock and sat down to dinner with a fairly good appetite.

The drive out has done me good.

What if I were to get well again!

How strongly the sight of the lives and happiness of others renews the will to live of those who, only the day before, alone with their souls in the darkness of the sickroom, wanted nothing better than to die soon!

10 January

My hopes of recovery were an illusion. Here I am once more confined to my bed, my body swathed in burning poultices. Go out now and try hawking this body of yours which used to fetch such a pretty price, and see what you would get for it today!

We must have committed very wicked deeds before we were born, or else we are to enjoy very great felicity after we are dead, for God to allow us to know in this life all the agony of atonement and all the pain of our time of trial.

12 January

I am still ill.

Count de N*** sent me money yesterday, but I did not take it. I want nothing from that man. He is the reason why you are not with me now.

Oh ! happy days at Bougival! where are you now?

If I get out of this bedroom alive, it will be to go on a

pilgrimage to the house where we lived together. But the next time I leave here, I shall be dead.

Who knows if I shall write to you tomorrow?

25 January

For eleven nights now, I have not slept, I have not been able to breathe, and I have thought that I was about to die at any moment. The doctor has left instructions that I was not to be permitted to touch a pen. Still, Julie Duprat, who sits up with me, has allowed me to write you these few lines. Will you not return, then, before I die? Is everything between us finished forever? I have a feeling that if you did come back, I should get better. But what would be the point of getting better?

28 January

This morning, I was awakened by a loud commotion. Julie, who was sleeping in my room, rushed into the dining room. I heard men's voices, and hers battling vainly against them. She came back in tears.

They had come to repossess their goods. I told her to let what they call justice be done. The bailiff came into my room, and he kept his hat on his head the whole time. He opened the drawers, made a note of everything he saw, and did not appear to notice that there was a woman dying in the bed which the charity of the law fortunately lets me keep.

As he was going he at least agreed to inform me that I had nine days in which to appeal, but he has left a watchman here! God, what is to become of me? This scene has made me more ill than ever. Prudence wanted to ask your father's friend for money, but I said no.

I received your letter this morning.* Oh, how I needed it to come! Will my reply reach you in time? Will you ever see me again? This is a happy day which has helped me forget the days which I have spent these last six weeks. It seems to me that I am a little better, in spite of the miserable feeling which was my mood when I wrote you my reply.

After all, we cannot be unhappy all the time.

And then I fall to thinking that perhaps I won't die, that you will come back, that I shall see the spring once more, that you love me still, and that we shall begin the life we had last year all over again . . . !

But this is madness! It is as much as I can do to hold the pen which writes to you of these wild longings of my heart.

Whatever the outcome, I loved you very much, Armand, and I should have already been dead a long time if I had not had the memory of my love to sustain me, and a kind of vague hope of seeing you by my side once more.

4 February

Count de G*** is back. His mistress has been unfaithful to him. His spirits are very low, for he loved her very much. He came and told me the whole story. The poor man's affairs are in a bad way, though this did not prevent him from paying off my bailiff and dismissing the watchman.

I talked to him about you, and he has promised to talk to you about me. It's strange but, as I spoke, I completely forgot that I used to be his mistress once and, no less strangely, he tried to make me forget too! He is a decent sort.

Yesterday, the Duke sent round to enquire after me, and he came himself this morning.* I cannot think what can keep the old man going. He sat with me for three hours, and did not say much above a score of words. Two great tears came to his eyes when he saw how pale I was. No doubt the memory of his daughter's death made him cry so.

He will have seen her die twice. His back is bent, his head is thrust forward and downward, his mouth is slack and his eyes are dull. The double weight of age and grief bears down upon his tired body. He did not say one word of reproach. It was as though he found some secret satisfaction in observing what ravages disease has produced in me. He seemed proud to be still standing, whereas I, who am still young, have been laid low by my sufferings.

The bad weather has returned. No one comes to see me now. Julie sits up with me as often as she can. I cannot give

Prudence as much money as I used to, and she has begun saying that she has business to attend to as an excuse for staying away.

Now that I am near to death—in spite of what the doctors say, for I have several,* which only shows how the disease is gaining on me—I am almost sorry I listened to your father. If I had known that I would have taken just one year out of your future, I would not have resisted my longing to spend that year with you, and then, at least, I should have died holding the hand of a friend. Yet it is clear that had we spent that year together, I should not have died so soon.

Let Thy will be done!

5 February

Oh, come to me, Armand, for I suffer torments! God, I am about to die! Yesterday, I was so low that I felt I wanted to be somewhere other than here for the evening, which promised to be as long as the one before. The Duke had been in the morning. I have a feeling that the sight of this old man, whom death has overlooked, brings my own death that much nearer.

Although I was burning with fever, I was dressed and taken to the Vaudeville.* Julie had rouged my cheeks, for otherwise I should have looked like a corpse. I took my place in the box where I gave you our first rendezvous. I kept my eyes fixed the whole time on the seat in the stalls where you sat that day: yesterday, it was occupied by some boorish man who laughed loudly at all the stupid things the actors said. I was brought home half dead and spat blood all night. Today I cannot speak and can hardly move my arms. God! God! I am going to die! I was expecting it, but I cannot reconcile myself to the thought that my greatest sufferings are still to come, and if . . .'

After this word, the few letters which Marguerite had tried to form were illegible, and the story had been taken up by Julie Duprat.*

'18 *February*

Monsieur Armand,

Since the day Marguerite insisted on going to the theatre, she has grown steadily worse. Her voice went completely, and then she lost the use of her limbs. What our poor friend has to bear is impossible to describe. I am not used to coping with such suffering, and I go in constant fear.

Oh, how I wish you were here with us! She is delirious for most of the time, but whether her mind is wandering or lucid, your name is the one which she says when she manages to say anything at all.

The doctor has told me that she does not have much longer to live. Since she has been so desperately ill, the old Duke has not been back.

He told the doctor that seeing her like this was too much for him.

Madame Duvernoy has not behaved very well. She thought she would still be able to go on getting money out of Marguerite, at whose expense she has been living on a more or less permanent basis, and she took on obligations which she cannot meet. Seeing that her neighbour is no further use to her, she does not even come to see her any more. Everyone has deserted her. Monsieur de G***, harried by his debts, has been forced to return to London. Before going, he sent us money. He has done all he could, but the men have been back with repossession orders, and the creditors are only waiting for her to die before selling her up.

I wanted to use the last of my own money to stop her things being taken back, but the bailiff told me there was no point, for he had other orders to serve on her. Since she is going to die, it is better to let everything go than to try and save it for her family, given that she does not want to see any of them and, in any case, they never cared for her. You can have no idea of the gilded poverty in which the poor girl lies dying. Yesterday, we had no money at all. Plate, jewels, Indian shawls—everything has been pawned and the rest has been sold or seized. Marguerite is still aware of what is happening around her, and she suffers in body, mind and heart. Great tears run down her cheeks which are now so thin and pale that, if you saw her now, you would not recognize the face of the woman you once loved so much. She made me promise to write to you when she was no longer able to do so herself, and she is watching as I write this. She turns her eyes in my direction, but she cannot see me, for her sight is already dimmed by approaching death. And yet she smiles, and all her thoughts, all her soul, are for you, I am sure.

Each time the door opens, her eyes light up, for each time she believes that you will walk in. Then, when she sees that it is not you, her face reverts to its expression of suffering, breaks into a cold sweat and her cheeks turn crimson.

19 February, midnight

Oh, poor Monsieur Armand! What a sad day today has been! This morning, Marguerite could not get her breath. The doctor bled her, and her voice came back a little. The doctor advised her to see a priest. She said she would, and he himself went off to find one at the Church of Saint Roch.

Meanwhile, Marguerite called me close to her bedside, asked me to open her wardrobe, pointed out a lace cap and a long shift, also richly decked with lace, and then said in a weakened voice:

"I shall die after I have made my confession. When it's over, you are to dress me in these things. It is the whim of a dying woman."

Then, weeping, she kissed me and added:

"I can speak, but I can't get my breath when I do. I can't breathe! Give me air!"

I burst into tears and opened the window. A few moments later, the priest walked in.

I went to greet him.

When he realized in whose apartment he was, he seemed afraid of the reception he might get.*

"Come in, father, there's nothing to fear," I said.

He stayed no time in the room where Marguerite lay so ill, and when he emerged, he said:

"She has lived a sinful life, but she will die a Christian death."

A few moments later, he returned with an altar-boy carrying a crucifix, and a sacristan who walked before them ringing a bell to announce that the Lord was coming to the house of the dying woman.

All three entered the bedroom which, in times gone by, had echoed with so many extravagant voices, and was now nothing less than a holy tabernacle.

I fell to my knees. I cannot say how long the effect of these proceedings on me will last, but I do not believe that any human thing will ever produce such an effect on me again until I myself reach the same pass.

The priest took the holy oils, anointed the dying woman's feet, hands and brow, read a short prayer, and Marguerite was ready for heaven, where she is surely bound if God has looked down on the tribulations of her life and the saintly character of her death.

Since that moment, she has not spoken or stirred. There were a score of times when I would have thought she was dead, had I not heard her laboured breathing.

*20 February, 5 o'clock in the afternoon**

It is all over.

Marguerite began her mortal agony last night, around two o'clock. No martyr ever suffered such torment, to judge by the screams she uttered. Two or three times, she sat bolt upright in her bed, as though she would snatch at the life which was winging its way back to God.

And two or three times she said your name. Then everything went quiet, and she slumped back on the bed exhausted. Silent tears welled up in her eyes, and she died.

I went close to her, called her name and, when she did not answer, I closed her eyes and kissed her on the forehead.

Poor, dear Marguerite! How I wished I had been a holy woman so that my kiss might commend your soul to God!

Then I dressed her as she had asked. I went to fetch a priest at Saint-Roch. I lit two candles for her, and stayed in the church for an hour to pray.

I gave money of hers to some poor people there.

I am not well versed in religion, but I believe that the good Lord will acknowledge that my tears were genuine, my prayers fervent and my charity sincere, and He will have pity on one who died young and beautiful, yet had only me to close her eyes and lay her in her grave.

22 February

The funeral was today. Many of Marguerite's women friends came to the church. A few wept honest tears. When the cortège set off for Montmartre, only two men followed the hearse: Count de G***, who had returned specially from London, and the Duke, who walked with the aid of two of his footmen.

I am writing to tell you of these happenings from Marguerite's apartment, with tears in my eyes, by the light of the lamp which burns mournfully and with my dinner untouched, as you might imagine, though Nanine had it sent up for me, for I have not eaten in more than twenty-four hours.

Life moves on and will not allow me to keep these distressing pictures clear in my mind for long, for my life is no more mine than Marguerite's was hers. Which is why I am writing down all these things here in the place where they happened, for I fear that if any length of time were to elapse between what has occurred and your return, I should not be able to give you an account of it in all its sorry detail.'

XXVII

'HAVE you finished it?' Armand asked me when I reached the end of the manuscript.

'I understand what you must have been through, my friend, if all that I've read is true!'

'My father vouches for it in a letter he wrote me.'

We talked for some while longer of the unhappy destiny which had just been played out, then I went home to get a little rest.

Armand, unhappy still, but a little easier now that his story was told, recovered quickly, and together we went to call on Prudence and Julie Duprat.

Prudence had just been declared bankrupt. She said that it was Marguerite's fault: during her final illness, she had loaned Marguerite considerable sums of money for which she, Prudence, had signed promissory notes. She had not been able to repay these notes because Marguerite had died without reimbursing her, nor had she signed any receipts which would have allowed Prudence to join the other creditors.

With the help of this unlikely tale, which Madame Duvernoy put about generally as an excuse for the mishandling of her own affairs, she succeeded in getting a thousand francs out of Armand who did not believe a word of it but wanted to appear as though he did, such was his respect for anyone and anything that had once been close to his mistress.

Next, we called on Julie Duprat, who went over the unhappy course of events which she had witnessed and wept sincerely as she remembered her dead friend.

Finally, we went to see Marguerite's grave over which the early rays of the April sun were uncurling the first leaves.

There remained one final call of duty for Armand to answer, which was to rejoin his father. Once more, he asked me to accompany him.

We arrived at C*** where I met Monsieur Duval, who looked exactly as I had pictured him from the description his son had given me: a tall, dignified, kindly man.

He welcomed Armand with tears of happiness, and shook my hand affectionately. I quickly realized that among the Collector's sentiments, fatherly feeling was by far the strongest.

His daughter, whose name was Blanche, had the clear-eyed gaze and serene mouth which point to a soul that conceives only saintly thoughts and lips that speak only pious words. She greeted her brother's return with smiles, unaware, chaste young woman that she was, that in a far country a courtesan had sacrificed her own happiness to the mere mention of her name.

I stayed for some time with this happy family which directed every waking thought to the son who had brought them a convalescent heart.

I returned to Paris where I wrote this story exactly as it had been told to me. It has just one quality to commend it, which may be contested: it is true.

From this tale, I do not draw the conclusion that all women of Marguerite's sort are capable of behaving as she did. Far from it. But I have learned that one such woman, once in her life, experienced deep love, that she suffered for it and that she died of it. I have told the reader what I learned. It was a duty.

I am not an advocate of vice, but I shall always be a sounding board for any noble heart in adversity wherever I hear its voice raised in prayer.

Marguerite's history is an exception, I say again. Had it been a commonplace, it would not have been worth writing down.

A NOTE ON MONEY

SINCE money plays an essential role in *La Dame aux Camélias*, readers may find it useful to have some guidance on contemporary currency and values.

The basic unit was the *franc* (of 100 centimes, or *sous*), though the older term *livre* was still in use. The *écu* was worth 5 frs. and the *louis* 20 frs. The exchange rate in the 1840s was around 25 francs to the pound. Armand's allowance of 3,000 frs. was the equivalent, therefore, of £120, and Marguerite's annual expenditure of 100,000 frs., £4,000. The 200,000 frs. which, according to Prudence, would not be enough to keep a mistress like Marguerite, mean £8,000 in contemporary sterling terms.

Given the high rates of inflation in our times, conversion tables have a limited value. The following costs and prices may help to put these and other sums into a broad cost-of-living context.

In London, around 1850, cabbies charged 6d. (old pence) a mile, and silk dress lengths cost 16s. (shillings) to £1 a yard. Bob Cratchit earned 15s. a week as a copying clerk. The average unskilled wage was about 12s. a week and £1 for craftsmen. A maid would expect between £7 and £10 a year, a footman £15 and a valet £20. A doctor with a superior practice earned £3,000 and the most successful lawyer £5,000. A man needed £1,000 a year to live like a gentleman, but £10,000 if he wished to run a country seat and keep a town season. Indian shawls could be had from £1 to £1,000.

In Paris, a workman's dinner of vegetables and meat cost 40 sous and the most expensive meal at the Café de Paris 500 frs., with Château Yquem at 25 frs. a bottle. The average worker's wage was 3–4 frs. a day (women earned about half this rate). A cook could be hired for 20–35 frs. a week (more for males) and turkeys fetched 20 frs. each in the shops. A primary school teacher was paid 300 frs. a year, curés 1,000, copying clerks 1,300, cabinet ministers 10 or 20,000, Senators 30,000. Corsets were normally in the 6–18 fr. range, but the most fashionable hats could cost 1,800 frs. A two-volume novel sold for 15 frs. (cheap editions 3 frs.), but newspapers in a highly competitive market were coming down to 6 or even 4 sous a copy. The annual subscription to the Jockey Club was 1,000 frs. The cheapest theatre seats were priced at 5 or 6 frs., but Marguerite's box at the Théâre-Italien, on a six-month lease, cost 5,475 frs. For her camellias she paid 3 frs. each, more than the daily wage of the vast majority of working men or women.

EXPLANATORY NOTES

1 *telling a tale*: cf. *Antonine* (1849): 'I have not gone to the
length of inventing this story: I have written it, or rather
copied it from models who are for the most part still alive';
La Dame aux Perles (1853): 'if I have not gone to the length
of inventing . . . it is to provide further proof that I have
observed for myself the story I tell'; *La Vie à Vingt Ans*
(1854): 'No one invents, my dear fellow; one retells tales.'
Many novelists, seeking to make their fiction respectable by
guaranteeing its reality, said as much. In Dumas's case, the
claim is more than justified: many of his novels and plays
draw directly on his own experience.

the rue Laffitte: in the 9ᵉ *arrondissement*, the financial centre
of Paris, was already becoming known for its art dealers and
galleries. Lola Montès lived for a time at no. 40, and
Offenbach later occupied no. 11. The *rue d'Antin*, in the
fashionable 2ᵉ *arrondissement*, crosses the Avenue de
l'Opéra. In fact, from 1844 until her death, Marie Duplessis
lived at no. 11 (now 15) Boulevard de la Madeleine, to the
west of the Opéra. The substitution of this new address is
one of a number of changes—the dates given here are
brought forward by two or three weeks—which Dumas
probably introduced to disguise the origins of his heroine.
Some of these changes were subsequently corrected: Marguerite was at first buried at Père Lachaise, but in the 1852
edition, Dumas reinstated Montmartre cemetery as her final
resting place.

Indian shawls: Indian cashmeres were an expensive status
symbol, the more ornate examples costing thousands of
francs. When Lucy Snowe arrives at Madame Beck's school
for girls in Belgium (Charlotte Brontë, *Villette* (1853), ch. 8),
she encounters the egregious Mrs Sweeney who has somehow acquired an impressive wardrobe: 'the chief item in the
inventory, the spell by which she struck a certain awe
through the household (was) *a real Indian shawl*, "un
véritable Cachmire" (sic), as Madame Beck said, with un-
mixed reverence and amaze. I feel that without this
"Cachmire", she would not have kept her footing in the

pensionnat for two days; by virtue of it, she maintained the same a month.'

2 *the Opera or the Théâtre-Italien*: the Paris Opera has occupied many sites. In 1794, it moved to the Salle Montansier in the rue de Richelieu and thence, in 1820, to the Salle Le Peletier, in the rue Le Peletier. The present building, which was begun in 1862, opened in 1875. The Théâtre-Italien moved from the Odéon on the Left Bank to the Salle Ventadour in the rue Méhul (2ᵉ *arrondissement*) in 1841. It was at the height of its vogue at this time and almost equalled the Opera as a venue for fashionable society. Donizetti was its mainstay in the 1830s, and Verdi was performed there in the 1840s.

3 *treasures of Aucoc and Odiot*: Casimir Aucoc, a goldsmith in the rue de la Paix, was especially known for his 'travelling desks', 'travelling bidets' and other *articles de voyage*. Jean-Baptiste-Claude Odiot (1763–1850), who had premises at 7 Place de la Madeleine, was the greatest exponent of the Empire style. Marie Duplessis's bills have survived and reveal that she gave most of her custom to Halphen.

6 *préfecture*: travel and other civil documents are still obtained from police headquarters. It is at the *préfecture* that Armand will meet the police superintendent in Ch. VI.

8 *the entrance to the Champs-Elysées*: was from the Place de la Concorde and was marked by two equestrian statues, the Marly horses. The first stage of the Avenue, as far as the Rond-Point about half way along its length, was a fashionable place of entertainment. The second stage, to the Étoile, was as yet still relatively countrified.

Alfred de Musset: (1810–1857), poet and playwright, and in many ways the archetypal Romantic.

9 *Vincent Vidal*: (1811–1887) had shown his first major collection of pastels in 1843. He drew Marie Duplessis several times and two of his drawings of her were sold in the 1847 auction. In the 1851 preface, Jules Janin particularly mentioned 'a radiant, chaste head of finished elegance' and noted that after Marie's death, Vidal drew only respectable ladies, 'having made an exception in her case which did no hurt to the budding fame of both artist and model'.

Lady of the Camellias . . . the name: in 1843 and 1844,

Marie Duplessis bought her camellias from Raconot, in the rue de la Paix. Dumas claimed responsibility for inventing the title, and Albert Vandam remarked that 'no one had ever thought of applying it to her while she was alive'. There were precedents, however, and Vandam mentions a Monsieur Latour-Mézerai who, because he was never without one in his button-hole, was known as 'l'Homme au caméllia'. More likely is the possibility that Dumas had read George Sand's *Isidora* (1846), the heroine of which is a courtesan with horticultural interests who is referred to as 'la dame aux camélias'. Dumas admitted that he had written 'camélia' (and not 'caméllia') not because he wished to contest the accepted spelling but because he knew no better. If he continued to write the word with one 'l', 'it is that since Madame Sand spells the word as I do, I prefer to be incorrect with her than correct with others'.

visit . . . to Bagnères: the 1872 edition specifies Bagnères-de-Bigorre (Hautes-Pyrénées) which catered for patients suffering from anaemia, rheumatism and digestive disorders. Bagnères-de-Luchon (Haute-Garonne) was more usually associated with the treatment of respiratory complaints.

elderly foreign duke: the 'Duke' was real enough. The Comte Stackelberg, a former Russian ambassador to Vienna, was eighty when he met Marie in 1844. It was widely believed that his attraction to her was her uncanny resemblance to his dead daughter. Dumas later asserted that Stackelberg had spread this story himself, to protect his reputation, and that his interest in her was sexual.

13 *. . . lastly Mademoiselle R****: it is likely that Dumas uses random initials, in order to castigate the 'fashionable vice' of his age. However, it is fairly certain that Mademoiselle R*** is the actress Rachel (1820–1858) whom Dumas knew through his father, a man of the theatre, who knew everyone. Tony was famous as a supplier of horses to elegant Paris. He attended the Church service held for Marie in the Church of La Madeleine on 5 February 1847 and, at the auction, bought her bay horse for 1,800 francs.

14 *Manon Lescaut*: (1731), by the abbé Prévost, tells how the
upright Des Grieux falls madly in love with the amoral
Manon who, remaining true through many infidelities, is
transported as a common prostitute and, followed to the end
by her lover, dies in an odour of sanctity. The parallel with
La Dame aux Camélias, which was based on Dumas's own
experience, is striking. Marie owned a copy of Prévost's
novel which, it was said, was annotated in her own hand.

16 *Marion Delorme*: a drama by Victor Hugo (1831); *Frédéric
et Bernerette*, a *conte* by Musset (1838); *Fernande*, a novel
by Dumas *père* (1844). It was not merely the Romantics
who showed an interest in the prostitute who, noble-hearted
or vicious, a victim of society or a predator on men, figures
largely in 19th-century French literature. Goncourt's *La
Fille Eliza* (1876), a semi-documentary study, and Zola's
Nana (1880), which shows the courtesan as the destroyer
of the Second Empire, are merely two of many examples.

17 *Voltaire*: (1694–1778), enjoyed mixed fortunes in the 19th
century. Some regarded him as the champion of rationalism.
Others saw in him a destructive force. In *La Dame aux Perles*
(1853), Dumas holds Voltaire responsible for the dangerous
habit of scepticism: 'we cannot believe any more completely
than we can doubt . . . The soul of every man today carries
a grain of the sorry seed so liberally scattered by our last
generation of philosophers, and, at the least provocation,
that seed germinates secretly.'

18 *the whole is in the part*: cf. *Antonine* (1849): 'I am with
those who believe that the whole is in the part. I am a
fatalist and believe that the great events of our lives emerge
from the smallest accidents of chance. Nothing is without
point in our destinies.' The notion that life is an unfolding of
preordained inevitabilities was a Romantic cliché. Henry
Murger, in ch. 12 of *Scènes de la Vie de Boheme* (1848),
mocks at a similar point of view: 'There is nothing futile in
the world; all is in all. The little streams make the great
rivers; the little syllables form the great Alexandrines; and
the mountains are composed of grains of dust. It's in "The
Wisdom of Nations". There is a copy of it on the *quais*.'

Unlike Prévost, however, who uses Fate as an excuse for his characters, Dumas makes little play with Fate as a mysterious, blind force. He later affirmed, however, in *Affaire Clémenceau* (1866), that the fatality of heredity was a force to be reckoned with. We have two personalities, one social and another that is instinctive: in moments of crisis, it may happen that the better, moral part of us is overcome by the natural and usually destructive self.

one hundred and fifty thousand francs: the records of the auction have survived and reveal that the sale realized 89,017 frs., of which Marie's creditors took 49,000. Dumas was only one of many who overestimated Marie's wealth. The sister, Delphine, now Madame Constant Paquet who still lived at Nonant, was the sole beneficiary: Marie had a niece, but no nephew.

28 *Montmartre cemetery*: (18ᵉ *arrondissement*) where Berlioz, Stendhal, Vigny, Gautier, Ernest Renan and Dumas himself are buried. Dumas's grave is located about a hundred yards from the plain marble block which commemorates Alphonsine Plessis.

35 *once I have seen, I shall see*: Armand-Jean le Bouthillier de Rancé (1626–1700) renounced the world and, as abbot of La Trappe, near Mortagne (Orne), revived the austerities of the Trappist Order. The allusion, of which he would not have approved, is to a letter in which he declares that creation 'importuned' him: 'Let us shut our eyes, o my soul! and let us stay far from the things of the world that we may see them and be seen by them.' Dumas probably found the remark in Chateaubriand's last book, the *Vie de Rancé* (1844), where it is quoted at the start of Book III. The evocation of Rancé is clearly intended to form part of the spiritual frame of reference which makes *La Dame aux Camélias* a novel of persecution, martyrdom and redemption. On a more personal level, Dumas identified with historical figures like Rancé and St Augustine who, after a misspent youth, saw the errors of their ways and reformed.

the rue Jean-Jacques Rousseau: (1ᵉ *arrondissement*), the home of the 'Messageries Générales' from which the mail coaches left each day at 6 o'clock. Each coach had room for two or three passengers, and it is from the rue Jean-Jacques Rousseau that Marguerite will leave for London.

36 *we should drive to the cemetery together*: it was Édouard de Perregaux who arranged for the exhumation at which he was present, on 16 February, with a friend. It has been suggested that the friend in question was Dumas, though whether the following pages derive from memory rather than from 'invention' is open to doubt.

42 *Théâtre des Variétés*: in 1807, Napoleon reclassified the theatres of Paris into the 'grands' (Comédie Française, Odéon, Opéra and Opéra-Comique) and the 'secondaires' (which were henceforth permitted to stage only certain kinds of plays). The Théâtre des Variétés was forced to move from the Palais Royal to the Boulevard Montmartre. It specialized in comedies interspersed with songs and was a fashionable meeting place for society ladies. It was to be the home of Offenbach in the 1860s. Dumas met Marie Duplessis here in September 1844 in almost exactly similar circumstances: he had spent the day at Saint-Germain with his father, met up with Ernest Dejazet (son of the actress and his model for Gaston) and went with him to the Variétés.

Michel-Victor Susse: (*c.* 1782–1853) was an art dealer, antiquary and supplier of paper and artist's materials. In addition to the shop at 31 Place de la Bourse, he had other premises at 7 and 8 Passage des Panoramas.

43 *the Opéra-Comique*: staged opera of the lighter kind—Auber, Halévy and Meyerbeer. It had moved home several times but returned to the Salle Favart, Place des Italiens, in 1840.

44 *Alphonse Karr*: (1808–1890) was a novelist and journalist with a sardonic turn of mind, as this story suggests. *Am Rauchen* (1842) was the fourth and final instalment of *Ce qu'il y a dans une bouteille d'encre* which began appearing in 1838. Karr once so irritated Louise Colet, Flaubert's importunate mistress, that she stabbed him with a kitchen knife. It was generally felt that the incident redounded to his credit.

45 *the Passage de l'Opéra*: a narrow, shop-lined street, was demolished to make way for the Boulevard des Italiens in Haussmann's reshaping of Paris in the 1860s.

48 *The Café Anglais; the Maison d'Or*: The Boulevard des Italiens boasted numerous cafés—the Grand Balcon, the Café de Paris, Tortoni's and so on—which made it the most fashionable street in Paris. The Café Anglais, at no. 13, had opened in 1822. It comprised an *entresol* and a first floor, and was divided into twenty-two private rooms. It was demolished in 1913. The Maison d'Or (more usually the Maison Dorée because of its gilt balconies) opened in 1840. A large room overlooking the street was used by casual patrons, but there were also a number of private rooms for habitués. It lost its vogue by the end of the 1860s. Among Marie's papers are bills for meals supplied by the Maison Dorée: it is likely to have been the source of the supper served in Ch. XI.

51 *Prudence Duvernoy*: Dumas acknowledged that Prudence was modelled closely on Clémence Prat, Marie's neighbour and go-between. Clémence was ostensibly a milliner, with premises at 17 Boulevard de la Madeleine. She was later arrested and imprisoned for the corruption of minors. Her theatrical ambitions outlasted Marie's death. In 1859, in a revival of *La Dame aux Camélias*, she played, very unconvincingly according to Dumas, the role of Prudence of which she was the original. However, it was Eugene Dejazet (Gaston) who knew Clémence, and not Dumas.

52 *the last [play]*: theatre-goers were frequently offered several kinds of entertainment and rarely complained of being given scant measure: Dumas *père's La Reine Margot* (20 February 1847) lasted nine hours. Jules Janin recalls seeing Marie Duplessis on one occasion at the Opera. When the opera was over, she left without waiting for the comedy and a ballet which were yet to come. Jerome K. Jerome (*My Life and Times*, Sutton, 1984, p. 73) recalled that an evening in the theatre in London in the 1880s lasted from six until twelve. The multiple programme 'began with a farce, included a drama and an opera, and ended up with a burlesque. After nine o'clock, half prices were charged for admission.' Half prices were not allowed by the French authorities, but patrons emerging at an earlyish stage of the proceedings resold their tickets to touts who offered them to new arrivals.

53 *Count de N****: it is likely that N*** was based on Comte
Édouard de Perregaux, a wealthy army officer, born in 1817,
who sacrificed much of his fortune to Marie between 1842
and 1844. He continued to give her money and married her
in 1846. He was near her when she died. He made the
funeral arrangements, requested the exhumation and identified the body. But if Perregaux was the model for N***, his
devotion is not dissimilar to that shown by Armand himself.
He was probably the man who loved Marie Duplessis the
most deeply.

61 *Carl Marie von Weber*: (1786–1826) was a favourite composer with the Romantics and remained popular throughout
the 19th century. *La dernière pensée* was another favourite.

63 *de G****: the initial hides Antoine-Alfred-Agénor de Guiche
(1819–1880) who, as the Duc de Gramont, was later to serve
briefly as Napoleon III's foreign minister. It was Agénor who
launched Marie Duplessis in 1840.

78 *The rue de Provence*: crosses the Chaussée d'Antin in the 9ᵉ
arrondissement. With the exception of the rue du Mont
Blanc, which disappeared in the creation of Haussman's Paris,
it is still possible to follow Armand's itinerary.

85 *cages which no one . . . tries to disguise with flowers*: a
hackneyed image. Cf. *Villette* (Ch. 14): 'a strange, frolicsome,
noisy little world was this school. Great pains were taken to
hide chains with flowers . . . Each mind was being raised in
slavery; but, to prevent reflection from dwelling on this fact,
every pretext for physical recreation was seized and made
the most of.'

88 *the Vaudeville*: the Théâtre du Vaudeville dated from 1772.
From 1840 its home was the Place de la Bourse and it moved
to the Boulevard des Capucines in 1869. It specialized in 'light
comedy with music', said Murray's *Handbook for Visitors
to Paris* (1874), which added sternly that 'the subjects and
treatment of many of the pieces render them unfit for the
ears of English ladies'.

98 *Saint-Denis*: to the north of Paris, was, according to Dumas
who coined the expression, a breeding ground for the *demi-
monde*. It was, he said, the home of daughters of the genteel
but impoverished families of Napoleon's officers who had
been killed in action. Educated above their station, but un-
marriageable since they had neither name nor dowry, they

infiltrated respectable society, manipulated their wealthy lovers and ruined families. Dumas had much more sympathy for the *grisettes*, who were decent working girls lured into prostitution by poverty and by men who should have known better. Marie Duplessis was a former *grisette*, and it was for this reason that Dumas, nostalgically no doubt, called her 'the last of the good-hearted courtesans'.

101 *this is what I wrote*: After Marie's death, Dumas managed to buy back the letter he had written to her in 1845. The letter, dated '30 August, midnight', ran as follows:

'My dear Marie, I am neither rich enough to love you as I should wish, nor poor enough to be loved as you would like. Let us both forget—you a name which must mean very little to you, and I, happiness which has become impossible for me to bear. There is no point in my telling how miserable I am, for you already know how much I love you. Farewell, then. You are not so heartless that you will not understand the reason for my letter, and you are too clear-headed not to forgive me. A thousand memories, A.D.'

On 28 January 1884, Dumas pasted the letter in a copy of the novel and sent it to Sarah Bernhardt as a souvenir of a memorable performance as Marguerite.

103 *The Café Foy . . . Véry's*: the Café Foy, on the Boulevard des Italiens. The Restaurant Véry opened in 1808 and was the first restaurant of standing to introduce fixed price menus. It was here, in 1871, that a patriotic waiter served coffee in a chamber pot to a Prussian officer who had demanded a cup from which no Frenchman had ever drunk.

117 *Frascati*: on the site of the present no. 23 Boulevard Montmartre, had opened in 1796. It was a conscious imitation of the Frascati gardens in Naples and comprised a hotel and a number of gaming rooms which became very popular after the closing, following the Revolution in July 1830, of the capital's gambling houses. Firework displays were given in its gardens.

120 *Bougival*: on the Seine, some eight miles along the carriage road from Paris to Saint-Germain. Later in the century, it was a haunt for shop-girls and their beaux. If Armand finds the name unattractive, it was because 'boue' means mud. Bernard Raffalli (*La Dame aux Camélias*, Gallimard, 1975,

p. 362) tentatively suggests that the *Point du Jour* may have been run by a Catherine Arnoult.

122 *lines by Lamartine . . . tunes by Scudo*: Alphonse de Lamartine (1790–1869), still thought of mainly as an elegaic love poet. The composer Paul Scudo (1806–1864) was also known as a harsh critic of Berlioz, Wagner and Schumann.

145 *St Margaret's Islands*: The Île Sainte-Marguerite lies off Cannes. It was there that the Man in the Iron Mask, stirringly brought to life by Dumas *père*, was long held prisoner.

148 *the Hôtel de Paris*: was in the rue de Richelieu (2e *arrondissement*).

159 *the Barrière de l'Étoile*: one of the ring of customs gates, built in 1788 by Ledoux, and still in use in 1863 as a collection point for dues levied on goods entering Paris.

160 *the Église Saint-Roch*: in the rue Saint Honoré (1e *arrondissement*). Dumas *père* married Ida Ferrier there in 1840.

167 *the rue Tronchet*: in the 8e *arrondissment*, runs north from the Place de la Madeleine as far as the Boulevard Haussmann. Chopin lived at no. 5 between 1839 and 1841. The character of Olympe was probably based on a woman Dumas had known, but no specific model has been proposed.

180 *Middle East*: after breaking with Marie, Dumas too travelled —but not for thirteen months—to Spain and North Africa. He returned to France on 15 January 1847 and was still at Marseilles when he learnt of her death on 10 February. He left for Paris immediately, perhaps for sentimental reasons but also because he had an urgent appointment with his publisher.

189 *I travelled over to join him*: after the end of her affair with Dumas, Marie continued her old life. She did, however, travel to London in February 1846, where she married Perregaux.

194 *I received your letter this morning*: Dumas heard of Marie's illness only after leaving Paris in October 1846 for Spain where he appears to have been happy. However, on 18 October, he wrote to Marie: 'Moutier has just arrived in Madrid and tells me that when he left Paris you were ill. I hope you will allow me to add my name to those who grieve to see you suffer.

'A week after you get this letter, I shall be in Algiers. If

I find a note for me at the poste-restante which forgives me for a mistake I made about a year ago, I shall return to France less sad, if I am absolved, and most happy, if you are better. Your friend, A.D.' No reply is known, but Dumas did not return to France and pressed ahead with his father to North Africa.

195 *the Duke . . . came himself this morning*: of all the contemporary witnesses, only Dumas suggests that Stackelberg returned to see her, though he did attend her funeral.

196 *I have several [doctors]*: Marie Duplessis was attended by a number of doctors who included the charlatan Dr Koreff. Dr Manec made thirty-nine calls between 18 September and 19 November 1846. She also consulted Dr Chomel, though, from May 1846, her main medical adviser was Dr Davaine who saw her 119 times between September and December.

to the Vaudeville: the final visit Marie paid to the theatre was in fact to the Palais Royal where she saw the popular *La Poudre de Coton* in the last week of December 1846.

Julie Duprat: who looks after Marguerite in her final illness, may be a reflection of Clotilde, Marie's maid. On the other hand, her name suggests that she may be based on the better side of Clémence Prat, who presumably had one.

198 *afraid of the reception he might get*: a priest was called to Marie from the Church of Madeleine nearby. He may have been alarmed, but he stayed long enough to be fed: 'Ham for the priest', says an entry made by a servant in Marie's account book, 'two francs'.

199 *20 February*: for reasons which are unclear Dumas has advanced events by seventeen days. Marie died on 3 February and was buried on 5 February; her remains were transferred on the 16th and the auction was held over four days, 24–27 February 1847. Marguerite died on 20 February, is buried on 22 February and exhumed around 8 March; her effects were sold on 16 March.

ÉMILE ZOLA

L'Assommoir
The Attack on the Mill
La Bête humaine
La Débâcle
Germinal
The Kill
The Ladies' Paradise
The Masterpiece
Nana
Pot Luck
Thérèse Raquin

A SELECTION OF   OXFORD WORLD'S CLASSICS

The Oxford World's Classics Website

www.worldsclassics.co.uk

- Information about new titles
- Explore the full range of Oxford World's Classics
- Links to other literary sites and the main OUP webpage
- Imaginative competitions, with bookish prizes
- Peruse the Oxford World's Classics Magazine
- Articles by editors
- Extracts from Introductions
- A forum for discussion and feedback on the series
- Special information for teachers and lecturers

www.worldsclassics.co.uk

American Literature

British and Irish Literature

Children's Literature

Classics and Ancient Literature

Colonial Literature

Eastern Literature

European Literature

History

Medieval Literature

Oxford English Drama

Poetry

Philosophy

Politics

Religion

The Oxford Shakespeare

A complete list of Oxford Paperbacks, including Oxford World's Classics, Oxford Shakespeare, Oxford Drama, and Oxford Paperback Reference, is available in the UK from the Academic Division Publicity Department, Oxford University Press, Great Clarendon Street, Oxford OX2 6DP.

In the USA, complete lists are available from the Paperbacks Marketing Manager, Oxford University Press, 198 Madison Avenue, New York, NY 10016.

Oxford Paperbacks are available from all good bookshops. In case of difficulty, customers in the UK can order direct from Oxford University Press Bookshop, Freepost, 116 High Street, Oxford OX1 4BR, enclosing full payment. Please add 10 per cent of published price for postage and packing.